Trekking in
BOLIVIA
A Traveler's Guide

YOSSI BRAIN,
ANDREW NORTH,
AND ISOBEL STODDART

THE
MOUNTAINEERS

Published by
The Mountaineers
1001 SW Klickitat Way, Suite 201
Seattle, WA 98134

© 1997 by Yossi Brain

10 9 8 7
5 4 3 2 1

Published simultaneously in Great Britain by Cordee, 3a DeMontfort Street, Leicester, England, LE1 7HD

Manufactured in Canada

Edited by Kris Fulsaas
Maps by Carmen Julia Arze
All photographs by Yossi Brain, unless otherwise noted
Cover design by The Mountaineers Books
Book design by The Mountaineers Books
Book layout by Gray Mouse Graphics

Cover photograph: *David Bandrowski descending pre-Hispanic paving on the Yunga Cruz trail with the east side of Illimani in the background.*
Frontispiece: *Peter Hutchinson on flexible bridge crossing over the Río Quimsa Chata, Takesi*

Library of Congress Cataloging-in-Publication Data
Brain, Yossi, 1967–
    Trekking in Bolivia : a traveler's guide / by Yossi Brain, Andrew North, and Isobel Stoddart.
        .p.   cm.
    Includes bibliographical references (p.   ).
    ISBN 0-89886-501-8
    1. Hiking—Bolivia—Guidebooks. 2. Backpacking—Bolivia—Guidebooks.
    3. Bolivia—Guidebooks. I. North, Andrew, 1969–   . II. Stoddart, Isobel. III. Title.
    GV199.44.B64B73   1997
    796.51'0984—dc21   97–2348
                                                              CIP

CONTENTS

Section II. TREKS 55

Section III. THE COUNTRY AND ITS PEOPLE 183

MAP KEY

🐚 Village/Settlement	🏠 Hut/Refuge
⛺ Camp or Bivouac Site	☁ Area above 5000m/16,000ft
—— Road	▲ Peak
—— Principal Road	⤨ Pass
——⊣ Roadhead	〰 River or Stream
⋯⋯ Track	⬭ Lake
⚒ Mine or Mining Settlement	▬ Tunnel

For scale see individual map.

ACKNOWLEDGMENTS

From Yossi Brain:
Thanks to the following people who shared the joys of routefinding on treks done for the first time in Bolivia: Daniel, Fabienne, and Bernard (France), Hank (U.S.A.), Alvaro Garrón, Lito Rojas, Laura Prömmel (Bolivia), Harold, Ulli Schatz (Germany), Peter Hutchison, Claire Mitchell (U.K.), Deanna Swaney (U.S.A.), Andy Ashton, Peter Corkill (and Ben and Oz for trying) (U.K.), Caroline and Marie-Alice (France), Valerie Lemieux (Canada), David Bandrowski, Will Fox, Karl Wolf (U.S.A.), Mark Ryle and Jason Currie, Alex Mitchell for trying (U.K.), Paul, Jodie, Jos, and Rob (Netherlands), Francisco and Gary (Bolivia).

For miscellaneous help: Louis Demers, Dr. John Triplett, formerly head of the U.S. Embassy medical unit in La Paz, Liam O'Brien, formerly head of the Defense Mapping Agency in La Paz, Peter Sutcliffe (New Zealand), Dr. Andy Ashton, Robert Strauss and Deanna Swaney, Mario Miranda, Dennis "Mongo" Moore, Peter Hutchison, Andy St. Pierre, Hans Müller of Centro Canadiense de Estudios y Cooperación Internacional La Paz, Clodagh Norton, Foto Linare, Alix Shand.

Special thanks to Ulli Schatz, Carmen Julia Arze, and whoever invented e-mail, without which this book would have taken several more years to appear.

From Andrew North and Isobel Stoddart:
Lars Hafsktolo, Joseph Vieria, José Velasco, Miguel, Adrian Waldmann, Rosa María Ruiz, Lucie Ruiz, and Amanda García.

Opposite: *Waterfall above Puina, Apolobamba North*

SECTION I
ABOUT TREKKING

Descending to the Sunchuli valley, Apolobamba South

Chapter 1

INTRODUCTION TO TREKKING IN BOLIVIA

B olivia is a landlocked country located in the heart of South America. It is about three-quarters the size of Alaska, or slightly larger than France and Spain put together.

On its western side, Bolivia shares a border with Chile and Peru. Its neighbor to the east and north is Brazil. To the south are Paraguay and Argentina. Bolivia has a population of some 7 million, and the highest percentage of indigenous Indian peoples of any country in South America. But in economic terms, it remains one of the poorest states on the continent.

However, Bolivia is a country of great natural wealth and diversity. It boasts world-class mountain ranges, barren highland plains, lush subtropical valleys, and vast expanses of tropical rain forest and grasslands. And because of the low population density and limited economic development, many of these areas are relatively untouched by human activity. Few other places can offer such varied and challenging trekking opportunities.

Trekking in the highlands involves following human- and animal-made paths and pre-Hispanic paved roads over passes up to 5,100 m (16,700 ft) high. Nighttime temperatures can drop below freezing, but days are hot and sunny and there is a danger of sunburn. The best pre-Hispanic paving is found on the trade routes which cross the Andes and link the Altiplano (the high plain stretching along western Bolivia) with the valley areas of the Yungas. Treks cross passes up to 5,000 m (16,400 ft) high before dropping, often steeply, into the warmer, more humid, and more vegetated areas below.

Although there are some well-known routes, there is a real pioneering flavor to lowland trekking in Bolivia. Some trails are rarely used by locals, let alone foreign trekkers. On some treks, you start in high mountains before descending through cloud forest and into the rain forest. Trekking in the lowlands can take you through tropical and subtropical forest as well as *pampas* grasslands and subtropical thornbush. Sometimes you follow wellworn or even pre-Hispanic tracks, but there may be whole days when you barely see a path at all and have to cut your way through with a machete.

A Trekking History

People have been "trekking" back and forth across the Andes mountain region of Bolivia, Peru, and northern Chile for centuries. Not, of course, in

BOLIVIA

POLITICAL DEPARTMENTS

1. LA PAZ
2. PANDO
3. BENI
4. SANTA CRUZ
5. COCHABAMBA
6. CHUQUISACA
7. TARIJA
8. POTOSI
9. ORURO

TREKS

1. ISLA DEL SOL
2,3,4. APOLOBAMBA
5. MAPIRI
6,21. CORDILLERA REAL
22. QUIMSA CRUZ
23. AMBORO
24,25. RURRENABAQUE AREA

Pre-Hispanic stone paving on way down to Pelechuco, Apolobamba South

search of wild and remote places, but to trade produce and to transport valuable minerals such as gold and silver. This has led to the development of a network of routes and trails across the region, linking Bolivia's Altiplano with its valleys and lowlands to the east and with Peru and Chile to the west.

The stone-paved, pre-Hispanic routes are the oldest surviving part of this network. However, it is not clear who constructed them. They are usually attributed to the Incas, who ruled what is now Bolivia during the fifteenth and sixteenth centuries from their capital of Cusco, in modern-day Peru. Paved roads were necessary for the expansionist Inca armies, enabling them to move easily around their empire—especially during the wet season.

Roads also played an important role in the Inca pacification process; once they had conquered a new area, the Incas introduced loyal Quechua communities from other parts of the empire. Since the native language in Bolivia at that time was Aymará, this explains why today there are non-contiguous Aymará- and Quechua-speaking areas. However, many historians point out that the Incas barely had time to build any roads in Bolivia, as they were only in power for about 80 years before the Spanish took over in the 1530s.

If the Incas did not build the ancient routes, it may have been their predecessors, the Aymará kings and the Tiwanacotas. The Tiwanacotas were based at Tiwanaku on the southeastern shores of Lake Titicaca, and controlled what is now Bolivia for 400 years until around 1200. However, they

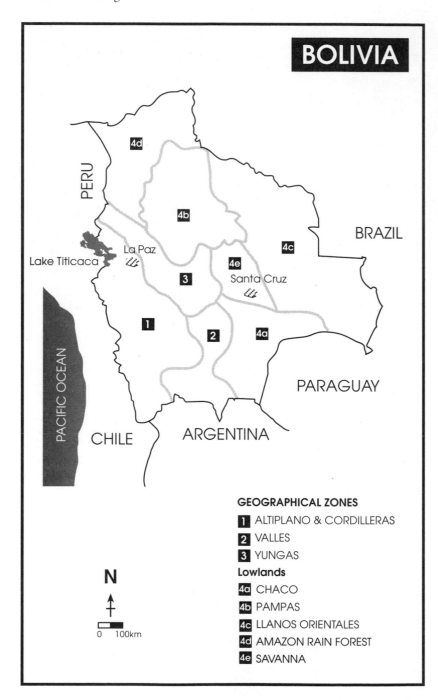

BOLIVIA

PERU

BRAZIL

Lake Titicaca

La Paz

4d

4b

4c

4e

Santa Cruz

3

1

2

4a

PACIFIC OCEAN

PARAGUAY

CHILE

ARGENTINA

GEOGRAPHICAL ZONES

1 ALTIPLANO & CORDILLERAS
2 VALLES
3 YUNGAS

Lowlands

4a CHACO
4b PAMPAS
4c LLANOS ORIENTALES
4d AMAZON RAIN FOREST
4e SAVANNA

N

0   100km

GEOLOGICAL ZONES
1 WESTERN CORDILLERA
2 ALTIPLANO
3 EASTERN CORDILLERA
4 SUB-ANDEAN ZONE
5 BENI-CHACO BASIN
6 PRE-CAMBRIAN SHIELD

BOLIVIA

N

0   100km

PERU

BRAZIL

Lake Titicaca

La Paz

Trinidad

Cochabamba

Santa Cruz

Oruro

Sucre

Potosí

Tarija

PARAGUAY

PACIFIC OCEAN

CHILE

ARGENTINA

had none of the empire-building desires of the Incas and were far less militaristic. So the Tiwanacotas would have had little reason to invest the considerable effort required to build a network of paved roads.

No matter who laid the stones, they were an impressive feat of engineering. The fact that many of the pre-Hispanic routes survive to this day testifies to the quality of their construction.

The Spanish built their own roads to transport gold and silver from

Pass and east side of Illimani near the start of the Reconquistada trail

Bolivia's mines. By far the most important mine was Potosí, which by the late sixteenth century had become the primary source of silver for the Spanish Empire. Silver mined in the Cerro Rico ("rich hill") was taken by llama train along these roads to the Chilean port of Arica or to Lima in what is now Peru, and from there to Spain.

The Spanish encouraged the miners to chew coca—it dulls feelings of tiredness and hunger—to increase their output. This led to the expansion of the road network between the Yungas coca-growing areas and the Altiplano. Tropical fruits, vegetables, cereal crops, and other agricultural products also reached the highlands along these routes.

Many of these trails are still used for trade and transport today, particularly in rural, outlying areas which have no access to motorized transport. However, modern road-building is destroying some of these trails, such as along the ancient Camino de Oro, the Gold Trail.

Season

The Bolivian trekking season runs from May to September, through the dry southern-hemisphere winter. The best and most stable weather is from June to August. Because Bolivia is in the tropics (i.e., close to the equator), there is less than 3 hours' difference between the longest and shortest days of the year—winter nights in Bolivia are 11 to 12 hours long.

For a week in August, the strong "Surazo" wind comes in from Argentina. The weather becomes less predictable, with occasional rain falling from September to December. December marks the start of the rainy season. The weather on the eastern side of the Cordilleras Real and Apolobamba gets worse earlier than on the western side, where it is possible to enjoy good weather into November. The rainy season lasts until March or April, with storms nearly every day, and many paths become streams.

Trekking Style

The issue is time versus money, as always—if you've got the money and not much time, book with a commercial trip; if it's the reverse, go to Bolivia and sort out your trekking when you arrive.

Commercial Expeditions Organized from Home

There are a number of well-established, specialized trekking companies in North America and Europe which arrange trips to Bolivia. The advantages of such treks are that everything is organized and paid for before you leave home; there is a high level of professionalism; the leader speaks your language; and there's nothing to worry about—relax, you're on vacation. The disadvantages are that, without exception, this is far more expensive than organizing a trip yourself, and they trek only the most popular routes.

Trips Organized on Arrival

There are good and bad trekking agencies in La Paz. The advantages of using agencies are that it is considerably cheaper than booking a trek before you leave home, and there is more flexibility and choice of treks. But you must find a reputable agency. For information on La Paz agencies, see "Getting Around in Bolivia" in chapter 3, Traveling in Bolivia.

Trekking Independently

Do it yourself: plan your trip at home and on arrival organize transport or whatever services you need. The advantages are that this is the cheapest option, you go where you want when you want, and you do treks not offered by any agency. The disadvantage is that it requires total self-responsibility.

Trekking for Women

Trekking alone (see below) is not advisable for anyone, but women trekking alone are asking for trouble. Even two women trekking together is no guarantee of safety. Don't do it.

Trekking Solo

This is dangerous. From a purely practical view, if you stumble and twist an ankle, you are in deep trouble if you are alone. Obviously, solo trekkers are an easier target for robbery or violence. It is not worth risking it.

Highland Trekking

Highland trekking in Bolivia follows ancient trade routes, some of them paved, some tracks, and some animal paths. Mountainous and highland areas are not covered by vegetation, so pathfinding is relatively straight-forward: you can normally see where you want to go and where the path is. However, the main problem is picking the right path; often there are many paths, which can be confusing. A well-used path is not necessarily the one you want; it could just be heading up to a currently cultivated set of fields. You can get caught by bad weather and/or poor visibility, so a compass (and the ability to use it) is essential. In most areas there are few people, so you should be capable of looking after yourself and other members of your group.

Mountaineering in Bolivia
There are almost 1,000 peaks over 5,000 m (16,000 ft) in Bolivia, some of them still unclimbed. Routes range from easy to extremely difficult, but none of them should be attempted unless you have experience in snow-, ice-, and rope-work and are properly acclimatized.

Lowland Trekking
Trekking in Bolivia's lowlands is a raw and challenging experience. Not only does it involve trails through thick jungle, but in many cases you are far removed from any kind of human habitation or assistance. Some routes have seen only a handful of foreign trekkers and others, such as the Apolo Trail, are rarely used even by locals. More exciting still, many lowland trails remain to be explored.

But don't be misled by the term "lowland." Some trails begin in high mountains, descending through luxuriant cloud forest and into tropical jungle. On some treks, you pass through dense Amazonian rain forest or subtropical jungle. In Amboró National Park, near Santa Cruz, you can experience all of these landscapes, as well as the subtropical thornbush of the Chaco, not to mention climbs of over 1,400 m (4,600 ft). From Rurrenabaque, you can try river trips into the jungle, or take jeeps into the *pampas* to see the diverse wildlife in these areas.

Admittedly, large swathes of Bolivia's lowlands are being cleared for agriculture or logged. But it is not happening on the same scale as in Brazil, and large areas remain untouched by any human activity.

This unspoiled remoteness is a special attraction of lowland trekking in Bolivia. But it is also one of its dangers. If you get into trouble, there is little chance of getting help. For many of the lowland routes described in this book, you are advised to hire a guide. Paths disappear in the dense jungle and, without a guide, you can easily become lost.

Getting to some treks and back again can be an adventure in itself due to Bolivia's often appalling roads. Some treks require several days of traveling. In the rainy season, many roads become impassable. The trails become similarly difficult, so it is best to restrict lowland trekking to the dry season, between May and mid-October.

Chapter 2

PRE-DEPARTURE PREPARATIONS

Getting to Bolivia

There are two major gateways to Bolivia: La Paz and the economic center of Santa Cruz.

Most air routes from North America to La Paz go via Miami and then on to Santa Cruz. From Europe there is a greater choice of routes via the United States or any of the major South American cities. Routes from the east, via São Paulo and Río de Janeiro in Brazil, and Buenos Aires in Argentina, often stop in Santa Cruz en route for La Paz. Those from the west, via Lima in Peru and Santiago in Chile, go to La Paz—the view of La Paz when coming down from the airport is unforgettable.

Weight allowances vary between airlines and tend to be more generous on North American airlines; stopover requirements also vary. A more expensive ticket might cost less in total than a cheaper ticket if you have to add excess baggage and stopover costs.

There is a US$20 departure tax on all international flights, payable in dollars or bolivianos at the airport. If you stay more than 3 months in Bolivia, there is an additional charge of US$30.

Visas

Tourists get a 30-day visa free of charge on entry to Bolivia. Europeans can try asking for a 90-day visa, but there is no guarantee it will be granted. If you need a longer visa, go to the immigration office on Calle Camacho corner Calle Loayza in La Paz before the 30 days are up. European Union citizens can get an extra 60 days free of charge; U.S. citizens and some others must pay US$20 for each extra 30 days.

Passports

Always carry your passport: it is a legal requirement, and you need it to claim mail from *post restante* ("general delivery"), for cashing travelers' checks, and for any other occasion when you need to prove your identity, e.g., at police and military checkpoints (see "Checkpoints, Registrations, and Charges" in "Getting Around in Bolivia" in chapter 3, Traveling in Bolivia).

Maps Outside Bolivia

Some Instituto Geográfico Militar (IGM) 1:50,000-scale maps are available in the United States and in the United Kingdom (see the list below). "A New Map of the Cordillera Real" by Liam O'Brien, scale 1:135,000, is excellent for planning trips in the Cordillera Real because it shows all the road accesses (though not all the roads shown in the area to the west of Chachacomani and Chearoco are passable). It is available direct from Liam O'Brien (see the list below) and also in La Paz. For maps that are available in Bolivia, see "Maps Available in Bolivia," in chapter 3, Traveling in Bolivia.

Note: All maps are metric. To convert meters to feet, multiply by 3.2808 (for a reasonably accurate estimate, multiply by 3 and add 10 percent). To convert feet to meters, divide by 3.2808.

Cordee, 3a DeMontfort Street, Leicester LE1 7HD, UK

Maplink, 25 East Mason Street, Department G, Santa Barbara, CA 93101, USA; telephone (805) 965-4402

Liam O'Brien, 28 Turner Terrace, Newtonville, MA 02160, USA

Omni Resources, 1004 South Mebane Street, P.O. Box 2096, Burlington, NC 27216, USA; telephone (910) 227-8300; fax (910) 227-3748

Stanfords, 12-14 Long Acre, London WC2E 9LP, UK; telephone 0171-836-1321; fax 0171-836-0189

Descending towards Sorata, Illampu Circuit

Spanish

You need some. Outside of tourist agencies and some hotels in La Paz, little English is spoken or understood. In the countryside, none is spoken at all or understood. It is a good idea to learn how to count, how to tell the time, and the days of the week in Spanish before coming to Bolivia. Get a dictionary and a phrasebook. See also "Language" in chapter 3, Traveling in Bolivia, and the appendix, Spanish for Trekkers.

Health Matters

Several months before you leave for Bolivia, contact a travel health specialist for up-to-date advice on health problems in Bolivia and vaccinations.

In the United States, call the "International Travelers Hotline," run by the Centers for Disease Control (404-332-4559). It also publishes an annual bulletin entitled "Health Information for International Travel." Your doctor may also be able to recommend travel health specialists in your area.

In the United Kingdom, contact the Nomad Travel Pharmacy (3-4 Turnpike Lane, London N8, telephone 0181-889-7014). They offer free consultations and administer vaccinations, as well as supplying the components of a medical kit. Nomad prefers people to arrange an appointment, rather than offering advice piecemeal over the phone.

At the Hospital for Tropical Diseases (0171-388-8989) in London, the Travel Clinic (0171-388-9600) runs a telephone and fax advice line covering every country in the world. They also administer vaccinations.

The Medical Advisory Services for Travellers Abroad, based in the United Kingdom, also runs an advice line, known as the Travellers Health Line (0891-224100).

There are some excellent wilderness first-aid courses available in the United States, where this form of medicine is most advanced, and also in Europe. In the United States contact the Wilderness Medical Society (P.O. Box 2462, Indianapolis, IN 46206, USA). In European countries, contact the national mountaineering organization, e.g., British Mountaineering Council, Club Alpin Français, Deutscher Alpenverein, etc.

When you get back home, have a feces and blood test to make sure you have not picked up anything you don't want living in you.

Immunizations and Prophylaxis

Bolivia is a tropical third-world country, so all appropriate immunizations should be taken. These include hepatitis A, tetanus, diphtheria, polio, typhoid, and rabies. If you plan to do just highland treks, there is no reason for worrying about lowland diseases. If you are planning on doing lowland treks below 2,000 m (6,500 ft), take these immunizations as well as those listed in the next section.

Hepatitis A: A course of injections is required, and it is possible to get 10-year protection if you have a booster one year later. Your specialist will advise.

Rabies: Although the vaccine does not give you full protection, it does allow you more time between being bitten and receiving treatment. The vaccine is administered in three doses, the second 7 days after the first and the final jab at 28 days. You can get a booster when you return to extend your protection.

Typhoid: Two vaccinations are necessary, 1 month apart, which give 3 years of protection.

Tetanus, diphtheria, and polio: Get boosters if you need them.

Cholera: A vaccine is available, but it offers minimal protection. Some health specialists suggest prophylaxis (preventive treatment) against cholera with Doxycycline. Doxycycline is also recommended by some as prophylaxis against travelers' diarrhea, and infections such as typhus. For advice on how to avoid cholera, see chapter 4, Staying Healthy in Bolivia.

Additional Immunizations and Prophylaxis for Lowland Treks

In addition to all the vaccinations listed in the previous section, you should be inoculated against yellow fever and also take prophylaxis against malaria.

Yellow fever: The vaccine confers 10 years of protection. Make sure you keep the certificate, in case border authorities demand proof that you have been vaccinated.

Malaria: Begin prophylaxis 2 weeks before entering Bolivia, and continue for 4 weeks afterward. However, be warned that no drug confers 100 percent protection, even methloquine (Lariam), and the parasite is constantly mutating. The only sure way to avoid getting malaria is to not get bitten by the *anopheles* mosquito. For precautions when you are in Bolivia, see chapter 4, Staying Healthy in Bolivia.

Malaria is caused by the blood parasite *plasmodium*, which is carried by the female *anopheles* mosquito. There are currently four strains of malaria: *Plasmodium falciparum* is the deadliest and can cause cerebral malaria; *Plasmodium malariae*; *Plasmodium vivax*; and *Plasmodium ovale*. Because of mutations, some strains are becoming increasingly resistant to antimalarial drugs such as chloroquine, and this is a problem in some parts of Bolivia. Consult specialists on the latest information and advice before you go.

Warning: Never mix methloquine with chloroquine treatments, as it can be highly poisonous. If you are tempted to take a risk and not bother with prophylactic protection, remember that cerebral malaria can be fatal.

Methloquine is controversial because of its alleged neurological side effects. In the most extreme cases, the drug has been accused of inducing severe mental illness. There have been many reports of people suffering nausea, vomiting, and weakness after beginning a prophylactic course.

Because of these alarming stories, many people refuse to take it, including some U.S. armed service personnel working in Bolivia. However, the company that manufactures methloquine claims that fewer than 1 in 10,000 suffer serious side effects. And few doubt that it is currently the most effective protection against malaria. Proponents of the drug also point out that people taking chloroquine have also suffered unpleasant side effects, especially when they have used it over a long period of time.

Consult your doctor or a malaria specialist before deciding whether to take it. Young children, people with certain medical conditions, and pregnant women should not take methloquine. Doctors advise pregnancy termination if you become pregnant while taking methloquine.

When one of the authors, Andrew North, first took methloquine, he noted, "It left me feeling cold and off-color for several days, as if I was about to suffer a bout of flu. My dreams became very strange and I woke up several times feeling nervous and anxious. However, these and other side effects disappeared within 2 weeks of starting the course." If you take methloquine and react badly, you should stop and consider avoiding the high-risk regions of the country.

Acclimatization

Landing at La Paz airport, at 4,000 m (13,100 ft), is a shock to the system. Make sure you are up to it. People with heart problems, diabetes, asthma, and other breathing problems should see a doctor before traveling to Bolivia.

The U.S. Embassy in La Paz recommends that people flying directly to the airport from sea level should take acetazolamide (Diamox) prophylactically. Acetazolamide speeds up acclimatization by acidifying the blood, which leads to an increase in breathing. It improves oxygen transport and sleep at altitude. Acetazolamide works directly to help prevent or reduce high-altitude pulmonary edema (see "Altitude Sickness" in the "Highland Trekking" section of chapter 4, Staying Healthy in Bolivia). It acts as a diuretic, so drink plenty of clear liquids (excluding alcohol). It sometimes causes a tingling sensation in the fingers and toes, and should not be taken by people with a sulfur allergy.

Physical Conditioning

You do not need to be super fit to trek, but the fitter you are, the easier the trekking will be and the more you will enjoy it. If you want to train before your trip, the best training is hill walking carrying a rucksack. Running, cycling, and swimming are all good general cardiopulmonary exercises, but they are not the same as hill walking with a rucksack.

The most common problem visiting trekkers suffer seems to be new boots. Buying a new pair of walking boots the week before you are going to live in them for 2 weeks or more is not a good idea. There is enough to deal with without blisters. If you are getting new boots, buy them several months before the trip and break them in.

Dental Precautions

Get your teeth checked before traveling. It is a waste of time having a tooth problem sorted out while on vacation, especially when it was more than likely evident 2 weeks earlier when you could visit your usual dentist.

Medical Kit

A good medical kit is essential. But don't go overboard in what you take. You cannot prepare for every eventuality. Otherwise, you might as well have an ambulance trundling along behind you. Before putting the medical kit together, decide how many people it is for. Make sure it is packed in a waterproof bag.

Many but not all of these drugs can be bought over the counter in pharmacies in Bolivia. However, you may wish to assemble your medical kit before traveling to Bolivia.

Acetazolamide: for high-altitude pulmonary edema

Dexamethasone: pills and injectable, plus 5 ml syringe and injection water (for high-altitude cerebral edema)

Painkillers: Paracetamol for headaches; Ibuprofen for sprains and muscle pain; Temgesic/Demerol for bone breaks

Antibiotics: Ciprofloxacin for general purposes and for persistent diarrhea (if symptoms persist, get specialist medical care); Tinidazole for giardiasis; Doxycycline for general purposes

Loperamide: blocking agent to deal with diarrhea or dysentery when you must travel on long journeys

Amethocaine eye drops: for relief of pain including snowblindness

Clove oil: for relief of tooth pain

Bonjela: for relief of gum pain

Oral rehydration salts: to restore mineral levels in the body after severe diarrhea or dysentery; these contain the correct balance of minerals and should be mixed with water, as directed on the packet; available from chemists in Bolivia—ask for *sales de rehidratación oral*

Space (survival) blanket

Bandages and elastic bandages: for securing large dressings

Suture strips

Adhesive bandages (plasters): a variety of different sizes to cover everything from sores and blisters to cuts; linen ones are the most durable, an important consideration for covering blisters because of the constant rubbing from boots and socks

Melolin pads: nonadherent, absorbent wound dressings for serious cuts; buy these in sealed packets and cut them to shape, securing them with micropore tape

Antiseptic cream

Micropore and zinc oxide tape

Safety pins (large): many uses, including for securing bandages, converting clothing into slings and bandages (create a triangular bandage effect by safety-pinning the victim's sleeve to the front of the shirt), and for temporary repairs of ripped clothing.

Additions to the Medical Kit for Lowland Treks

For a compact medical kit designed for two people on a 6-day trek starting in the mountains and descending to the jungle, add the following to the list in the previous section.

Large waterproof adhesive dressing: to keep a wound dry while allowing it to breathe; buy these in specialist shops

Tweezers: for pulling out ticks, among other things; stick the sharp end in a cork for traveling

Scissors: for cutting bandages and tape

Antiseptic wipes: for quick cleaning of wounds

Iodine antiseptic paint: better than cream because it does not leave a moist residue, which can attract bacteria

Syringes and needles: in case hospitals or clinics do not have clean needles

Two 5 ml syringes

Five short needles of 0.5 mm width

Five medium-length needles of 0.8 mm width

Saline drip needle

Fungicidal cream or powder: for dealing with athlete's foot and other fungal infections

Antihistamine tablets: to deal with allergic reactions, swellings, persistent itchings, severe insect bites, hay fever

Anti-inflammatories: to deal with muscle inflammations and other serious swellings

Anti-malarial tablets (see Vaccinations and Prophylaxis for Lowland Treks, above)

Equipment

You will probably assemble your equipment and clothing before you depart for Bolivia. However, if you need to obtain or replace any item while in Bolivia, the following lists, translated into Spanish, will be useful.

Clothing and Personal Equipment

Thermal top *(ropa interior termica)*

Fleece jacket *(chaqueta de frisa)*

Synthetic trousers *(pantalones sinteticas)*

Gore-Tex jacket with hood *(chaqueta de Gore-Tex con capucha)*

Boots (for lowland treks: lightweight, ankle-height, waterproof, lined with Gore-Tex) *(botines de caminar)*

Sunscreen *(crema contra el sol)*

Sunhat *(sombrero)*

Sunglasses *(gafas)*

Medical kit *(botiquín de primeros auxilios)*

75-plus-liter rucksack *(mochila)*
Head flashlight, battery *(linterna frontal y pila de repuesto)*
Three-season down sleeping bag *(saco de dormir de pluma)*
Sleeping bag liner *(saco de dormir interno)*
Sleeping mat *(aislante)*
Tent (for lowland treks: the lightest you can afford, with fine-mesh lining to keep out mosquitoes) *(carpa)*
Multifuel stove that runs on leaded or unleaded gasoline, as well as kerosene (essential; virtually impossible to find white gas, and gas canisters are rarely available outside La Paz) *(cocinilla)*
Large 975-ml (33-fl-oz) fuel bottle *(botella de combustible)*
Cooking pans, mug, spoon (pack in a compact bag) *(ollas, taza, cuchara)*
Food *(comida)*
Iodine tablets or liquid tincture for purifying water (tincture available in La Paz) *(iodo)*
Robust 1-ltr (qt) water bottle with carrying case to attach to belt *(cantimplora)*
Two 2-ltr (2-qt) water bags for backup supplies when water is scarce *(bolsas de agua de dos litros)*
Lighters *(encendedores)*
Pocket multipurpose knife *(cortapluma)*
Duct tape for temporary repairs to tents and rucksacks *(cinta de embalaje)*
Map *(mapa)*
Pocket compass with cord *(brujula)*
Whistle *(silbato)*
Money (B5, B10 denominations) *(dinero)*
Passport (legal requirement) *(pasaporte)*

Optional equipment:
Camera and spare batteries *(máquina fotográfica, pilas de repuesto)*
Film *(película)*
Notebook, pen, pencil *(libreta, bolígrafo, lapiz)*

Equipment for longer trips:
Sewing kit *(kit de costura)*
Second rucksack *(segunda mochila)*
Smaller backup fuel bottle *(botella de combustible extra)*
Book *(libro)*
Vitamin C and iron tablets *(tabletas de vitamina C y hierro)*
Waterproof stuff sacks *(bolsas impermeables)*
Spare laces *(cordones extras)*
Toothbrush, paste, soap, comb *(cepillo y pasta de dientes, jabón, peine)*

Additional Equipment for Highland Treks
Thermal top and bottom *(ropa interior termica)*
Balaclava *(pasamontaña)*

Thin synthetic socks *(calcetines delgados sinteticos)*
Thick wool socks *(calcetines gruesos de lana)*
Thin gloves *(guantes delgados)*
Inner gloves *(guantes interiores)*
Sunglasses (100 percent UV-proof) *(gafas con protección UV)*
Gore-Tex bivi bag *(bolsa de biviouac de Gore-Tex)*
Fleece trousers *(pantalones de frisa)*
Down jacket *(chaqueta de pluma)*

Additional Equipment for Lowland Treks

Clothing: Because many of the lowland treks start in mountain areas, you need two types of clothing. For higher altitudes, take a thermal top, plus a warm fleece. In the jungle, cover as much of your body as possible, while keeping your clothing loose and light. Cotton is the best material. Take two pairs of lightweight trousers; the second is to wear when your clothes get soaked.

However, there is no need to buy the latest high-tech, high-cost walking clothing. You can buy perfectly adequate lightweight trousers and shirt in La Paz. Head for Calle Sagárnaga in central La Paz, just off the Prado, where there is a succession of shops and stalls selling locally made clothes. It is also a good place for gift-shopping before you return home.

A pair of cotton trousers costs around US$4 and a long-sleeved shirt about the same. But you might have to hunt around to find the right size, especially if you are over 1.82 m (6 ft) tall. You can buy floppy hats along the street, useful for protecting against sunburn and insects falling out of trees in the jungle. You will also need:
Light cotton scarf
Waterproof bottom layer, ideally Gore-Tex
Two T-shirts: the second is to wear when your clothes get soaked
Two long-sleeved shirts: the second is to wear when your clothes get
   soaked
Equipment: Many lowland treks in this book start in the mountains, so you need some equipment for colder temperatures as well as for the jungle. Start with the basic lists at the beginning of the Equipment section, then add the items below.
Permethrin-impregnated mosquito net: optional if your tent has fine-mesh
   lining
Machete: useful for clearing vegetation which has overgrown the trail, but
   don't plan on cutting your way through the jungle
Roll of string
Insect repellent: Neat DEET (Diethyltoluamide) or equivalent, for impreg-
   nating cotton clothing; it should not be used on synthetics
Optional equipment: To avoid theft on long journeys, disguise your ruck-
sack inside a large flour sack, which you can buy from stalls in markets.
Small rucksack or daysack: for carrying food when you employ mules; you
   may be able to make do with a fanny pack

Map case with neck strap

Sunglasses

Water filter: some people prefer using pumps to tablets or tincture because of concerns about the effects of iodine; however, they are heavy in comparison and relatively slow

Cooking knife, 12 cm (5 in)

Fishing gear: monofilament line, range of hooks from size 8 to 4, a couple of floats, a few weights, and a hand-winding reel (a basic fishing kit takes up very little room and there are plenty of fishing opportunities in Bolivia's rivers; even in upland areas, there is good fishing potential—see the Camino de Oro trail; worms work fine as bait for a variety of different fish, including trout)

Sandals: to give your feet a rest from hot boots

Small padlocks: for locking up rucksack pockets and keeping out opportunistic thieves

Extra straps for attaching things to outside of rucksacks

Photography

From the cities to the mountains to the jungle, everything in Bolivia seems highly photogenic. But control your shutter mania and try to be selective about what you take. You will end up with a far more interesting collection of shots than if you just snap everything. There is nothing more boring than going through endless shots of green jungle or llamas.

Equipment

What camera equipment you bring depends entirely on what standard of pictures you want to bring back. If you are happy with color snapshots, a compact 35 mm camera, or one of the newer and smaller APS (Advanced Photographic System) models, will suffice. You can carry a compact easily on a hip belt. If you have just bought a new camera, shoot a roll of film and get it developed before traveling.

If you are aiming higher, you will need a robust 35 mm single lens reflex (SLR) camera with a selection of good quality lenses. Ideally, your SLR camera body will have the minimum of electronics because it will be less susceptible to the cold, damp, dirt, and knocks that are an inevitable part of trekking. In extreme cold, batteries often fail, so it is worth having a camera that has the capacity to work without batteries. They are more expensive, but they do exist.

For the same reasons, manual focus lenses are also preferable. But autofocus models will work fine as long as you look after them. Bring spare batteries. Remember that lithium batteries are difficult to find in Bolivia and very expensive.

For most purposes, a wide angle lens—24 mm/f2 or 35 mm/f2—and an 85 mm/f1.8 portrait lens will do. If you have space, pack a 200 mm telephoto or a zoom lens to deal with more distant subjects. Fit skylight

Illampu and Ancohuma from the path above Sorata, Illampu Circuit,
Lagunas Chillata and Glaciar

filters to the front end of your lenses for protection. Alternatively, fit warming
filters such as an 81A or 81B. If you are really serious about getting good
close-ups of birds and other wildlife, you will need to lug even more powerful lenses around, such as a 300 mm/f2.8. It is all a question of how much
weight you can bear. If you have room, pack a flash.

If you walk along with your camera dangling around your neck, it can
quickly become covered in sweat and dust. Far better to keep it in a small
shoulder bag, bringing it out when you need it. I always leave my lens caps
off so I can start photographing immediately. I use a small waterproof cycle
courier bag to carry my gear, lined with two plastic bags to give added protection from rain and dust. I find ready-made camera bags very cumber-
some, and they also tend to be an obvious attraction for thieves.

Film
It is worth packing some faster-speed films, of 200 or 400 ASA, because
light levels in the jungle, under the tree canopy, can be very low, even when
the sun is shining above. As always, however, it is a balance between image
quality and speed. If you want sharp color slides of jungle flora and fauna,
with the minimum of grain, stick to films of 100 ASA or below.

North American- and European-quality film and processing are available
in La Paz, at similar or lower prices. All types of film are available, but check

the sell-by date. It is possible to develop slides without having them mounted *(solo revellado)* for US$3, which are easy to take home and avoids the risk of carrying exposed film.

Try Agfa Center (Calle Loayza 250) and Foto Linares (Calle Loayza three doors above the Agfa Center). Foto Linares is the best place for anything out of the ordinary, e.g., slides to prints, black-and-white developing, and repairs; ask for Señor Rolando Calla, who speaks English but is only at the shop in the mornings from 10:30 A.M. to 12:30 P.M.

Techniques

The best times for taking pictures in Bolivia are during the first hours of sunlight and the final hours before sunset, which produce the most saturated colors. That does not mean you should not take pictures between these times, but the bright, tropical daytime sun can produce very washed-out results if you are not careful with exposure settings. The higher in altitude you go, the more this applies, as the atmosphere thins.

When taking pictures in bright sunlight and/or of highly reflective scenes such as snow-covered mountains, remember that cameras' internal (built-in) light meters often overcompensate and set a smaller aperture than is really warranted. The result is dark or rather muddy pictures.

To deal with this, set your camera to manual and shoot bracket exposures. This means shooting a couple of frames on a larger aperture setting than that suggested by the camera. For instance, if the camera light meter sets an aperture of f11 with a shutter speed of 1/250th of a second and you feel this may result in underexposure, shoot another frame a half stop wider at f9.5, followed by another at f8.

Under the tree canopy, the reverse can apply. Some cameras open up too much to compensate for the lower light, resulting in washed-out images. Bracketing is again the solution, except this time you experiment with smaller apertures than the meter suggests.

In the jungle, also be careful about strong light coming from behind your subject. Known as backlight, this can result in underexposure. For instance, in photographing a flower growing on a branch above you, with a fair amount of sunlight coming through the tree canopy, the camera light meter will expose for the brightest light source—the sunlight—not the flower. You can compensate for this either by taking an exposure reading for the flower or, better still, using fill-in flash. This lights up the flower, allowing the camera to choose the ideal aperture setting for the background.

When trying to photograph Bolivian people, especially women, be extremely sensitive. Many Bolivians resent tourists brandishing their cameras and snapping everything in sight. The only thing you can do is ask politely, and you may be lucky. Do not try to snatch shots. Not only is this grossly insensitive and rude, but it can evoke an angry reaction. In the end, though, it is up to your own judgment as to when it is appropriate to take pictures and how best to approach a situation you want to photograph.

Chapter 3

TRAVELING IN BOLIVIA

Language

Normally, Bolivians show great patience with foreigners trying to speak Spanish; don't be frightened, give it a try. For useful phrases and words, see Spanish for Trekkers, at the back of this book.

As with the rest of Latin America, there is no lisping as in Castilian Spanish. The Spanish language in Bolivia is, relative to other Spanish-speaking countries, spoken slowly and clearly. The main reason is that it was not until the 1970s that the majority of the Bolivian population actually spoke Spanish as a first, second, or third language: Today, Spanish is the second language of the majority of people who speak it. Only 42 percent of Bolivians speak only Spanish.

You might meet people in the *campo* (countryside) who do not speak any Spanish at all but one of the native languages. Aymará is spoken in the highland areas of the Cordilleras Real, Quimsa Cruz, and Occidental, plus the northern and central Altiplano down to Potosí. Quechua is the main language of the Cordillera Apolobamba and Cochabamba and the southern Altiplano from Potosí down. In the lowlands, there are currently forty-three other recognized native languages, the main one being Guaraní. Aymará and

Climbing up to Paso Suches on the Apolobamba North and Pelechuco to Apolo trails (Andrew North)

Quechua speakers normally count in Spanish, and place names, if your pronunciation is close enough, are the same in any language.

The term *gringo* (or *gringa* for females) is less and less often used pejoratively. *Gringo* is a nickname for any Bolivian who does not have black hair, and is a very useful term covering in one word "white-skinned citizens of the United States, Canada, Europe, Israel, South Africa, and Australia." It does not mean "white," but "white tourist" (there being few black or Asian tourists). Blacks are called *negrito/a* and Asians *morrenito/a*. These and other terms westerners might consider pejorative are not considered negative; fat people in Bolivia are often called *gordo/a* by their friends.

Local Expressions and Terms

To express the diminutive, Bolivians often add *-ito* to masculine nouns and *-ita* to feminine nouns, as in *señorita* (literally "little woman," Miss) and *cholita* (little chola, Miss). However, this is also done when it has no significance at all, e.g., *un pesito* (literally, "a little peso"), *un minutito* ("a little minute"), *ahorita* ("really now"), *pancito, cafecito,* etc.

Never use the term *indio* to describe a native person; it is an insult and was banned following the 1952 revolution. Use *boliviano* or *boliviana* in general or *campesino/a* if referring to a peasant.

Money

For the last few years, the boliviano has been constantly but slowly devaluing against the U.S. dollar—the rate normally changes by one centavo every week or so. Boliviano prices are subject to inflation, but because of devaluation prices measured in U.S. dollars stay pretty much the same. (This is why dollar prices are used throughout this book.)

Changing cash dollars to bolivianos is easy in La Paz and other major cities and tourist areas. Make sure you are getting the official rate whether you are changing on the street or in a *casa de cambio*. Always count your money in front of the money changer before walking away. There is no black market rate.

In the major cities and tourist centers, U.S. dollars are widely accepted by just about anyone for just about anything, though check the exchange rate, which will be lower than the official rate. However, even slightly damaged U.S. dollar notes are not accepted, so do not accept them yourself.

The boliviano is the only known currency backed by Scotch tape—a huge number of Bolivian notes are repaired. If you rip a note, just tape it back together. There are problems if part of the note is missing, however small and insignificant. Do not accept this sort of note; no one else will either.

Visa, Mastercard, and other credit, debit, and charge cards are rarely accepted outside expensive hotels and restaurants even when there is a sign saying "WE ACCEPT VISA/MASTERCARD." Where they are accepted, there is often a 7 percent surcharge. These cards are most useful for obtaining bolivianos directly from automatic cash dispensers in the centers of the major cities.

There is an endemic and unexplained shortage of change throughout Bolivia. The biggest currency note, B200 (US$40), is virtually unusable unless you are paying for flight tickets, or an expensive hotel or meal. On the street and in most shops, and in the entire *campo*, the B200 note is unchangeable. Do not accept it. The B100 note is difficult to break in La Paz and impossible in the countryside. This means that, before going on a trip, you should collect B5 and B10 notes, which reduce but do not eliminate your problems.

Note: Many older people refer to "pesos," which is the same as bolivianos.

Shopping

Always ask the price before buying something or getting into a taxi. By doing this you force the vendor to declare a price, which gives you the choice of accepting or refusing. However, there is widespread "tourist pricing" on the streets and in markets: vendors come up with a ridiculously high price because they know that a certain percentage of tourists will pay up.

While you can disagree with a price, refuse to pay it, or walk over to the next stall that sells exactly the same items, you can rarely haggle for anything other than tourist goods (mainly handicrafts and clothes) bought on the streets, where the starting price is often 50 percent higher than the final selling price. If you are buying more than one item, ask for a discount on the total.

Begging

You can tell when you are on a popular trail because children will run across fields to yell, *"Regálame dulces/plata/bolis"* ("give me sweets/money/ballpoint pens"). The worst areas for this are the Isla del Sol and the Río Choquekhota valley on the way up to the Takesi trail.

This is just opportunistic begging. If you give in, you are helping create a dependency culture that at present does not exist, and encouraging beggars to hassle future trekkers. A polite but firm "No" normally puts an end to such requests without any hard feelings.

You will see quite a few beggars on the streets of La Paz and there is little doubt that for some it is a profession. Many of the physically injured beggars—some quite horribly maimed—are miners, victims of dynamite accidents. Sometimes children are sent to beg by their parents to supplement the family income.

How you react to such encounters is up to you. The dilemma is the same wherever you come across beggars in less-developed countries. There is the argument that giving encourages begging, which it does. But there is an equally strong argument that you should give, because there is no social security system worth speaking of in Bolivia.

Two occupations only marginally removed from begging are lemon selling and shoe shining. Lemon sellers in their traditional *campesino* clothes tend to look completely out of place in the big city and will ask anybody to buy lemons. Shoe shine boys *(lustrabotas)* do occasionally look at your foot-wear before asking, and dirty boots are a definite target. In a couple of min-utes for US$0.10 you can have the shiniest walking boots around. The face masks are to prevent them being recognized by classmates or teachers who know they should be at school.

Food

Packaged food, including soups, powdered drinks, noodles, biscuits, and chocolate, can be bought in La Paz from shops and stalls in Calle Isaac Tamayo near the junction with *(esquina)* Calle Tumusla. Fresh food (and a lot of packaged food) can be bought at the main market around Calle Rodriguez *esquina* Calle Max Paredes. Ready pasta meals and other North American luxuries can be bought at North American prices from Zatt su-permarket in Calle Sanchez Lima corner Calle Belisario Salinas in Sopocachi. A better selection is available from Gava in Avenida Ballivian, Calacoto, in the Zona Sur and Ketal, Calle 21, San Miguel.

Outside La Paz, Santa Cruz, and Cochabamba, there is very little choice in food. The basics normally available in most medium to large villages are pasta, canned sardines and tuna, cooking oil, powdered milk, and canned tomato concentrate. If you are lucky, you might be able to get fresh bread and fruit.

Try to eat as quickly as possible after setting up camp; if you eat carbohy-drates within one hour of finishing exercise, your muscles will recover in the shortest possible time. If you don't eat within 3 hours of finishing exercise, your muscles will deteriorate. I work on a 7-day menu based on the follow-ing (translated for your dining pleasure). The claims for portion sizes on all packaged foods—especially pasta meals—should be treated with derision.

Breakfast: *(desayuno)*

instant oats *(avena instantánea)*	powdered milk *(leche en polvo)*
sugar *(azucar)*	tea/coffee *(té/café)*
cereal *(cereal)*	

Lunch: *(almuerzo)*

bread for first 4 days *(pan)*	mayonnaise *(mayonesa)*
dry biscuits thereafter *(galletas de agua)*	chocolate *(tableta de chocolate)*
	crushed peanut bar *(tableta de mani)*
tomatoes for first 2 days *(tomates)*	powdered drink *(refresco en polvo)*
avocados for first 2 days *(paltas)*	dried fruit and nuts *(fruta seca y nueces)*
cheese *(queso)*	
jam *(mermelada)*	boiled sweets *(caramelos)*
condensed milk with sugar *(manjar)*	

Dinner: *(cena)*

dried soup *(sopa de paquete)*	pasta meals *(comida lista de fideo, e.g., Insalata, Caracoquesos, Lipton)*
dried cheese tortellini *(Tortellini relleno con queso)*	

Chinese noodles (two packets/
person/meal) *(fideos chinos)*
mashed potato mix *(pure de papa)*

canned cream *(crema en lata)*
canned tomato extract *(extrato de
tomate en lata)*

Maps Available in Bolivia

The Bolivian Instituto Geográfico Militar (IGM) produces 1:50,000-scale maps for much of the country. The main exceptions are everywhere east of the Cordilleras Real and Apolobamba, the Cordillera Apolobamba itself, and the Cordillera Real between Sorata and Laguna Khara Khota.

Note that glacial retreat means that the blue ice contours on maps exaggerate the area of permanent snow and ice cover. Names are often wrong on the IGM maps and, unless they have been updated recently, many roads are missing.

IGM maps are available with 24 hours' notice from the IGM sales office in La Paz (at Oficina 5, Calle Juan XXIII 100, a dead end behind the central post office off Calle Rodriguez between Calle Murillo and Calle Linares), open Monday to Friday, 8:30 A.M. to 12:00 P.M. and 2:30 P.M. to 6:00 P.M. If you want maps immediately, go to the IGM headquarters (Estado Mayor, Avenida Bautista Saavedra, Miraflores), open Monday to Friday, 9:00 A.M. to 11:00 A.M. and 3:00 P.M. to 5:00 P.M. It is a military base and they will only let you in with your passport. If the original color map (US$7) is not available, the IGM will provide a black-and-white photocopy (US$5), which is of limited use.

"A New Map of the Cordillera Real" by Liam O'Brien, scale 1:135,000, is excellent for planning trips in the Cordillera Real because it shows all the road accesses (though not all the roads shown in the area to the west of Chachacomani and Chearoco are passable). It is available in La Paz for US$10 from various outlets, including the Club Andino Boliviano (Calle México 1648) and Los Amigos del Libro (Calle Mercado 1315).

Walter Guzmán Córdova produces 1:50,000-scale maps on glossy, tear-resistant paper to Condoriri-Negruni, Huayna Potosí, Mururata-Illimani, Sajama, and several Inca Trails (Choro, Takesi, and Yunga Cruz Trails). These are available from Los Amigos del Libro (see address above).

The German Alpine Club produces two excellent 1:50,000-scale maps, one to Illimani and the other to Ancohuma-Illampu, which are sometimes available from Los Amigos del Libro in La Paz.

Note: All maps are metric. To convert meters to feet, multiply by 3.2808 (for a reasonably accurate estimate, multiply by 3 and add 10 percent). To convert feet to meters, divide by 3.2808.

Alternative Names and Spellings

IGM maps are covered in mountains called "Cerro Illampu" and "Cerro Condoriri." There are many places called "Uma Palca," which simply means "river crossing." IGM maps sometimes give completely unused names. The O'Brien map uses the current standard Aymará spelling of names, which is

often confusing, e.g., for "Ancohuma," it uses "Janq'uma." You will dis-
cover that local peasants often have completely different names from those
used by map makers.

The hard "c" sound, as in "cold," can be spelt with "c" or "k." "Khota"
is often spelled "kkota," and O'Brien uses "q'uta." The letters "q" and
"k" appear to be interchangeable, with the current fashion being to use "k",
e.g., "Takesi" for "Taquesi." "Hui" and "wi" are also different spellings of
the same sound.

Equipment Available in Bolivia

A limited but growing amount of new gear is on sale in La Paz, including
rucksacks, fleece jackets, gas cannisters (including Epigas and camping gaz),
and headlamp batteries. Prices are high due to transport costs and import
duty, e.g., Duracell MN1203 battery for a headlamp is US$10. Condoriri
(Calle Sagárnaga 339, telephone 319369) offers the best selection.
Condoriri also does an excellent repair service for all types of clothing and
sewable gear, including zipper, strap, and buckle replacement.

The alternative is to buy second-hand gear from departing trekkers and
climbers with an airline baggage-weight problem. The best noticeboards
for buying and selling (plus finding partners for trekking or transport) are
in the Hotel Torino in Calle Socabaya, Hostal Austria in Calle Yanacocha,
and the Club Andino in Calle México.

All specialist mountaineering and trekking agencies have some gear for
hire. Colibri has the biggest selection (for the address, see La Paz Agencies, in "Getting Around in Bolivia," later in this chapter).

Fuel

Epigas and gaz cannisters are available from a number of La Paz trekking
agencies, including Condoriri. Leaded gas only is available from gas stations.
Kerosene is available from a limited number of places, as is paraffin. Meth-
ylated alcohol spirit *(alcohol potable)* is available from street stalls at the
corner of Calle Sagárnaga and Calle Illampu in La Paz and in village shops
all over the country. White gas *(gasolina blanca)* is often but not always
available from Colibri at US$5 per liter; it is also available in Santa Cruz.

Getting Around in Bolivia

Whatever form of transportation you are using, rice, flour, and sugar sacks
that are available from markets and shops make ideal rucksack protectors.
Your sack will look just like any other piece of luggage and not a tourist
sack worth stealing.

La Paz Agencies

Many agencies in La Paz offer guides, transport, cooks, and porters, as much
or as little as you want. Most trekking guides speak only Spanish, though

there a few who speak English, French, or German. If you are paying for a cook and food, ask to see the menu to make sure you like what you will be getting. There are also a number of specialist trekking and mountaineering agencies in La Paz.

Andean Summits (Calle Sagárnaga 189, Casilla 6976; telephone and fax 317497)—French and some English spoken.

Andes Expediciones (Edificio Santa Ana office 314, Plaza Alonso de Mendoza; telephone 320901, fax 392344).

Club Andino Boliviano (Calle México 1638, Casilla 1346; telephone and fax La Paz 324682)—basically a ski organization that runs the Chacaltaya ski lift and hut.

Colibri (Calle Sagárnaga 309, Casilla 7456; telephone 371936, fax 323274)—run by the very experienced Oscar Sainz, who speaks some English and fluent French.

Colonial Tours (Hostal Austria, Calle Yanacocha, Casilla 5108; telephone and fax 316073)—English-speaking.

EcoBolivia Foundation (Casilla 8505; telephone 315974, fax 325776, e-mail ECOB@megalink.com)—treks in Madidi National Park; English-speaking; owns and operates its own facilities.

Ozono (Avenida Ballivian 786, Calacoto, Casilla 7243; telephone and fax 722240, e-mail bolivia@ozono.bo)—English-speaking, run by British-born, La Paz-based guide Yossi Brain, also German and French speakers.

Refugio Huayna Potosí (Hotel Continental, Avenida Illampu 626, Casilla 731; telephone 323584, fax 378226)—run by Dr. Hugo Berrios (fluent English and French), who has done many different treks in the country.

TAWA (Calle Sagárnaga 161, Casilla 8662; telephone 325796, fax 391175)—French- and English-speaking.

Public Transportation

"The rich fly, a tiny minority own cars, and the rest of Bolivia jostles at mega bus-terminals. A huge network of risk-taking, enterprising, endlessly ingenious bus operators, whose achievement should rank among the legends of transport history, grapple with washed-out roads and icy Andean passes to keep those who must, moving between cities," says Matthew Parris writing in *The Times*, January 17, 1994.

It is possible to get within walking distance of most—but not all—of the treks by using public transportation (detailed information is included under "Start" and "Finish" for each trek).

Buses are by far the cheapest but most uncomfortable way to get around—most southern winter journeys are a dust-filled nightmare. Anyone over 172 cm (5 ft, 8 in) is likely to spend the journey jamming their kneecaps into the back of the seat in front and arrive needing a night's rest!

Outside the bigger villages and towns, public transport is normally in the back of a truck *(camión)* or pickup *(wagoneta)*, which is cheap but slow and incredibly dirty. When traveling by pickup, have warm and windproof gear with you and be prepared to get covered in dust. During the wet season, roads are often flooded or washed away and vehicles frequently get stuck in the mud, adding anything from hours to days to the journey. Only 5 percent of Bolivia's roads are asphalted and only 20 percent can be used all year.

Jeeps are by far the most expensive, but the most comfortable, means of getting around. The standard vehicle for getting around in Bolivia is the four-wheel-drive Toyota Land Cruiser, with up to nine seats and a large roof rack to take all the gear. They are usually driver-owned. If you just want transport, it is cheaper to contact a driver directly and thereby avoid paying agency fees, normally an additional 30 percent. However, an agency might have other people going to the same area during peak season and could then arrange a ride share, which would be cheaper.

There are a number of very experienced and reliable drivers, but many others will offer to take you somewhere without actually knowing where it is and then, not surprisingly, get lost. Make sure your driver knows the way. A good driver also knows where to stop for photos and to eat, and for interesting side visits. It is normal to pay drivers for the outward trip when they drop you off and for the return when you get back in La Paz.

Recommended La Paz-based drivers include Oscar Vera (telephone and fax 230453), who speaks English and some French; Vitaliano Ramos (telephone 416013); Jorge Escobari (telephone 417353); and Ramon Flores (telephone 721789).

If you try hitchhiking, most people with space will pick you up, but normally expect to be paid. However, they often give you a price: a kind of fare system exists, because many drivers do the routes on a regular basis.

Planes and Boats

In the lowlands, planes are often an attractive option, given the arduous nature of road travel, especially in the rainy season. Lloyd Aereo Boliviano (LAB) flies to most of the main towns and cities in the country. The military airline Transportes Aereos Militares (TAM) also provides cheap flights to many of the more remote locations, such as Apolo and Riberalta. Both operators have good safety records and are reliable. There is a weight limit of 20 kg (44 lbs). Both LAB and TAM have offices in most major towns and cities around Bolivia (in La Paz: LAB, telephone 353606; TAM, telephone 379285).

In the lowlands, boats are a common form of transportation and come in all shapes and sizes. For short river crossings where there are settlements, you might find a boatman, who will skillfully pole you across on his raft *(balsa)*. For longer river trips, there are motorized dugouts. There is even talk of introducing high-speed inflatables on the Río Tuichi.

Porters and Pack Animals

Porters are available for hire at the start of many treks. But on some routes, you may need to organize them in advance. Standard pay is US$10 per day.

Llamas can carry more than 20 kg (44 lbs). Mules carry 40 kg (88 lbs) each. Unless prearranged, the muleteers *(arrieros)* normally have to get the animals from their grazing fields 3 or 4 hours away.

For a 1-day trip using any of the above, it is normal to agree on a price beforehand and pay in full at the end of the day. For longer trips, things are slightly more complex. You should agree on a price for the whole trip, but you will normally then be asked for a deposit. Do not pay more than 25 percent up front. Pay the full amount on arrival. Do not submit to any requests for payment during the trip—the *arrieros* sometimes decide they have had enough. If you pay them the balance of what they are owed, they will leave. If they decide to go early, there is no reason to pay them any more than the deposit already paid.

While Bolivian guides are expected to have their own equipment, *arrieros* are not. So you will sometimes have to provide an *arriero* with a tent, a stove, and food. Make sure this is all sorted out before you leave.

Beast of burden: preparing a mule for the Camino de Oro (Andrew North)

A written contract is a useful way of making things clear to everyone. An example of wording in Spanish (translated to English, below) is as follows:

Contrato de Trabajo
Yo, _____, con C.I. _____ me comprometo a
realizar el siguiente servicio para _____ como porteador/
arriero/cocinero/ayudante/chofer
De _____ a_____, la fecha _____
De _____ a _____, la fecha _____
De _____ a _____, la fecha _____
De _____ a_____, la fecha _____
Con _____ porteador(es) @ Bolivianos _____ cada uno
Con _____ mula(s)/llama(s) @ Bolivianos _____ cada una
Con _____ cocinero(s) @ Bolivianos _____ cada uno
Con _____ ayudante(s) @ Bolivianos _____ cada uno
Con _____ coche(s)
@ US$/Bolivianos _____ para la ida y US$/Bolivianos _____ para la vuelta
Firma _____ Firma _____
_____ de _____ de 19___

Translation:
Work Contract
I, _____, I.D. card number _____ promise to carry out
the following service for _____ as porter/muleteer/cook/
helper/driver
From _____ to _____, date _____
From _____ to _____, date _____
From _____ to _____, date _____
From _____ to _____, date _____
With _____ porter(s) @ Bolivianos _____ each
With _____ mule(s)/llama(s) @ Bolivianos _____ each
With _____ cook(s) @ Bolivianos _____ each
With _____ helper(s) @ Bolivianos _____ each
With _____ car(s)
@ US$/Bolivianos _____ for the outward journey
and US$/Bolivianos _____ for the return
Signed _____ Signed _____
(Place of signing, e.g., La Paz) (day) of (month) of (year)

Asking for Directions, Travel Times, and Distances
If you need to ask directions, you are in trouble. It seems to be a Bolivian trait never to admit that they don't know the way, even if they have never heard of the place. They will almost never say "I don't know." The general

rule is: ask three people, and if two come up with the same answer, then give it a try.

Do not ask questions about directions that can be answered "Yes," because Bolivians tend to say "Yes"; e.g., ask "Where is Santa Ana?" not "Is this the road to Santa Ana?"

There is no point asking someone without a watch how long it takes to get somewhere. Another problem is that a *campesino* is able to get from A to B somewhat faster than a visiting trekker, so most time estimates are not applicable even if accurate. If someone has not been to the place in question, they will simply say "*lejos*" or "*muy lejos*" ("far" or "very far"), even if it is a couple of hours' walk away.

Distance estimates are even more inaccurate, because of variations in terrain—a 5-km (3-mi) flat section of road might take an hour, as would 1 km (0.6 mi) of steep ascent or thick vegetation.

Checkpoints, Registrations, and Charges

Police and military checkpoints are a tedious but unavoidable feature of traveling in Bolivia. They serve little purpose, but you will normally be asked to show your passport. You may also be asked for your profession and reason for visiting, and often your marital status.

Do not leave anything on the bus when you get off at police and military checkpoints. It might not be there when you get back.

Be patient and polite to the guards. Don't be overly concerned about the details they put down. If you try to ensure they are all correct, you could be there for ages. The worst part of the process is that there is a bus full of Bolivians waiting for you to hurry up and get back on the bus.

Various nonmilitary/nonpolice types often ask you to register when passing through their village. Ask to see their authority: "*Puedo ver su autorización, por favor.*" If they can't show you, there is no need to comply. There is never any legal basis for paying for the privilege of having your details written down.

On some treks, locals might try to charge you to pass through. There is no legal basis for these charges, which are mentioned in the text as appropriate. Decide your plan of action beforehand. The charges exist because foreign visitors have paid up before. You might need to feign incomprehension or show anger. Be prepared to storm off. If your Spanish is good enough you can argue.

Strikes, Demonstrations, and States of Siege

Strikes and demonstrations are a feature of Bolivian political life and you may well find your travels affected by them. Most sectors of the Bolivian work force have been provoked into protesting at one time or another. Such events, and the level of support they enjoy, provide a kind of barometer measurement of the public mood.

General strikes are called several times a year, but the level of support varies. Sometimes they collapse within a day or so. However, bus and mini-bus drivers are well organized politically and usually support strikes, so public transportation is one of the first industrial sectors affected.

Demonstrations in La Paz are common and normally involve marches through the city center. It is a dramatic sight to see thousands of *campesinos* blocking the streets and causing traffic chaos. On occasion, police react in a heavy-handed way and employ tear gas—very unpleasant in the thin atmosphere of the city. Keep out of the way if such clashes develop.

Under prolonged pressure from public protests, Bolivian governments sometimes resort to declaring a state of siege *(estado del sitio)*. Such declarations suspend a whole range of political rights. If a curfew *(toque de queda)* is introduced, it becomes illegal to be outside during certain hours (usually between midnight and 6 A.M.). You may also need written permission to leave the city during such times. If a state of siege is declared while you are in Bolivia, contact your embassy or consulate for advice.

Personal Security

You are very unlikely to face threats to your personal security, but a few simple precautions will minimize the risk even further.

Do not camp in sight of a village or settlement if at all possible. If you must camp near, camp above rather than below. If you have to camp really close, ask for permission to stay next to someone's house. All your belongings should be inside the tent; anything left outside is unlikely to be there in the morning. Do not camp on the trail unless you really have to—people use trails late at night and, more often, very early in the morning.

You might be approached by someone demanding money for any number of reasons. Keep walking, smile, and feign incomprehension. It is possible but extremely unusual that the person will become angry or violent. Think in advance about what you will do: running away is not an option unless you are prepared to dump your rucksack. If you produce your money, the whole lot might be snatched from you. Keep some stashed.

Some Bolivians get very drunk on Friday nights and during fiestas, especially in the *campo*. It can make them very confrontational, so avoid them. If you do get caught in such a situation, smile, nod, and get away.

It is impolite to refuse a drink, but it is even more impolite to spit out a drink you have just been given. Some of the local drinks are definitely an acquired taste, e.g., *chicha*, made by peasants masticating grain and then spitting it out into a vat, which starts the fermentation process. *Singani* has a similar effect to tequila on most people. It is more like a drug than a drink and gives you a hangover from hell.

Your gear is most at risk of being stolen when you are waiting for transportation, loading, and unloading. You are very unlikely to get mugged in Bolivia, but if you put something down and turn around, it might not be there when you turn back. Do not leave cameras lying around.

Have a small bag for things you need for the journey—water bottle, camera, spare jacket—so you can load your rucksack onto the top of the bus or jeep, where it is normally safe—except from the dirt and rain.

Dogs

Bolivian dogs seem to enjoy making a lot of noise if anyone passes their territory, but they rarely get physical. However, some will go for you and it is worth remembering that rabies is endemic in Bolivia; avoid being bitten at all costs.

The first rule about dogs is the oldest and the most useful: do not show fear. Whenever a dog starts barking and comes toward you, pick up a stone or any object lying around which can be thrown. This warns the dog you are armed, and dissuades most of them from coming nearer.

If the dog continues to advance, lift up your arm as though you are about to throw. The vast majority of dogs will then back off. (This works even if you don't have anything to throw.)

Should the dog still continue to advance—and especially if it draws back its top lip to bare its teeth—you have a problem. Remember, we are not talking about auntie's pooch. We are talking teeth, possibly rabies, and a lot of pain. Throw whatever you have. Do not aim to frighten the dog, aim to hit it and hurt it. Keep your eyes on it as you make your getaway—they can move very quickly if you turn around. Keep moving and keep throwing. The dog might follow for a while, but once you are off its turf, it will normally give up the chase.

If you are bitten, forget about catching the dog and taking it to be tested for rabies; where you are likely to be trekking, there will be no such centers for days. You will have to assume you have rabies and get to La Paz, Santa Cruz, or Cochabamba as quickly as possible to have the (costly) injections (assuming the dog has not done serious physical damage). In La Paz many dogs wear fluorescent tags showing they have been inoculated under that year's anti-rabies inoculation. Unfortunately, the anti-rabies program rarely reaches the countryside. If you are bitten, follow the advice in the "Rabies" section in chapter 4, Staying Healthy in Bolivia.

Environmental Impacts
Litter

There appears to be little concern about litter among Bolivians. You will frequently see people drop litter on the street or throw it out of bus windows, without a second thought. Only in the major cities is there organized rubbish collection and disposal. In smaller places, rubbish is normally dumped at the edge of the village. In such a large country, with so few people, Bolivians feel that their rubbish has little impact. They certainly find it hard to understand foreign visitors who make a fuss about the issue. Carry out your own litter, regardless of what other people do.

Road Building

Most of the trails described in this book were created by people wanting to get from point A to B on foot or with animal transport. Although many are still in use, the gradual development of Bolivia's road network is undermining their role. For outlying communities, the roads are an important change. Journey times to the major cities are no longer measured in days but in hours, providing access not just to markets but to health care.

However, as a result, fewer people are using the old trails. Some trails have been lost already; others are disappearing under choking vegetation. So it is important to cut back vegetation that obstructs the trail when you are trekking—you are helping to preserve the trail.

Another problem with building new roads is the complete lack of concern for its impact on the older trails. Two examples of this are in the Cordillera Real: much of the Zongo Valley has been destoyed by the construction of roads and dams, in the interest of providing electricity. It is no longer worth trekking in the area. In the Amaguaya valley, a road was dynamited and bulldozed through in the second half of 1995, leaving the pre-Hispanic road to collect the debris. It is no longer possible to follow the ancient trail.

Extractive Industries

There are mining operations all over Bolivia and, as with mining all over the world, they are environmentally destructive. Logging is increasing in many lowland areas, for example near Rurrenabaque, although the scale of production is currently limited by the poor infrastructure.

Subsistence Methods

Some of the subsistence practices of local communities are also responsible for environmental degradation. Burning hillsides to trap animals and dynamite fishing are commonly employed. Overhunting is a problem in many national parks and reserves. These areas are also suffering the effects of encroachment by migrant farmers (see chapter 9, Amboró National Park) or people forced to move under government resettlement programs.

Slash-and-burn agricultural techniques are used to clear large areas of forest. However, the soils are naturally very thin in rain-forest areas and are typically unable to sustain farming for more than a couple of years. Clearing large areas of forest affects the local ecosystem, reducing rain capture and therefore water flows to adjacent farming areas. *Campesinos* invariably pay little heed to arguments that conserving natural resources is in their own interest.

Ecotourism: A Possible Solution

In spite of their social and environmental costs in rural areas, activities such as logging and mining obviously provide an essential source of income for the Bolivian economy. However, some hope "ecotourism" could eventually provide an alternative source of income to logging and mining in the more ecologically sensitive areas. This might in turn encourage the Bolivian government to take more steps to protect the country's rich natural heritage. Bolivia's tourism industry is still undeveloped compared to that of other countries in the region, such as Peru, Ecuador, Chile, and Brazil. However, it is currently growing at an exponential rate, largely based on ecotourism-type activities, such as trekking in highland and lowland areas.

Ecotourism has been a buzzword in the tourism industry for several years. It can be broadly defined as tourism that is environmentally sustainable and whose focus of interest is natural landscape or wildlife. However, it raises a lot of questions: What is meant exactly by "sustainable?" Is this just another example of opportunists jumping on the ecological bandwagon, while paying lip service to environmental concerns? Is a true ecotourist actually an armchair traveler, searching for new experiences in books and films rather than consuming resources by traveling around the world?

Whatever the answers to such questions, it is imperative that, at this early stage of ecotourism's development, proper attempts are made to ensure the industry really is sustainable. Bolivia has the chance to learn from the mistakes countries such as Nepal are currently trying to rectify, i.e., overuse and exploitation of resources by the tourism industry. Opportunities include involving local communities in planning and decision making, conducting careful estimates of the carrying capacities of national parks, and the introduction and enforcement of environmental laws and conservation policies.

But for any conservation policy to be sustainable, it requires significant changes in human attitudes (those of both locals and outsiders) through education and general awareness. At the same time, other economic alternatives need to be provided, such as ecotourism and sustainable harvesting techniques. There also needs to be a firm scientific "backup" which can monitor, protect, and breed species. Finally, tighter controls on the export of flora and fauna are needed.

There are several encouraging signs that such ideals are being taken seriously in Bolivia. One independent group of tour operators has formed an organization—Associación Boliviano de Ecoturismo (ABET)—specifically to address ecotourism issues. They are currently working on a trial eco-village with the North American charity Conservation International at Chalalan, near Rurrenabaque (see chapter 10, Rurrenabaque and the Western Amazon Basin). If you want more information, write to some of the organizations listed in the appendix, Contacts.

Finally, remember that, although you are making a valuable contribution to Bolivia's economy, you are also capable of leaving long-term environmental and social scars.

Chapter 4

STAYING HEALTHY IN BOLIVIA

Research shows that, for travelers anywhere in the world, accidents involving cars or falls are by far and away the most common cause of death. Violence comes second, infectious disease third, and natural causes fourth.

Acclimatization

Acclimatization is necessary whether you are going to trek in the highlands or the lowlands. Bolivia is very different from home in terms of altitude or heat and humidity, unless you live 4,000 m (13,100 ft) up a mountain or in a jungle. Whether you are going high or low, give your body time to adjust. Be sure to read the "Acclimatization" section of "Health Matters" in chapter 2, Pre-departure Preparations, and the information on page 48 of this chapter.

Most people feel ill on arrival in La Paz. The city is at 3,100 m to 4,100 m (10,200 to 13,400 ft), depending on where you are; the center is at 3,600 m (11,800 ft). When you arrive, your body must adjust to the lower air pressure, which means you must breathe 50 percent more often than at sea level to get the same amount of oxygen into your blood. Full acclimatization to the height of La Paz involves increasing your red blood cell count by 50 percent and takes about 5 months. However, a week at the height of La Paz or the Altiplano is normallly sufficient before doing a trek that crosses passes over 5,000 m (16,000 ft) high.

Some new arrivals collapse while just carrying their luggage from the arrivals lounge at La Paz airport. Common symptoms of what is mild altitude sickness include breathlessness, racing pulse, lethargy, tiredness, inability to sleep, loss of appetite, headache, and dehydration. These will normally last for a couple of days. No one knows for sure what causes altitude sickness, but the answer seems to be to take it really easy when you arrive. People who rush their acclimatization invariably regret it later.

Do nothing on the first day in La Paz apart from lying down and letting your body adapt. Day 2 can be spent moving slowly around or getting a bus or jeep out to somewhere like Tiwanaku or Copacabana for a bit of sightseeing. Spend the rest of your first week in Bolivia getting mild or moderate exercise without gaining altitude; this can be done by trekking on the Isla del Sol or visiting the Salar de Uyuni. Most but not all trekkers will then be ready to go.

Nonetheless, it is still possible to get altitude sickness if you ascend too

Illimani from the southwest, Cohoni Loop

fast. This cannot be predicted; different individuals react in different ways and at different rates to going high. Here are some things you can do to help the acclimatization process.

Drink much more water than you would at sea level. Because you will be breathing air that is drier than you may be used to, you lose a lot of water. Bottled mineral water is widely available in La Paz. At 5,000 m (16,000 ft), you need more than five liters (five quarts) a day. Check the color of your urine; specialists say it should be "gin clear"—the more yellow the urine, the more dehydrated you are. You should also eat light meals high in carbohydrates and low in fat.

Note: There is no medical evidence that "Sorojchi" pills, on sale in La Paz and given out by some of the hotels, have any impact on altitude sickness. Similarly, there is no medical evidence that the traditional coca tea helps beyond being another excuse for consuming liquids and a very mild painkiller.

Food Poisoning and Gut Infections

The most commonly occuring problem for visitors to Bolivia—as with any third-world country—is gut infections. They are mostly caused by ingesting food or water which has been contaminated with sewage effluent or other sources of feces. Diarrhea is the most common gut ailment, but they also include infections such as dysentery and giardiasis, as well as larval tapeworms.

Gut infections can be avoided by taking simple precautions: Do not eat salad unless you know it has been prepared with the tourist stomach in mind, i.e., washed in treated water. (The major offender in Bolivia appears to be lettuce, which picks up more water than other vegetables. Also, do not eat raw mushrooms unless you want to be really ill.) Only eat cooked vegetables; only eat fruit you peel yourself; do not eat ice cream; and do not eat raw fish dishes *(ceviche)*. Wash your hands after going to the toilet. Treat all water other than bottled mineral water before drinking it.

Street food is not necessarily contaminated; yes, hygiene standards are not what they might be. But food sold in street stalls is rarely kept overnight. Normally they stay open until everything is sold.

If you get diarrhea, drink plenty of fluids and oral rehydration salts *(sales de rehidratación oral)*. If it persists for more than a couple of days, take a general antibiotic such as Ciprofloxacin. Do not take Loperamide, which stops your digestive system from working—it traps the bug in your system—unless you have started taking antibiotics or really have to take that bus or plane.

Giardiasis

A more unpleasant form of diarrhea is giardiasis, which is caused by ingesting the protozoa *Giardia lamblia,* often in contaminated water. It can be picked up anywhere animals are present (which often pollute water sources). Remember, llamas are quite happy up to 5,000 m (16,000 ft). The main indicator of giardiasis is diarrhea together with a huge and painful buildup of gas in the stomach and intestines and "farting through your mouth."

To avoid giardiasis, use iodine-based water purification tablets or tincture, or a filter pump, to treat all water while out trekking. Tincture of iodine works better than pills in the cold, and 30 ml bottles can be bought from pharmacies in La Paz (ask for *iodo)*.

The manufacturers of iodine-based purification tablets state that the pills should not be used on a "continuous" basis, but fail to define what this means (and fail to reply to letters asking them for this information). The situation is not clear, but on balance it appears to be better to take iodine than risk giardiasis.

If you get giardiasis, take Tinidazole or Metronidazole antibiotics. Do not ignore it; the symptoms might appear to go away by themselves, but the bug is capable of moving to your liver. This is serious and you need to see a specialist.

If you don't like the taste of iodine, add vitamin C powder or a powdered drink *after* the iodine has had its effect. If you add it at the same time, the iodine is deactivated. Note: If you add iodine-treated water to starchy water such as pasta or potato cooking water, it will initially go blue.

Dysentery

If you start getting bloody diarrhea or diarrhea with pus, coupled with stomach cramping and fever, you might have bacterial dysentery. This is more serious than diarrhea and is caused by the *Shingella* bacterium. Like diarrhea, dysentery starts abruptly, but the symptoms can last much longer. Treat it with a week-long course of Ciprofloxacin.

Long-term travelers might catch the amoebic form of dysentery, which is caused by a waterborne protozoa known as *Endamoeba histolytica*. Initially, it may seem like normal diarrhea, but then chronic diarrhea sets in, forcing you to make frequent charges to the toilet, but producing very little feces. Sometimes blood and pus are present and it can be very painful. Flagyl and Tinidazole are recommended as antibiotic treatments. As with diarrhea, keep drinking plenty of fluids. Take oral rehydration salts to maintain your body's mineral levels. It is best to consult a doctor if you think you have amoebic dysentery.

Cholera

It is possible to get cholera in any built-up area in Bolivia. Cholera is transmitted by contaminated food and water and is particularly associated with poor wastewater treatment. Guard against it by being careful about what you eat and drink. And wash your hands after visiting the toilet.

Take the same precautions as above for diarrhea to minimize the risk. Occasionally there are cholera outbreaks, during which you should avoid all uncooked food (especially the raw fish dish *ceviche*). Cholera leads to massive dehydration and death.

Rabies

The rabies virus attacks the brain and is fatal if untreated. It is transmitted in the saliva of infected animals. Dogs, bats, rodents, and other small animals throughout Bolivia carry the rabies virus. Vampire bats, which are found in the Amazon basin, are notorious carriers, so make sure your body is fully covered if you are camping in this region.

Consider yourself at risk of developing the disease if you are bitten, scratched, or even licked by any animal in the country. Should this happen, do the following immediately, whether or not you have had the rabies vaccine: scrub the bite for at least 5 minutes under running water, with soap, then treat with a disinfectant such as iodine. Research shows that this reduces the chances of contracting rabies by 90 percent. Then get an anti-rabies injection as soon as possible. The best hospitals are in La Paz, Santa Cruz, and Cochabamba.

Accidents

You're on your own. There is no formal rescue service in Bolivia. In the words of 3-year resident Liam O'Brien, "If you break a leg, learn how to hop." Transport is so poor that by the time anyone who isn't already in the vicinity gets to you, it's probably too late. There are few helicopters. If you can get access to a telephone, phone your embassy or consulate. Insurance is expensive but essential for air-evacuation home; medical care is limited in Bolivia and any serious injuries should be treated in North America or Europe.

Medical Care in Bolivia

If you need medical treatment while in Bolivia, contact your embassy or consulate, which can provide you with the names and telephone numbers of doctors, dentists, and specialists who speak your language. There are a number of very good U.S.- and European-trained medics in La Paz and Santa Cruz.

Health Hazards During Highland Treks

The Bolivian Andes are considerably higher than the Rockies or the Alps, and acclimatization is essential before doing any of the high-altitude treks. Fitness is no substitute for acclimatization; indeed, fit young men appear to have more problems than other people.

Altitude Sickness

Two forms of altitude sickness are fatal if unrecognised and untreated. In the case of either, if the symptoms are severe, the victim should be taken to lower altitudes immediately, even if it is in the middle of the night: it is easier to help an ill person down than to carry an unconscious body.

High-altitude pulmonary edema (HAPE): This occurs when the blood-gas barrier in the lungs starts breaking up due to the difference in pressure between the pulmonary artery and the air inside the lungs. If untreated, the victim will drown. Symptoms include pink, frothy sputum; blue lips; severe breathlessness; and gargling in the lungs. Treatment is to descend and to take acetazolamide, per prescription instructions.

High-altitude cerebral edema (HACE): This is caused by the brain swelling up and crushing against the skull. If untreated, it leads to brain hemorrhage, coma, and death. Symptoms include severe headache, vomiting, loss of balance, disorientation, vision problems, incoherent speech, behavioral changes, and coma. Treatment is to descend immediately to lower altitudes. Dexamethasone (Decadron) is a steroid that works directly to reduce the size of the brain. If someone is in a coma, it is necessary to inject them in the upper outer quadrant of the buttock with 8 g dexamethasone phosphate in 2 ml. If the victim merely has a debilitating headache, give them 2 mg dexamethasone pills, four immediately in an emergency, then one four times a day while descending to a lower altitude.

Sleep Disturbances

A common occurrence during sleep at high altitude is periodic (Cheyne-Stokes) breathing, in which the sleeper stops breathing during every cycle. You sleep poorly at high altitude, with more wakeful periods and less REM (dream-state) sleep. The more frequent wakenings lead to people waking up in the middle of a dream. Consequently, dreams often seem more vivid than at sea level.

Overexposure to Sunlight

Ultraviolet light at high altitude is very, very strong. Without proper eye protection, it is possible to get snowblindness after as little as 15 minutes above 5,000 m (16,000 ft). It does not matter if it is sunny or cloudy. In fact, more UV light is reflected on cloudy days. Snowblindness is not normally apparent until the night after the damage has been done. The pain has been described as like having acid or boiling water poured into your eyes. The next day, the victim often cannot see and has to be led. Amethocaine eye drops help relieve the pain. Snowblindness counts as a permanent eye injury—part of the retina is burnt out—which means victims are more susceptible in the future. Wear sunglasses that give 100 percent protection against UV light.

Sunburn is a serious business at high altitude and happens even on completely overcast days. A hat is essential to avoid sunstroke. A high sunscreen protection factor (SPF) suntan lotion should be used on all exposed skin, with sunblock on the lips and nose.

Hypothermia

Excess heat loss, above what the body can replace—hypothermia—is a result of four factors: convection by wind or water, conduction through direct contact with a colder surface or medium, loss of heat by evaporation of sweat or water from the body's surface, and radiation of body heat to the surrounding environment. Hypothermia typically occurs when people get tired, wet, and cold.

When the body loses more heat than it can generate, this leads to a fall in the core body temperature from the normal 37.5°C (99.5°F) to 35°C (95°F or less). The only accurate temperature reading it is possible to take in the field is rectal, and this is rarely practical if the victim is already cold. Therefore, it is important that all members of a group can recognize the symptoms of hypothermia; the victim will not. Symptoms include loss of judgment, disorientation, uncontrollable shivering, slurred speech, inability to walk straight, uncooperativeness, apathy, end of shivering, and unconsciousness.

When hypothermia is recognized, further heat loss must be stopped. Find shelter immediately (put up the tent); get wet clothes off and dry clothes on the victim while insulating him or her from the ground. It is important to maintain the victim's hydration (especially at high altitudes) and give high-energy food and drinks.

The old advice is to get into a sleeping bag with the victim. But this is currently under debate in medical circles; as some believe it may stop the victim's shivering, which is the most effective way of rewarming in the field. The amount of heat transmitted from body to body is pretty minimal, and certainly a lot less than the victim will generate by shivering. Studies show that even if all the heat generated by the rescuer were transmitted to the victim, it would be insufficient.

Chemical heating pads are heavy and expensive, and will not do more than rewarm cold hands or feet. There is no evidence they will rewarm a hypothermic victim, and they might stop shivering. Airway gas warming apparatus is the most effective way of rewarming, but simply is not practical for the average trekker to carry.

If the victim is unconscious from hypothermia (e.g., after immersion in cold water or snow), it is extremely difficult to do anything at all. The standard medical advice is that someone is not cold and dead until they have been warm and dead (i.e., they have been found cold and unconscious and have been rewarmed). However, in the field, days from a hospital, rewarming is difficult at best, and might lead to potentially fatal ventricular fibrillation.

Hypothermia is completely avoidable. Hence, the best cure is prevention. Wear a hat and have a fleece and waterproof/windproof jacket with you; do not have all your spare clothes in a pack on a mule. Pack all spare clothing and your sleeping bag inside waterproof bags inside your rucksack.

Health Hazards During Lowland Treks

With sensible precautions and common-sense behavior, the risks of jungle trekking can be kept to the minimum. When you return from your jungle trekking trip, it is a good idea to have a checkup with a tropical diseases specialist, just in case any nasties have penetrated your system.

Below is a list of common ailments from which trekkers in lowland areas might suffer and for which they can treat themselves. This list cannot cover every possible condition, and cannot advise on treating serious illnesses. In addition to "Further Reading" at the back of this book, see "Additional Immunizations and Prophylaxis for Lowland Treks" in the "Health Matters " section of chapter 2, Pre-departure Preparations.

Malaria

There is a risk of contracting malaria in all areas of the country below 2,500 m (8,200 ft). If you are staying above these altitudes, the threat is negligible. Experts divide up the risk into three different regions. (For precautions to take before you leave for Bolivia, see "Vaccinations and Prophylaxis for Lowland Trekking" in the "Health Matters" section of chapter 2, Predeparture Preparations.)

Border of Brazil: *P. falciparum*; high risk. The potentially fatal *falciparum* strain exists in this jungle region, and there is widespread resistance to chloroquine. If you visit this region, experts advise prophylaxis with the more powerful drug methloquine, also known as Lariam. It is taken weekly and is only available with a doctor's prescription.

Beni and Pando Departments: Moderate risk. Chloroquine and proguanil prophylaxis is recommended as a minimum. But take methloquine for extra protection.

Other rural areas at less than 2,500 m (8,200 ft): *P. vivax*; low risk. Chloroquine and proguanil are recommended.

The only way to be sure of avoiding malaria is to prevent being bitten by the *anopheles* mosquito. When you are in Bolivia, wear long-sleeved clothing dawn to dusk and use insect repellents. A fully lined tent and/or a robust, permethrin-impregnated mosquito net is essential.

For soaking one shirt, manufacturers recommend a solution of 25 ml neat DEET to 200 ml water. That is equivalent to about 5 tsp DEET to ½ pt water. Mix well, because DEET is insoluble in water. Hang the shirt to dry after soaking, and store in a sealed bag. For added protection, wear ankle, wrist, and head bands impregnated with DEET. Soak them in about 4 ml (slightly less than 1 tsp or 0.1 fl oz) DEET. You can also apply it neat on skin, but sweat will gradually wash it off.

Some people find using DEET too much hassle and make do with insect repellent gel. This comes in tubes and you can quickly smear it over hands and face when the swarms descend. Even if you use DEET, pack some gel as backup.

Blisters

Most trekkers suffer blisters, however well-fitting their boots. It is best to cover them with adhesive bandages (Band-Aids, or plasters) before they rub open and become infected. But change the bandages regularly because they get damp with sweat, which slows the healing of the wound and invites infection. If your feet get wet as well, dry them thoroughly as soon as possible, and dust with talcum powder. It may sound like a bit of a chore, but damp blisters against wet socks rub open much more quickly, leading to painful infections.

Athlete's Foot

If you allow your feet to stay damp and sweaty for long periods without drying and airing them, you can develop this unpleasant fungal infection. Rather than dealing with it once it has taken hold, take precautions. Shake talc into your socks every morning, and dry wet feet as soon as possible. If you do get athlete's foot, apply anti-fungal powder to the infected areas.

Sores and Skin Infections

Bacteria thrive in the moist conditions of the jungle and can easily infect the smallest sore or cut. Wash them with soap and water or an antiseptic wipe. If necessary, apply a plaster, but change it if it becomes damp, because this will encourage bacterial growth. If infection does develop and the wound becomes tender and inflamed, take a general-purpose antibiotic such as Ciprofloxacin. But exercise care in taking these drugs because indiscriminate use allows bacteria to build up immunity.

Heat Complaints

The longer you spend in jungle areas, the more you will become acclimatized to the heat. The body is much better at losing heat than retaining it, so it acclimatizes to extremes of heat more rapidly than to cold. But never underestimate the danger of hot temperatures. Maintain a constant intake of fluids. Rest regularly when you are trekking in very hot temperatures, perhaps taking a siesta in the shade during the hot midday hours. For more detailed information, consult *Practical Guidelines for Wilderness Emergency Care* by the Wilderness Medical Society (see "Further Reading" at the back of this book), from which some of the following information is taken.

Heat cramps: These are muscle spasms caused by overwork in hot temperatures and inadequate consumption of fluids, resulting in electrolyte depletion. They normally occur in heavily exercised muscle groups such as the legs. If you suffer, the best treatment is to rest and drink fluids with added salt. Taking extra salt each day helps to prevent heat cramps.

Heat rash: This is caused by excessive sweat trapped under the skin and is also known as prickly heat. Sweat glands become blocked often because clothing is too tight against the skin, and the accumulated sweat is forced into adjacent tissue, leading to inflammation. Tightly fastened padded rucksack hip belts are a common cause. The skin underneath cannot breathe and, as you walk, the belt rubs and irritates. Sometimes the inflamed skin can be broken open, leading to infection. If this happens, dab with iodine solution and cover it with an absorbent pad. Keep the clothing around it as loose as possible.

Heat syncopes or faints: This is a temporary loss of consciousness in hot temperatures. It tends to occur after strenuous exercise, but people normally regain consciousness quickly. Again, rest is the best treatment.

Heat exhaustion: Heat exhaustion occurs when the body's salt and/or water levels drop too low. Symptoms include weakness, lethargy, headaches, mild confusion, nausea, and rapid pulse. Sufferers should rest in a cool area and drink cool, lightly salted water or an oral rehydration solution. Cooling the skin by fanning or wetting can also help. Full recovery can take more than 24 hours.

Heat stroke: This is a serious medical emergency that occurs when the body's core temperature rises too high, above 40.5°C (105°F), causing damage to the renal, hepatic, and nervous systems. People who are overweight, elderly, or suffering from other diseases are the most susceptible. But unfit and unacclimatized trekkers can be at risk too. Disorientation, unusual behavior, ataxia (loss of control of bodily functions), rapid pulse, and hot, red skin are preliminary symptoms, followed by convulsions and collapse. The death rate for heat stroke victims is high, so rapid cooling and, if possible, immediate evacuation are essential. Remove excess clothing and get the patient into shade. Cool with water and rapid fanning. Massage the patient's extremities to move cooler peripheral blood to the core of the body. If available, apply ice packs to the neck, armpits, and groin.

Ticks

Ticks transmit several unpleasant diseases to humans, including typhus, and are found throughout the lowland areas of Bolivia. The precautions against them are the same as for other insects: long-sleeved clothing covering the limbs, and regular application of insect repellent. Also check yourself and fellow trekkers regularly for ticks. Light-colored clothing helps, because it is easier to see the little nasties.

If you do find a tick embedded in your skin, you might not have been infected, because transmission is often delayed. However, the tick should be removed as soon as possible. Unfortunately, there is no foolproof method for this. If you have discovered the tick before it is deeply imbedded, and if you have a pair of tweezers, gently grasp the beastie as close as possible to the point of attachment and pull it out very carefully. A bit of skin may come off with the tick, but that normally means it has been successfully removed. If its mouth parts have been left behind, try to pry them out with a needle. Note that removing the tick with tweezers is often not recommended, because leaving part of it is sure to cause infection. An alternative is to suffocate the tick by covering it with an oil, such as kerosene, so that it will disengage itself and be easy to remove. Afterward, wash the wound with soap and water or an antiseptic wipe, and cover with a bandage.

Rare Medical Problems and Diseases

Snake bites: The jungle conjures up visions of serpents and vipers just waiting to pounce. There are a couple of venomous snakes in the Bolivian jungle, such as the bushmaster and the coral snake. But the reality is that your chances of seeing any snake, let alone being bitten by one, are very small. They are shy and retiring creatures and will slither quietly away when they sense the approaching thump of a trekker's boots.

Only if they are surprised and cornered are snakes likely to bite. Even then, fatal bites are rare. Poisonous snakes often fail to deliver their full quota of venom when they strike. But take care not to plunge your hands into rock holes, or any other potential hiding place for snakes.

If you do get bitten, forget about sucking out the venom. And don't bother with a snake bite kit. Unless you have specialist training, you can do more harm to yourself than the original bite. Most snake experts and travel health specialists now advise against them.

The best procedure is to wash the wound carefully to clean off any sprayed venom that might subsequently enter it, and then bandage as much of the affected limb as possible. The bandage should be wrapped tightly enough to restrict, but not cut off, the blood flow. If possible, keep the bitten area lower than the heart. Then get the victim to a hospital.

Leishmaniasis: Villagers living in both upland and lowland areas can suffer from Leishmaniasis, which is transmitted by bites from the sandfly. The less serious form manifests itself as ulcers around the bite sites, but there is another strain which attacks the mucous membranes in the face.

Travelers rarely contract the disease, but seek medical attention if you suspect it. As always with insect-delivered infections, the best treatment is avoiding the bites, which means covering your limbs and using DEET or other insect repellents.

Dengue fever: Found throughout the lowland areas of Bolivia, dengue fever is a virus affecting joints, muscles, and blood vessels. It is transmitted by the bite of the *Aedes* mosquito and is also known as "Break Bone Fever." There is no treatment, so avoid being bitten. Follow the usual rules on covering up and applying insect repellent.

Chagas: This fatal disease is an old travelers' scare story, but the risk of contracting it is very small. Chagas causes progressive constriction of the blood vessels over a period of years and eventually leads to heart attacks and death. There is no cure. It is caused by a parasite that lives in the feces of the Vinchuca beetle, also known as the "Assassin Bug." The beetle lives in lowland areas, typically in mud brick and thatch huts, and transmits the parasite through its nasty bite.

If you do sleep in mud brick and thatch huts, make sure you use a mosquito net. Should you be bitten by the beetle, wash the wound carefully and seek medical attention urgently. Don't scratch, as this could rub the parasite into your blood.

Hemorrhagic fever: There have been reports of people contracting hemorrhagic fever in lowland jungle areas of Bolivia. The disease has similarities with the Ebola virus found in Africa and is transmitted by mosquitoes. Early indicators include chills, fatigue, and other flulike symptoms, followed by hemorrhaging of the capillaries. If you think you or any other member of your group has got it, get to a hospital.

A Note About Safety

Safety is an important concern in all outdoor activities. No guidebook can alert you to every hazard or anticipate the limitations of every reader. Therefore, the descriptions of roads, trails, routes, and natural features in this book are not representations that a particular place or excursion will be safe for your party. When you follow any of the routes described in this book, you assume responsibility for your own safety. Under normal conditions, such excursions require the usual attention to traffic, road and trail conditions, weather, terrain, the capabilities of your party, and other factors. Keeping informed on current conditions and exercising common sense are the keys to a safe, enjoyable outing.

Political conditions may add to the risks of travel in Bolivia in ways that this book cannot predict. When you travel, you assume this risk, and should keep informed of political developments that may make safe travel difficult or impossible.

—*The Mountaineers*

Opposite: *Illimani from the southwest, Cohoni Loop*

SECTION II
TREKS

Using the Trek Descriptions

The start and end point of each trek is listed below the title, followed by the number of days required. The next few paragraphs give an overview of the trek.

Start and Finish

The information given next is normally the nearest village to the start and/or end of the trek, plus information on accommodations, supplies, and services available at those locations.

The best-known details about transportation are given. Note that regular departure times for public transportation are often changed to take into account national, regional, and local fiestas, strikes, etc. Check before traveling. Travel times are approximate and dependent on the state of the road, vehicle, and driver.

Itinerary

This is an overview of suggested aims for each day of the trek. However, possible camping places are also mentioned in the trek description, so it is not essential to meet each day's target destination.

Maps

Available maps are listed in order of usefulness.

Other Trekking Possibilities

Here, other treks that link in to either the start or end of the trek are mentioned, as well as possible side trips.

Route Description

"Left" and "right" refer to the way you are looking as you trek in the direction the trek is described.

Travel times, indicated in bold, are for trekking without any breaks. Where possible, travel times with mules have been used. It is a good idea to take a 10-minute break every hour, or 5 minutes every ½ hour, when it is steep or hard going.

Recommended campsites are flat and dry, and have clear running water nearby. Ideally, campsites are a good distance from any settlement or habitation. However, on lowland treks there is often less choice. Good camping places are mentioned in the text as they come up.

Chapter 5

LAKE TITICACA

Walking along the edge of the cobalt-blue Lake Titicaca, it is difficult to believe that the lake is 3,810 m (12,500 ft) above sea level—until you look east and see the snowcapped peaks of the Cordillera Real. A bizarre experience is stopping to fill your water bottle while going along a sandy beach—the water is fresh.

1. Isla del Sol
Copacabana to Isla del Sol
(1–3 days)

This is a beautiful location for easy trekking. The island is held to be the birthplace of the sun, the moon, and the first Inca. All sorts of legends and superstitions are associated with the area. For instance, the god Thunupa rebelled against the first Inca. Thunupa was condemned to death here and

Chincana ruins, Isla del Sol

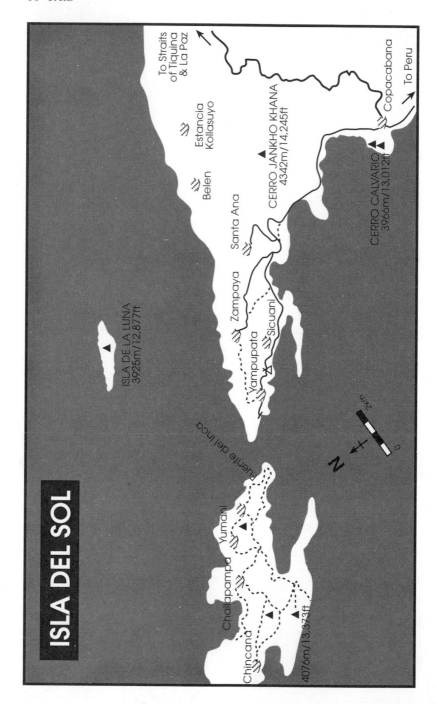

ISLA DEL SOL

Isla de la Luna 3925m/12,877ft

Challapampa

Chincana

Yumani

4076m/13,373ft

Puente del Inca

Estancia Kollasuyo

To Straits of Tiquina & La Paz

Belen

Santa Ana

Zampaya

Sicuani

Yampupata

Cerro Jankho Khana 4342m/14,245ft

Copacabana

To Peru

Cerro Calvario 3966m/13,012ft

N

2km

tied to a raft which was sent across the lake to crash against the rocks. But the rocks opened, allowing Thunupa to escape along what is now the Río Desaguadero, the lake's main outlet. There are stories of an underground tunnel from the island direct to Machu Picchu in Peru. Off the northern end of the island there are underwater ruins which are thought to be Incan.

Be warned: begging—especially by children—on the Isla del Sol is widespread.

Start and Finish

Copacabana is a beautiful lakeside town with an ornate church of great religious significance to Bolivian Catholics. Around Easter (and also during the Copacabana fiesta August 5–8), thousands of pilgrims make the journey to Copacabana—some of them walking across the Altiplano from La Paz—to pay their respects to the Dark Virgin of the Lake. At these times, you may find that all transportation and lodgings are full. For places to stay, check out Hotel Emperador and La Cupula (an excellent place to eat). Most restaurants serve trout fresh from the lake, and fresh bread is available.

To reach Copacabana from La Paz, daily buses leave from Cementerio (US$2.25). Get off at the Straits of Tiquina near the Bolivian navy base. From here, you must get a launch (US$0.20) to the other side, where you rejoin the bus, which has been taken across by pontoon; total journey time is about 4½ hours. If you travel to Copacabana on a Friday, buy a ticket in advance; do the same if coming back to La Paz on a Sunday. Conversely, during the week, buses are often canceled because there are not enough passengers. Buses to La Paz leave several times daily from the main square (US$2.25, 4½ hours journey time).

Itinerary

Day 1, to Yampupata and the Isla del Sol. Day 2, exploring the Isla del Sol. (You could spend longer on the island if you wanted.) Day 3, back to Copacabana.

Maps

IGM Copacabana 5745 I.

Other Trekking Possibilities

You can start the trek from the Straits of Tiquina and follow a pre-Hispanic road through Parquipujio, Chisi (which has some ancient ruins), the stone village of Zampaya, and other villages to reach Yampupata. This trek (5 days total) gives fantastic views of the Cordillera Real across the lake. From the Isla del Sol, follow the coastal road to Copacabana.

Alternatively, hire a boat from Copacabana to the island.

Route Description

It is 17 km (11 mi) along the west side of the peninsula from Copacabana to Yampupata. Walk out of Copacabana along the lakeside road, which is rarely used by vehicles. After **2½ hours,** cross the stream below a grotto and then follow a short paved section of pre-Hispanic path, which rejoins the road. In another **30 minutes,** reach the very strung-out village of Sicuani. Camping is possible 1 hour beyond Sicuani where there is an *alojamiento.* Alternatively, continue to the fishing village of Yampupata in **another hour**.

Take a motor launch from Yampupata to Fuente del Inca (also known as Las Escaleras, "the Steps") on the southern end of the Isla del Sol (US$8). A rowboat (US$3, or US$1 per person) takes 40 minutes. Arrange the time and day of your return.

The traditional reed boats still exist, but just for the tourists: a reed boat takes 3 days to build and lasts 7 to 8 months; a wooden boat takes longer to build but lasts 7 or 8 years. Allegedly, if fishermen fall overboard, they are left to drown, as an offering to the earth goddess Pachamama. The huge sealike lake is often hit by storms, so Pachamama has a regular supply of offerings, averaging four fishermen a year.

Once you're on the island, it is up to you. The island is, by Bolivian standards, densely populated (an estimated 5,000 people live there) and intensively cultivated, and so it is covered in trails. The west side is far less populated and has the highest point on the island.

The most impressive ruins are in the far north at Chincana and the Labyrinth, which can be reached by motor launch. From there, you can walk back across to the other end of the island and be picked up at the Inca Steps, where there is a second set of ruins, including Pilcocaina and the Inca Spring. Walking from one end of the island to the other takes **5 hours.**

There is a museum in Challapampa, which is occasionally open, and a basic *alojamiento.* There are also a number of places to stay in Yumani, plus plenty of places to camp, especially on the secluded western side of the island.

When you are through exploring Isla del Sol, make the prearranged boat trip back to Yampupata. From Yampupata going back to Copacabana, it is possible to avoid the road. Find the path leading directly to Zampaya, or follow the road out of Yampupata for **20 minutes** until the terracing on the left ends, and then head uphill to the ridge. From the top of the ridge you can see the road to Zampaya, which is **1 hour** away by foot. It takes **another hour** to reach Santa Ana and then **50 minutes** to drop down to the grotto. If you've got the time, you can stay in the hills, deciding when to return to the coastal road and Copacabana.

Chapter 6

CORDILLERA APOLOBAMBA

T here are three treks through the Cordillera Apolobamba, which stretches northwest into Peru. Trekking the Apolobamba North route (trek 2), heading north from Curva (trek 4, Apolobamba South), or straight toward Apolo (trek 3, Apolo Trail), you start or finish in Pelechuco at the heart of the rarely visited Cordillera Apolobamba.

Pelechuco, at 3,600 m (11,800 ft), is set in a steep valley formed by the river of the same name. The name is derived from the Quechua *puyu kuchu*, which means "cloudy corner." Pelechuco was founded in 1560 and many fine colonial buildings remain. Today, the main economic activity is gold mining.

Every year, for the week around July 25, Pelechuco holds a big fiesta to

Looking down on Pelechuco (Andrew North)

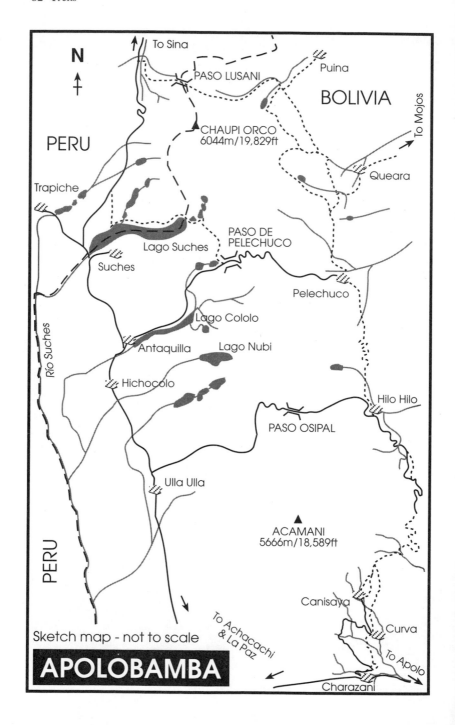

To Sina

PASO LUSANI

Puina

BOLIVIA

To Mojos

N

PERU

▲ CHAUPI ORCO
6044m/19,829ft

Queara

Trapiche

Lago Suches

PASO DE
PELECHUCO

Suches

Pelechuco

Río Suches

Lago Cololo

Lago Nubi

Antaquilla

Hichocolo

Hilo Hilo

PASO OSIPAL

Ulla Ulla

▲ ACAMANI
5666m/18,589ft

PERU

Canisaya

Curva

To Achacachi
& La Paz

To Apolo

Sketch map - not to scale

APOLOBAMBA

Charazani

celebrate its foundation. But there are smaller fiestas every month. The locals support each one enthusiastically and with energetic drinking.

Journeys both to and from the trek's starting point are spectacular. On the way out of Achacachi, look out for the roadside adobe brick buildings called *putucos*, which are used for storing and drying animal manure so it can be used as fuel.

Note: Overnight journeys across the Altiplano in less than state-of-the-art transport are extremely cold. Take your sleeping bag onto the bus with you.

The journey through the Río Pelechuco valley is well worth doing in daylight. If returning by jeep, a visit to the thermal baths 2 hours by jeep from Pelechuco near Antaquilla is a must, followed by a daylight trip through the vicuña reserve of Ulla Ulla. If you have time on the way out or back, visit some of the first colonial churches built in Bolivia in the villages of Carabuco and Escoma.

2. Apolobamba North
Pelechuco to Pelechuco
(6–7 days)

This is a fantastic trek through unexplored, unmapped, and largely uninhabited countryside, crossing a series of high passes and involving camps above 4,000 m (13,000 ft) every night. While few people live in the area, the wildlife is abundant: llamas, *viscachas,* and wild horses, and it is often possible to see condors. There are no villages en route and only a few isolated farms and hamlets.

Start early and finish early—clouds can come in from midday and reduce visibility at 4,000 m (13,000 ft) to under 30 m (100 ft), making it difficult to follow the route and impossible to see the views.

Start and Finish

You will find various small shops and cafes around Pelechuco's square. The village has a number of basic *alojamientos:* Rumillajta (US$1.40 per person per night), behind the church, and Pension México (US$1 per night) plus Chujlla Wasi (US$1 per night), on the main square. The village is basic—no phone, no electricity, and no latrine system, but there is a medical post that is often staffed. If you have time to kill, pay a visit to the the single-table Pelechuco pool hall.

Bus from La Paz to Pelechuco from Calle Reyes Cardona corner Avenida Kollasuyo, three blocks up from Cementerio, Wednesdays at 11:00 A.M. for US$6; the trip takes 18 to 24 hours. Outbound tickets should be bought in advance from the small La Paz office in Calle Reyes Cardona, corner Avenida Kollasuyo, or from the buses themselves, which park in the afternoon before departure in Calle Reyes Cardona. To (or from) Pelechuco by

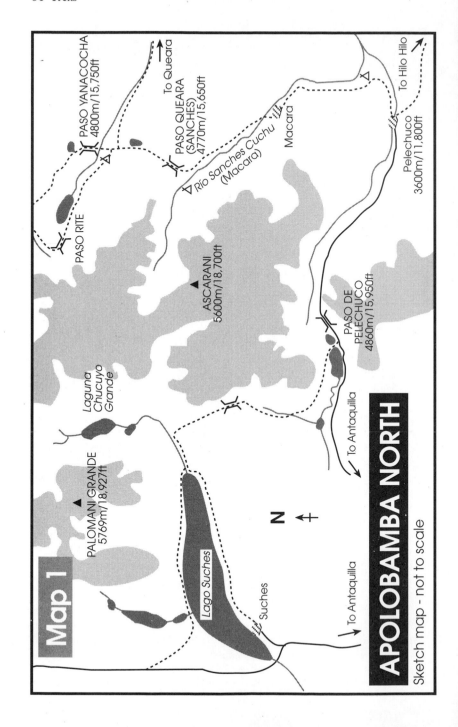

Map 1

APOLOBAMBA NORTH

Sketch map - not to scale

N

PASO YANACOCHA
4800m/15,750ft

To Queara

PASO QUEARA
(SANCHES)
4770m/15,650ft

Río Sanches Cuchu
(Macara)

Macara

To Hilo Hilo

Pelechuco
3600m/11,800ft

PASO RITE

ASCARANI
5600m/18,700ft

PASO DE
PELECHUCO
4860m/15,950ft

Laguna
Chucuyo
Grande

To Antaquilla

PALOMANI GRANDE
5769m/18,927ft

Lago Suches

Suches

To Antaquilla

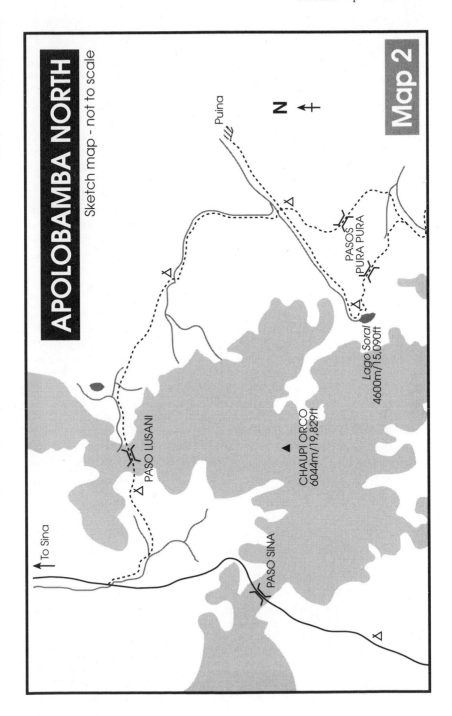

APOLOBAMBA NORTH

Sketch map - not to scale

Map 2

N

Puina

PASOS
PURA PURA

Lago Soral
4600m/15,090ft

PASO LUSANI

CHAUPI ORCO
6044m/19,829ft

To Sina

PASO SINA

jeep costs US$300 and takes 10 hours or more. Spend the night in Pelechuco and start trekking the next day.

Return tickets should be organized when you get to Pelechuco. Return bus leaves Pelechuco Fridays at 8:00 P.M. and Saturdays at 4:00 P.M.

Itinerary

Day 1, to between the Queara and Yanacocha Passes. Day 2, to above Lago Soral or the waterfall downvalley. Day 3, to the Peruvian side of Paso Lusani. Day 4, to the other side of Paso Sina. Day 5, to above Lago Suches. Day 6, to the Paso de Pelechuco or to Pelechuco. Day 7, to Pelechuco.

Maps

None are published in Bolivia. The best available map is the one first published by the British Royal Geographic Society in 1911–13, and updated by Paul Hudson in 1993. However, it does have mistakes and omissions. For instance, it does not show the Paso Lusani north of the peak of Chaupi Orco. White space on the map indicates lack of surveying.

Other Trekking Possibilities

In terms of elevation gain, it makes sense to do the trek in the reverse direction to that described and start the trek at Paso de Pelechuco (off the road to Pelechuco). This saves 1,500 m (5,000 ft) of ascent. The trek is described starting in Pelechuco because at the time I did the trek, we didn't know where the pass was north of the peak of Chaupi Orco—it is unmarked on the map. However, doing the trek in reverse means you cannot hire mules in Pelechuco or recover from the 18- to 24-hour bus journey from La Paz.

If you do start at Paso de Pelechuco, camp at the head of Lago Suches. Second campsite is around the lakes before Paso Sina; third camp is below Paso Lusani; fourth camp is above or below the waterfall above Puina; and last camp is at the derelict houses near Paso Yanacocha, before walking back down to Pelechuco.

For a long and extremely challenging trek, you could do trek 4, Apolobamba South, arrive in Pelechuco, rest and restock, and then continue straight on to do trek 2, Apolobamba North.

Pelechuco is also the base for trek 3, Apolo Trail, which can be done in combination with either trek 2, Apolobamba North, or trek 4, Apolobamba South.

Route Description

With your back to the Pelechuco church, exit the square via the far right-hand corner, head down the street, and cross the river, near the medical center. Follow the wide path down and then up, left, into the valley of the Río Sanches Cuchu (Macara). Camping is possible 1 hour out of Pelechuco to the right of the path. Continue on up to the left of the near-deserted village of Upine (30 minutes). It takes another hour to reach the small village of Macara. About **20 minutes** above the village, cross a bridge to the right-hand side of the valley. When the path starts to rise up away from the valley floor **20 minutes** later, it is possible to camp off to the left at the end of the Río Sanches Cuchu valley.

The slog up to Paso Queara, at 4,770 m (15,650 ft), also known locally as Paso Sanches, takes **2½ hours**, gives great views of the Río Sanches Cuchu valley, and passes a large square *apacheta* (cairn) built below the highest point. It is not a pass marker but shows the division between the Pelechuco and Queara Districts.

Stay on the left while crossing the broad pass area and descend, staying left of a deep blue mountain lake, to excellent camping near derelict farm buildings, **5½ hours from Pelechuco.** The path heading to the right **1 hour below the pass** goes to Queara.

From the derelict buildings, there are two options. The first takes you farther west, avoiding Paso Yanacocha but crossing Paso Rite, then heads over the westernmost of the two Pasos Pura Pura and along the shores of Lago Soral. The second option, which is the main route described here, first climbs Paso Yanacocha and then the easternmost Paso Pura Pura, and

Pelechuco from below

bypasses Lago Soral to reach a track from the village of Puina, where the two options rejoin.

Option 1, via Paso Rite: From the derelict buildings, head up to the end of the valley, staying on the left-hand side—do not cross the stream until you are above the lake. Paso Rite is reached in **2 hours.** Drop down to the river below, staying on the right-hand side of the valley.

Option 2, via Paso Yanacocha: From the derelict buildings, descend to the stream and start moving up to the obvious pass, which takes **40 minutes.** Go through Paso Yanacocha, 4,800 m (15,750 ft), which means "Black Lake Pass." Black Lake is on the other side of the pass, and it is possible to camp 25 minutes below the pass and above the lake.

Descend through a notch in the ridge **45 minutes** below the pass, for views of Chaupi Orco, at 6,044 m (19,829 ft) the highest peak in the Apolobamba range. Steep zigzags bring you to a river (and camping sites) in **50 minutes.**

From the river crossing, there are two possibilities. The first option takes you over the westernmost Paso Pura Pura, joining with the first route option after Paso Rite. The second option takes you over the easternmost Paso Pura Pura, joining with the other route option without passing near Lago Soral.

Option 1: Climb up on the other side, stay on the left-hand side of the valley, and follow a rising traverse. This enters a valley, which can be followed on the left-hand side up to the western Paso Pura Pura (**1½ hours**). Descend to a lake, go around the left-hand side of it, and follow the exit stream until you are above the large and sedimented Lago Soral (excellent camping next to the clear exit stream **1¼ hours** below the pass). Drop diagonally down to the right (bottom) end of Lago Soral (possible camping). (Base camp for Chaupi Orco is above the other end of Lago Soral, at the head of the valley.) From Lago Soral, continue downvalley until you see a farm next to a bridge before a waterfall (**1 hour**).

Option 2: From the river crossing, descend on the left-hand side of the valley until you can see a derelict farm to the left above the section where the valley starts to drop steeply. Go through the farm, cross a boggy flat section to reach ideal camping, or continue up a paved stone path which rises up onto the ridge in front via a series of steps (**50 minutes**). Follow the narrow but well-defined path along the ridge and then go right to arrive at the broad pass area which is also called Pura Pura (**50 minutes**). There is a path on the right-hand side of the valley, a house after **1 hour,** and a bridge **5 minutes** later. Cross the bridge and follow the path as it goes right. Leave the path to drop more directly to the valley floor, zigzagging through the myriad llama paths (**15 minutes**). There is a farm and a bridge leading to a waterfall on the other side of the valley.

All the route options join at this bridge. Cross the bridge and follow paths on either side of the waterfall up to a *pampa* above (excellent camping) in **25 minutes.** At the end of the valley, go up the left-hand side of the waterfall and then follow the broad main valley as it curves first right and then left. There is excellent camping all the way up the valley until you reach a lake below Paso Lusani. It takes **5½ hours** to reach the pass, where there is a large *apacheta* marking the border between Bolivia and Peru.

Descend on the right-hand side of the valley close to the glacier with views of the glaciated peak of Ananea before crossing to the left-hand side of the stream. Camping is possible **40 minutes** below the pass; the main stream is full of glacial sediment but there are clear side streams.

After a series of waterfalls on the left-hand side of the valley, cross to the right-hand side and follow the main valley out until you reach a big valley with a road in it. The road goes down (right) to the Peruvian village of Sina. Go up (left) and follow paths, and in places the road, to Paso Sina **(5 hours)**. There are plenty of camping possibilities all the way up the valley.

From the pass, follow the new road down. (You can arrive at excellent lakeside camping by following the old road off to the left.) Continue following the road as it rises up and goes around a ridge, giving views of the village of Trapiche in the distance. When the road starts dropping into wide Altiplano, **2 hours** after the old road rejoins the new, head off left

Lake reflection below Paso Sina on Peruvian section of Apolobamba North

(southeast) cross-country until you reach Lago Suches, which marks the border between Peru and Bolivia.

From here there are two options: around the northern (Peruvian) side of the lake or the southern (Bolivian) side of the lake.

Option 1: There are a number of very small, traditional hamlets along the northern (Peruvian) shore of the lake, dependent on llama herding. There is also a small boat, which makes it a higher navigable water course than Lake Titicaca! Lago Suches drains into Lake Titicaca via the Río Suches. Camping is possible at a number of sites along the northern shore before you arrive at a white concrete post after **3½ hours** of lakeside walking. This is the official border marker. Camping is also possible at the eastern end of the lake, which seems to appear from under some rocks—there is no aboveground stream feeding the lake.

Option 2: It is a longer route around the southern (Bolivian) side of the lake (**4½ hours**), but the road takes you through the small village of Suches, which has a number of small shops. Continue walking along the lake's southern edge to the abandoned colonial village of San Antonio. None of the buildings have roofs but the walls are intact. Continue walking beside the lake until you are forced up, and then drop down to the lake's eastern end.

From the end of the lake, both route options now head upvalley toward Laguna Chucuyo Grande. There is excellent camping to the right of the stream **1 hour** above the lake end.

Head up (right), aiming for the area to the right of the snowcapped Point 5600, where there is an unnamed pass (**1 hour**). This leads to a more leisurely descent on the other side, with the Matchu Suchi Cuchu ridge up to the left and possible camping. Cross the stream to the left-hand side of the valley and follow the valley down until you reach the Paso de Pelechuco area (**1½ hours**).

From here it is a **5½-hour**, 1,200-m (4,000-ft) descent, and 19 km (12 mi) to Pelechuco. Follow the old road, which allows you to cut off many of the corners of the new road. Occasionally vehicles pass by. But don't bank on it.

3. Apolo Trail
Pelechuco to Apolo
(7–8 days)

The trek from Pelechuco to the lowland town of Apolo is for people with plenty of time and a lot of determination. Depending on weather conditions and how overgrown the route has become, it can take over 8 days. When you add on the 20-hour bus journey to Pelechuco from La Paz, the likelihood of having to wait a day or two for a guide before you can start, and the possibility of a 2- or 3-day journey back to La Paz from Apolo, the whole trek can take the best part of 2 weeks.

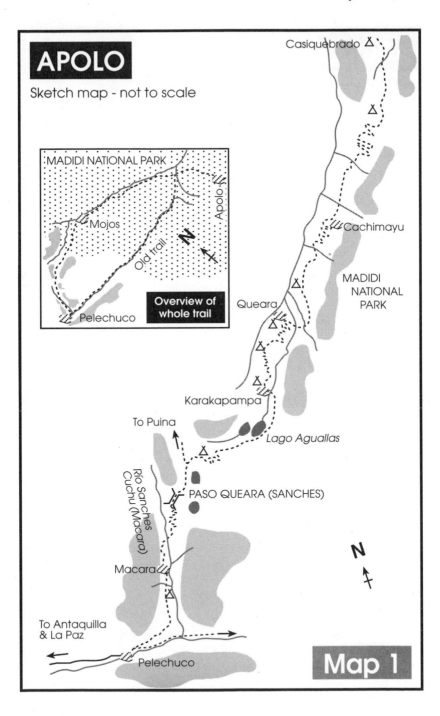

APOLO

Sketch map - not to scale

Casiquebrado

MADIDI NATIONAL PARK

Mojos

Apolo

Old trail

N

Overview of whole trail

Pelechuco

Cachimayu

MADIDI
NATIONAL
PARK

Queara

Karakapampa

Lago Aguallas

To Puina

Río Sanches
Cuchu (Macara)

PASO QUEARA (SANCHES)

Macara

To Antaquilla
& La Paz

Pelechuco

N

Map 1

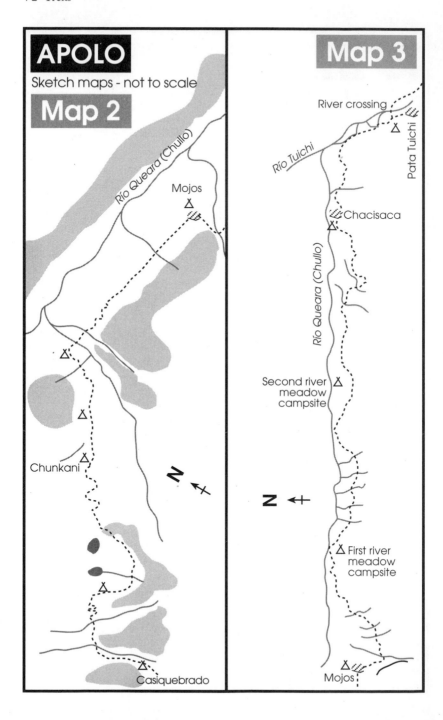

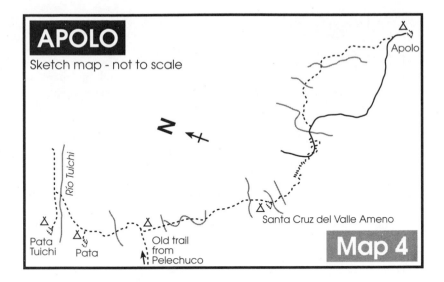

This is actually the long way to Apolo. There is a shorter route, built in pre-Hispanic times, which heads almost due east from Pelechuco, and this could be done in 4 days. Unfortunately, it has now become impassable due to the collapse of several key river bridges. Instead, you have to make a huge semicircular detour, starting with a climb to Paso Queara (Sanches) at 4,770 m (15,650 ft). Most of the route is inside the newly established Madidi National Park, which is home to the endangered spectacled bear as well as myriad birds. It is a rarely used route, and the jungle sections can become very overgrown, necessitating frequent machete hacking.

Before you go, get in touch with EcoBolivia Foundation, instrumental in establishing the park. The foundation's director, Rosa María Ruiz, has done the route herself. For contact details, see "La Paz Agencies" in the "Getting Around in Bolivia" section of chapter 3, Traveling in Bolivia. Also see chapter 10, Rurrenabaque and the Western Amazon Basin.

Start

For information about Pelechuco, how to get there, its accommodations, and guides there, see "Start and Finish" for trek 2, Apolobamba North. For the trail as far as Paso Queara, see "Route Description" for trek 2, Apolobamba North.

For this trek, you are advised to hire a guide. But finding one with the necessary experience is hit and miss. Ask for Freddy Delgado, who lives in the town. He is a guide and also serves as a contact point for other guides. If you want to do the Apolo Trail, ask for Modesto and his brother Policarpio. They live in the area and know the route well.

Finish

Apolo is a slightly forlorn colonial town, situated on a plain midway between two rows of hills. Its focus is a peaceful square with a whitewashed church. It is also a military town, housing over 1,000 young conscripts. The Hotel Tri Centenario, on the main square, is the only hotel, but there are several pensions to choose from in the streets around the main square.

The choice of eating places is limited. There is an Entel telephone office on the corner of the square, to the right of the Hotel Tri Centenario, which opens in the mornings. Alternatively, you can make a radio-telephone call at Radio Communidades Serrano, which is normally open until late in the evening. But interference can be a problem. The office is just off the main square.

One of Apolo's attractions is the mandarin wine (US$1 a bottle) vinted by the nuns of Apolo's Cistercian convent. They also sell a variety of fresh fruit and vegetables. The convent shop is open Monday through Friday from 8:30 to 11:00 A.M. and from 1:30 to 5:00 P.M., and on Saturday from 8:30 to 11:00 A.M.

Getting out of Apolo can be quite an exercise. In theory, *camionetas* (pickup trucks) and four-wheel-drive station wagons leave for La Paz every day except Sunday. In practice, it depends on the state of the road and

Santa Cruz del Valle Ameno, Pelechuco to Apolo (Andrew North)

whether any vehicle is available. The road becomes impassable if hit by rain, and even when it is dry, it can be extremely slow going; 2- to 3-day journeys back to La Paz are not uncommon. To find out who is going and when, ask at Radio Communidades Serrano. Expect to pay US$16 for the trip.

The alternative is the Transportes Aereos Militares (TAM) flight to Rurrenabaque and La Paz, which leaves Mondays at 11:45 A.M. Book your tickets as far in advance as possible, as the flight fills up quickly. The TAM office is on the northwest side of the town, about a 5-minute walk from the square. Tickets to Rurrenabaque are US$20; to La Paz, US$38. The luggage limit is 25 kg (55 lbs) per person. You can get a *camioneta* lift to the runway *(pista)*, situated to the south of the town, from the main square at around 10:30 A.M. for US$0.20. From Rurrenabaque there are regular buses to La Paz. Rurrenabaque is also one of the best centers for trips into the jungle and *pampas* (see chapter 10, Rurrenabaque and the Western Amazon Basin).

Itinerary

Day 1, to Karakapampa/Queara. Day 2, to Casiquebrado. Day 3, to thatch shelter campsite after Chunkani, or to Mojos. Day 4, to Mojos or to river camp. Day 5, to river camp or to Pata. Day 6, to Pata (including Río Tuichi crossing) or to Santa Cruz del Valle Ameno. Day 7, to Santa Cruz del Valle Ameno or to Apolo. Day 8, to Apolo.

Maps

There are no published maps of the route.

Other Trekking Possiblities

From Pelechuco: If you have time before you set off, you could attempt the first part of the old route to Apolo. With your back to the Pelechuco church, exit the square via the far right-hand corner, head down the street, and cross the river, near the medical center. Soon after, take the right-hand path leading down to the Río Pelechuco. It follows the course of the river, staying on the left-hand bank all the way down. An hour's walking takes you to a magnificent vegetation-covered bridge over a tributary waterfall. You have to retrace to get back to Pelechuco.

Before trekking the Apolo Trail, you can do the Apolobamba North or South treks (treks 2 and 4), which both finish in Pelechuco.

From Apolo: If you have the energy once you reach Apolo, there is a beautiful 5- to 7-day trek to San José, on the Río Tuichi. Find a guide and take all the food you will need. When you arrive at the Tuichi, hire a raft *(balsa)* to cross the river. You can then continue up- or downriver. There is water and camping en route. Along the trail, there are a few Quechua communities where you might be able to buy basic foodstuffs, such as rice and corn, although the vendors might not speak Spanish.

Route Description

The first part of the route, from Pelechuco to the other side of Paso Queara (Sanches), follows that of trek 2, Apolobamba North. After reaching the flat top of Paso Queara (Sanches), you come to a boggy hollow. Heading north to northwest, the main trail stays to the left while crossing the broad pass area and descends, staying left of a deep blue mountain lake, to excellent camping near derelict farm buildings, **5½ hours** from Pelechuco. Above and to the right is a black rock peak. Just after you pass it, the path splits, with one route heading left to Puina (this is the route for trek 2, Apolobamba North). Take the narrower, less distinct right-hand path heading downward.

It soon joins a larger, paved path, along which there are camping possibilities. **Forty minutes** later, reach two interconnected lakes, known as Lago Aguallas by the locals. As you descend, watch out for the terminal moraines in the basin below. The track circles the right-hand lake before zigzagging steeply downward. Cross a small ridge before descending again to a small settlement, **1½ hours** from the split in the path at Paso Queara (Sanches).

Heading north past these huts, descend for another **5 to 10 minutes** to the village of Karakapampa. Here, the path crosses a stream and continues descending steeply, with the village above you on the left. The stream passes over a high waterfall. A short way below the waterfall, a path leads off to the left from the main descent. It takes you to an open patch where you can camp and which offers wonderful views of the valley and the partly abandoned settlement of Queara below. There is another stream in a gorge to the left of the campsite.

Continue descending on the main route, where the closely packed stones of the original pre-Hispanic trail are still intact. Pass through Queara and on to a wide meadow created by a meander in the Río Queara (also known as the Río Chullo), **40 minutes** beyond Karakapampa. The river runs on your left. Once past Queara, you are inside Madidi National Park.

An hour beyond the meander, a small log bridge crosses a stream. From here, the trail climbs for **1½ hours** until you reach two huts and some fields. This is Cachimayu.

About **1½ hours** beyond Cachimayu, climb up to an open, grassy stretch. You then face another series of ups and downs, reaching a hollow **1 hour** later—a possible campsite. Head east from here, and **40 minutes** of walking brings you down to a more sheltered campsite at Casiquebrado. This is marked by a thatched shelter in a clearing.

The trail leads straight down from here, with the stream to your right. Just after crossing the stream, the path bears east. **Forty minutes** from Casiquebrado, there is a steep climb to the top of a wooded hill. There is a brief descent before climbing again to a patch of open grassland, where there are camping possibilities. Then scramble across a gently sloping rock face embedded in the hillside, bearing northeast, and the trail then leads up to a ridge. The trail continues on the other side of the ridge. When you reach the end of the ridge, about 1¾ hours from Casiquebrado, you should be able to make out the village of Pata, if it is a clear day. But you will not reach it for at least another 3 days!

A **half hour** below the ridge, there is a small clearing. The trail leads off from the right of the clearing, bearing north and descending steeply. This is one of the most exciting sections of the trail, as you pass through rich cloud forest and down a series of deep and narrow gullies and stone staircases.

After **1½ hours** of steep descent, the gradient becomes less severe and the trail passes through thick jungle. **Half an hour** of walking from here brings you to a clearing known as Chunkani, just after a short and gentle climb. There is a tiny stone shelter on the left. You can camp here, and there is a small stream on the east side of the clearing, at the bottom of the slope.

From the clearing, the trail heads north and again descends, passing through more gullies. In places, the path has been laid with logs to make walking easier in wet conditions. **An hour** from Chunkani, come to another clearing where there is a thatched shelter. This makes a good campsite and there is a stream a few minutes farther down the path.

Río Tuichi, Pelechuco to Apolo (Andrew North)

Heading east out of the clearing, the trail goes through thick jungle and reaches another clearing **1 hour** later. Another **hour** of descending brings you to a clearing just above the Río Queara, which makes a good campsite. Just beyond, the path crosses the river as it foams through a narrow and spectacular gorge. **Fifteen minutes** farther on, cross a smaller feeder stream, a good place to stock up on water before the subsequent **50-minute climb.**

At the top, there is a clearing and the path heads southeast around the hill. Below is a group of huts. Another **1½ hours** of fairly easy walking gets you to Mojos, the largest settlement since Pelechuco. It is distinguished by its thatch-roofed bell tower, on one side of the soccer field. There are no shops here, but you might be able to buy bananas or yucca. You can camp on the field, but ask one of the residents for permission. There is water about 10 minutes farther down the trail, which heads southwest out of Mojos.

A **half hour** beyond Mojos a path goes up to the right; stay to the left. Keep straight when you see another path going off to the left a little farther on. After crossing a stream **1¼ hours** out of Mojos, climb to an open, cleared section of hillside. It is then a boring trudge for the next **45 minutes** until you descend closer to the Rió Queara. Large areas of jungle have been cleared on this side of the valley.

The path becomes very narrow near the river, and you have to watch your footing. The rattan thickets that grow here can become very overgrown and you might need the machete in places. Eventually, you come right down to river level. **Half an hour** later, after crossing several side channels, reach a large meadow next to the river, where it is possible to camp. The insects can be intolerable here, although the butterflies are spectacular.

Heading east, the trail plunges back into another rattan thicket before climbing up into jungle again. Bear east, with the river to your left. About **1½ hours** from the meadow campsite, a log crosses a larger stream. Soon after, cross another stream and the trail bears southeast.

Another **1½ hours** farther, you come down to the river again and into a second meadow. This makes a good campsite, except for the ever-present horseflies and other flying nasties. Jaguars are known to live in the surrounding jungle, and you might hear their distinctive whistle.

The trail heads southeast across the meadow and up the hillside. The trail descends the other side of the ridge, then climbs again, following the same pattern for the **next hour** or so. **An hour and 45 minutes** from the meadow, the path splits, with the left-hand route staying close to the river. This has become impossibly overgrown, so take the right-hand, uphill route, which brings you back down to river level again **15 minutes** later. Then pass above a large meander in the river's course, before descending **a half hour** later to an open grassy stretch.

You have to struggle through another section of bush before coming out next to the river in a large meadow with good camping. After another rattan thicket, reach two huts, **half an hour** from the open grassy stretch. This is Chacisaca. Turn left here, heading back into the jungle. **Ten minutes** farther, there is a hard climb up to a ridge, and at the top you get your first view of the Río Tuichi, flowing northeast.

Then descend down to the Tuichi floodplain and a large, open stretch of gravel and mud bisected by a side stream. Wade across this several times to reach the main shore, 1¼ hours from Chacisaca. The trail then climbs up over a bluff before dropping down to river level again. Twenty minutes farther, the trail crosses a soccer field on the floodplain. You could camp here or just beyond, at the river crossing point, but don't pitch too close to the river. It can rise incredibly fast when rain hits the region. Ten minutes up the path is the village of Pata Tuichi Communidad Virgen del Rosario, where you might be able to buy fruit or vegetables. If the Tuichi is low, you can swim across, but be prepared for the cold water.

When the river is in flood, ask in the village for one of the local boatmen to take you and your gear across. They use a long log raft, which they maneuver by pole. The rate for the crossing depends on the number of people. Getting our group of six people and their belongings across took seven journeys and cost US$9. The mules had to swim. If the raft is not available or the river is too high, you might have to wait until the next day, in which case you can camp anywhere along the bank.

There is a small beach on the other side. The path goes up the hillside and follows the river until it crosses a small feeder stream about 20 minutes farther on. Stock up with water at this stream, because you then face a 3-hour climb up a series of hills and ridges with no reliable water sources. Two hours up, heading southeast, reach a soccer field (possible camping) and just beyond it is a path down to the right leading to the village of Pata. Here you can camp and may be able to stock up on water and buy fruit. When you reach a line of fencing, followed by a flat section along the right-hand side of a ridge, you have completed the main climb, another hour from Pata.

Twenty minutes farther is a grassy ridge. Head south from the ridge. The path goes through a series of ups and downs before reaching a smaller grassy ridge 1 hour later. From here, it is a 15-minute descent into a small wooded valley, with a stream at the bottom. By this point, you have rejoined the old Pelechuco-to-Apolo trail, and parts of the track are again laid with stone. About 1 hour later, the trail passes a small grassy patch on the right, at the top of a forested ridge. Camping is possible here.

It is then downhill to Santa Cruz del Valle Ameno, heading east to northeast and passing through a stretch of dense jungle. A stream crosses back and forth across the path several times. Around 1 hour from the grassy patch on the ridgetop, the vegetation opens out and the trail comes to a soccer field (possible camping) and a village. By this point, the track is wide enough to take jeeps. Beyond is another bridge and banana plantations on either side of the path.

Another 20 minutes brings you to Santa Cruz del Valle Ameno. A high, arched wooden bridge over the river marks the beginning of the town. It is a quiet and attractive place, all the streets and the main square are covered in grass. There are a number of shops selling basics like bread, tuna, pasta, and canned milk, as well as beer. Make sure you indulge in the wonderful oranges they grow in this area and buy some to take with you. There are no accommodations in the town, but if you ask, one of the locals may offer to put you up or give you camping space outside their house. Otherwise, ask for permission to camp in the main square.

The track heads east out of Santa Cruz del Valle Ameno, crosses the river just outside, and then goes south. You may encounter a jeep or pickup heading to Apolo, but don't bank on getting a lift. A **half hour** out of town, cross a stream and just afterward there are two paths leading up the hillside to the right. This is a shortcut up to the next section of road to avoid the long slog around the hill. It is about **20 minutes** to the top and you then follow it for a short stretch before taking another shortcut downhill. A **half hour** farther down, the road crosses a small river and then runs parallel with it for a few hundred yards. **Fifteen minutes** from the river crossing, turn left off the road, just before a white hut. This is what the locals call the mule track; it is much shorter than the road.

Head almost due east until you reach a soccer field, where the path bears to the right and down into a small valley. Here the landscape is heavily eroded, with little vegetation. Cross a small bridge and then bear southeast as you climb to the top of the hill. The trail crosses another stream and then comes onto a ridge, **half an hour** from the beginning of the mule track. You can then see the path out in front of you, with huts and small plantations below to the left.

At the top of this ridge, you can see the distinctive church tower of Apolo, in the middle of a plain. Hills on either side stretch southward. From here, it is just over **1 hour** to Apolo.

4. Apolobamba South
Charazani or Curva to Pelechuco
(5 days)

This is one of the best mountain treks in Bolivia, passing through traditional villages and then up into the heights of the southern Cordillera Apolobamba. There are more people living in this area than in the northern half of the range. But after the villages of Curva or Canisaya, you are unlikely to see more than a few people a day and no other tourists. The first language of the few people here is Quechua, followed by Aymará and then Spanish.

You can start the trek in Charazani or Curva in the south, or Pelechuco in the north. The advantages of starting in Charazani or Curva are that these villages are relatively easy to get to; the trekking is better starting in the south because the passes have steep ascents and easier descents. If you finish in Pelechuco you can combine this trek with trek 2, Apolobamba North, or

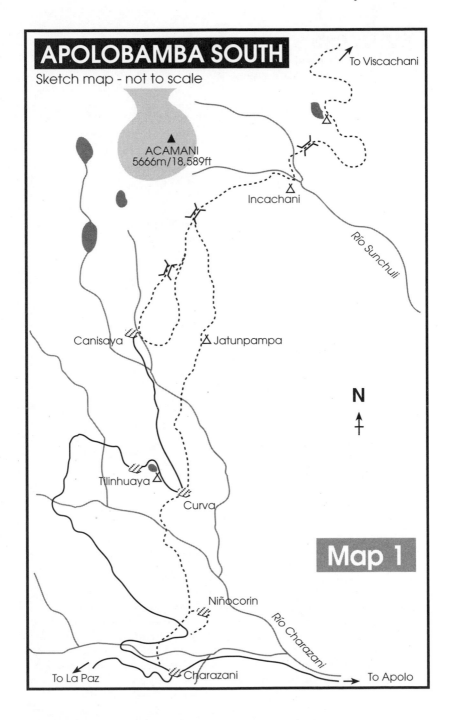

APOLOBAMBA SOUTH
Sketch map - not to scale

To Viscachani

ACAMANI
5666m/18,589ft

Incachani

Río Sunchuli

Canisaya

Jatunpampa

N

Tilinhuaya

Curva

Map 1

Niñocorin

Río Charazani

To La Paz

Charazani

To Apolo

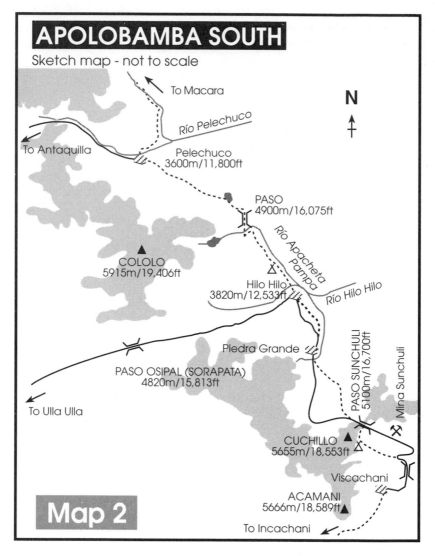

trek 3, Apolo Trail; and you can check out the thermal baths near Antaquilla on the way out of Pelechuco. The disadvantage is that there is normally only one bus a week out of Pelechuco, entailing a long wait if you miss it.

If you start in Pelechuco, it is easier to hire a guide/muleteer and mule (US$8 per mule per day plus US$8 per day for the muleteer), and at the end of the trek, there is transport out of Charazani four times a week, so you need only wait a maximum of 2 days. Moreover, it is far more comfortable waiting in Charazani because food and accommodations are better than in Pelechuco. There are hot baths only 10 minutes from the village. The disadvantage is that, from the north, the ascents of the passes are longer and the descents shorter and steeper.

In summary, if you are using public transport, start in Pelechuco. If you are hiring a jeep, start in Charazani or Curva. This trek is described from south to north.

Start

Charazani (official name Villa Juan J. Perez) is the largest village in the region. At 3,200 m (10,500 ft), it is noticeably warmer than La Paz, and there are thermal baths (entrance US$1) 10 minutes below the village in which to cool off. There are some small shops and eateries (which often serve trout for *cenar*) around the square and a number of *alojamientos,* the best of which is Hotel Kallawaya, for US$1.40–$2 per night. There is a medical post but no telephone and since 1994 there has been no electricity. The road to Apolo follows the left-hand side of the valley, dropping below Charazani. There is a big fiesta

View down Río Apacheta Pampa valley, Apolobamba South

around July 16 which is famous for its highland music and nonstop dancing (and drinking) for 3 days.

Curva is an attractive hilltop village at 3,900 m (12,800 ft). It is the capital village of the Kallawayas, the traveling witch doctors of the area, and is situated below their sacred mountain of Acamani. Its fiesta is particularly well supported by the local population for most of the week around June 29. However, Curva has nothing to offer in terms of accommodations or food.

Buses leave from La Paz for Charazani from Calle Reyes Cardona, corner Avenida Kollasuyo above Cementerio, on Wednesdays, Fridays, Saturdays, Sundays, and Mondays at 6:00 A.M. (US$4.40). The trip takes 10 hours. The bus sometimes goes up to Curva (1½ hours, US$1.60) to pick up passengers for the return trip to La Paz.

A jeep from La Paz to Curva (or vice versa) costs US$250 and takes 8 hours (6½ hours to Charazani). Ask the driver to go via the village of

Amarete, which is reminiscent of Nepal. Leaving La Paz by jeep at 6:00 A.M., with rest stops, you should arrive in Curva at between 3:00 and 4:00 P.M., which gives you enough time to get to the first campsite on the trek.

To return to La Paz from Charazani, the bus leaves Fridays, Sundays, Mondays, and Wednesdays at 4:00 A.M., and Mondays at 7:00 P.M.

Note: Overnight bus journeys across the Altiplano are extremely cold; take your sleeping bag with you.

Finish

For details on Pelechuco, see "Start and Finish" for trek 2, Apolobamba North.

Itinerary

Day 1, to beyond Curva. Day 2, to Incachani. Day 3, to Sunchuli. Day 4, to above Hilo Hilo. Day 5, to Pelechuco.

Maps

None are published in Bolivia. The best available map is the one first published by Britain's Royal Geographic Society in 1911–13, and updated by Paul Hudson in 1993. However, it does have mistakes and omissions. The relative positions of the southern Apolobamba villages are wrong. White space on the map indicates lack of surveying.

Other Trekking Possibilities

From Pelechuco you can do trek 2, Apolobamba North, or head off to the jungle for trek 3, Apolo Trail.

A rarely tried but worthwhile alternative route for this trek is through the village of Canisaya, upvalley from Curva. The stonework is of a particularly high quality, with almost smooth house walls and, unusual for Bolivia, many dry stone walls. From Curva, take the road that comes up from the lake near Tilinhuaya, and follow it to the col and then left, away from Curva. Arrive in Canisaya square after 1¼ **hours.** Make your way to the river and cross it, then head for a path that rises diagonally up the hillside on the right. Cross the col and contour along the path for **1 hour** to arrive at a small group of farms and a lake. Head toward the lake and then go around it counterclockwise, climbing steeply to join a well-defined path. This continues up through a notch and then follows the contours for **2 hours** until it arrives at a large cairn. From here it is **15 minutes** up to the broad col, where you rejoin the normal route. (Coming from Pelechuco, **10 minutes** below the broad col, reach a large cairn and follow the path to the right to Canisaya; then follow the rest of this alternative route in reverse to Curva.)

Route Description

If you start in Charazani rather than Curva, it takes **4 hours** to walk to Curva. Do not follow the road all the way; it takes forever. Instead, follow the road to Curva out of the village, drop down to the thermal baths, cross the river, and follow paths up the other side to rejoin the road. Follow the road until you are opposite the village, and then look for a path heading up (left) to the church with the white tower and yellow body on the hill. Down to your right, you can see the village of Niñocorin, where in 1970 the remains of a Kallawaya medicine man were found, carbon-dated to 800 or 1000 B.C. From the church, go down the other side of the hill and turn left when you reach the better path, which follows the contours and drops through terraced wheat fields to a bridge. Cross the river and head up to Curva, arriving in the main square.

From the square in Curva you can see a cross on the hill to the north overlooking the village. Contour around the hill, keeping the cross on your left, and descend to a stream crossing in **1 hour.**

Move up toward the first valley on the right through walled fields. Stay to the right of the stream and continue upward. There are a number of possible camping sites, but if there is time, continue up until you cross the stream above some small walled fields and join a well-defined path coming into the valley from the left. Follow this up and in another **1¼ hours** reach an excellent camping spot in a narrow but flat *pampa*. This is known locally as Jatunpampa, at 4,200 m (13,800 ft), and there is a stream nearby.

Continue upvalley and across a second *pampa* to reach a pass in **1 hour.** It takes **another 20 minutes** to reach the pass at 4,700 m (15,400 ft), which gives fantastic views of the peak Acamani to the left. At the cairn, head off downhill to the right to reach a camping spot near the waterfall of Incachani at 4,100 m (13,450 ft) in **1¼ hours.** There are plenty of places to stop for lunch on the way down. An early camp gives plenty of time to wash in the cold, fast-moving stream, to spot wild horses and *viscachas*, and to examine the ascent that faces you first thing next morning.

Cross the stream at the bridge below the waterfall and follow the zigzag path up into a scree gully, which is often frozen over and remains in the shade until 10:00 A.M. It takes **1¼ hours** to get to the col. From this point, you may be able to see the peaks of Ancohuma and Illampu, which mark the northwest end of the Cordillera Real, to the south before reaching the pass at 4,800 m (15,750 ft) in another **15 minutes.**

Contour left and gently up until you join the ridge in **20 minutes,** which gives views of Ancohuma, Illampu, and the Cordillera Real to the south and Sunchuli mountain to the north. Follow the path down and pass a small lake before arriving at a second larger lake in **30 minutes,** which gives fantastic views of Acamani and where it is possible to camp.

From the lake, rise up another ridge before descending left to the small mining settlement of Viscachani in **30 minutes,** where the dirt road to Hilo Hilo (Illo Illo) starts. Follow the road **45 minutes** to the pass at 4,900 m (16,075 ft). From here you can see the Cordillera Real stretching away to the south, Sunchuli mountain, and the other mountains surrounding the Sunchuli valley to the north and west.

As the road drops down into the valley and bears right, look for a path that leads off to the left. The path drops quite quickly toward the gold mine of Sunchuli and then contours along the side of the valley, staying above the aqueduct until you arrive at an ideal camping spot at 4,600 m (15,100 ft) in **1 hour,** below the Cuchillo peak.

The next section is possibly the best part of the trek but you will be heading north all the way (equivalent to south in the northern hemisphere), so the sun is in your face all day. From here on, there is a good path, once used by Inca gold miners.

From camp, head up to the road, which reaches Paso Sunchuli via a series of switchbacks. The plod uphill can be shortened and made more exciting by cutting off the corners. It takes **1¼ hours** to reach the pass, which is the highest of the trek at 5,100 m (16,700 ft) and gives excellent views. It is possible to scramble up to a cairn above the road for even better views dominated by Cololo, the highest mountain in the southern Cordillera Apolobamba at 5,915 m (19,406 ft).

Follow the road down from the pass for a couple of minutes and then head right, down a steep path. After **15 minutes** it crosses a stream opposite the glacier lake below Sunchuli mountain. Continue down to the bottom of the valley, which takes **1 hour.** Turn right and join the road a couple of minutes above the picturesque stone and thatch village of Piedra Grande, reached in **15 minutes.**

Stay on the road until a pre-Hispanic paved path leads off downhill to the right after **1 hour.** Cross a bridge and follow the path up (right) to reach the village of Hilo Hilo in **1 hour.** There are a couple of small shops selling provisions such as crackers, pasta, tuna, soft drinks, beer, candles, matches, and batteries. But fresh goods are rare.

When leaving Hilo Hilo, do not follow the path up to the left, which leads west to Ulla Ulla and the Altiplano. Walk out of the village between the *baño* and the cemetery, where newer and richer graves are roofed with corrugated iron. Follow the path above the new school and then pick a route through walled fields and llama pastures before the path becomes clear again, crosses a bridge, and heads up the valley with a pointed rock peak at its head. It takes **2 hours** passing through two flat areas *(pampas)* to reach a bend in the valley with large fallen stones where there is good camping; it is also possible to camp in either of the *pampas.*

Continue upvalley to reach a bridge across the stream after **30 minutes.** Then climb up to the final pass at 4,900 m (16,075 ft), which takes **1 hour.** From here it is downhill all the way via a lake after **20 minutes,** through llama and alpaca pastures, and along some pre-Hispanic paving before arriving in Pelechuco at 3,600 m (11,800 ft) in **1½ hours.**

If you do this trek in reverse direction, from Pelechuco to Curva, leave Pelechuco's square by facing the church and heading up the cobbled street to the right of the church. After 30 m (100 ft), the street does a ninety-degree left turn. Continue along it until, after a few minutes, you cross a

Downtown Hilo Hilo, Apolobamba South

stream. After the stream, immediately turn right and up. From here the route is clear—follow the description above in reverse.

Pelechuco-to-Charazani times are as follows: Pelechuco to first pass, **3 hours**; descent to first possible camping, **30 minutes**; to last camping before Hilo Hilo, **1 hour**. Up to Hilo Hilo, **30 minutes**; up to the road, **40 minutes**; along the road to Piedra Grande, **45 minutes**; to Sunchuli pass, **3 hours**; descent to camping in Sunchuli valley, **45 minutes**. Up to the pass above Viscachani, **1 hour**; descent to Viscachani, **30 minutes**; ascent to lake and possible camping, **45 minutes**. To top of scree slope from hell, **40 minutes**; unpleasant descent to Incachani and camping, **1½ hours**. Ascent to broad col, **2 hours**; descent to Jatunpampa, **1 hour**; descent to river crossing, **1 hour**; up to Curva, with possible camping near marshy lake outside Curva, **1 hour**.

To find the start of the path from Curva to Charazani, with your back to the church in Curva, leave the square via the far right-hand corner, where there are some broad paved steps heading downward. The path is then clear; cross the bridge (fill up water bottles), head up, and **20 minutes** later leave the broad path and head up the path on the right that leads to the church on the hill. Descent from Curva to bridge, **1 hour**; rise to church, **1½ hours**; down to road and along until opposite red-roofed thermal baths below Charazani, **30 minutes**; down to river, **20 minutes**; up other side and into Charazani, **40 minutes**.

Chapter 7

CORDILLERA REAL

The Cordillera Real stretches for 160 km (100 mi), from the Illampu–Ancohuma massif at the northwest end to Illimani, southeast of La Paz. Recorded heights for Illampu, formally known as Mount Sorata, have reached the unbelievable figure of 7,621 m (25,003 ft). But the currently accepted figure is a "mere" 6,368 m (20,892 ft). The gap between Illampu and Acamani, the south end of the Cordillera Apolobamba, is filled by the virtually unvisited Cordillera Muñecas (reached from Sorata via the Consata road).

Sorata from above

5. Illampu Circuit
Sorata to Sorata
(5–7 days)

This trek is a tour around the entire Illampu–Ancohuma massif. It is hard work: three passes over 4,000 m (13,000 ft) and one over 5,000 m (16,000 ft), involving a total of 4,260 m (14,980 ft) of ascent and descent. But it is well worth the effort, with stunning mountain views and the chance to see condors, *viscachas,* and Andean geese, among others.

The Illampu Circuit is normally done in 7 days. The trek starts with a solid 2,063 m (6,768 ft) of ascent from Sorata to Abra Illampu at 4,741 m (15,554 ft). If you go via Paso Huila Khota, at 4,886 m (16,030 ft), there is an ascent of 2,208 m (7,244 ft). This first section normally takes 1½ days. A fit and acclimatized group using mules to Lakathiya could do the circuit in 4½ days. For this route, campsites after Abra Illampu (or Aguas Calientes) would be in the Quebrada Illampu, after Cocoyo, well above Chajolpaya, at the top of Laguna San Francisco, and (if necessary) after Loriacani.

Start and Finish

The Illampu Circuit starts and finishes in Sorata, a beautiful colonial town at a pleasant 2,678 m (8,786 ft). It is noticeably warmer than La Paz which is 1,000 m (3,300 ft) higher. Sorata has, at various times during its history, been a center for coca, quinine, and rubber production and was made a *ciudad* (city) in 1900. From among the giant palm trees of the main square, it is possible to see Illampu.

There is a selection of hotels. Justifiably the most popular is the rambling Residencial Sorata on the plaza (great breakfasts for US$2). Slightly out of town is the more modern and expensive German-run Hotel Copacabana. There are a number of restaurants, mainly on the plaza. But above the town is the not-to-be-missed Ristorante Italiano where the food is as good as the service is slow. You can use the time to watch the sunset over the valley of the Río San Cristobal from the terrace.

Residencial Sorata, Sorata

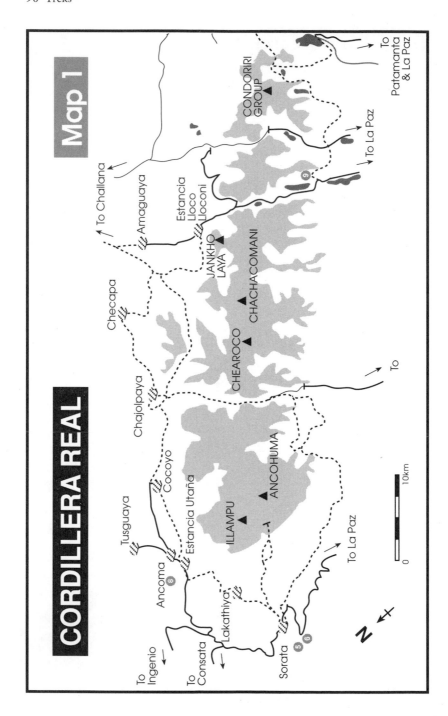

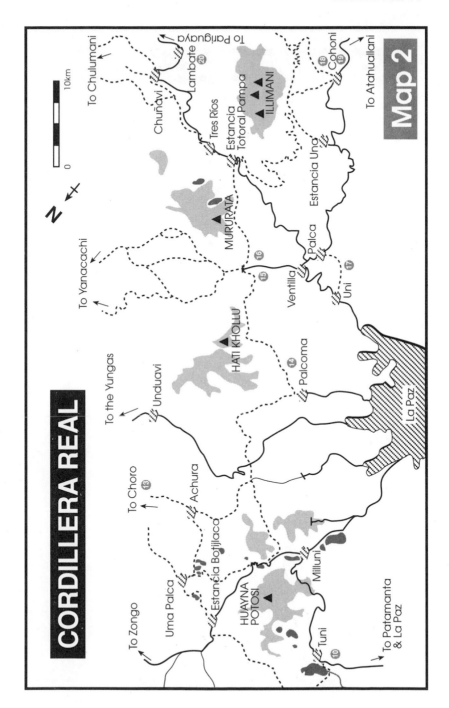

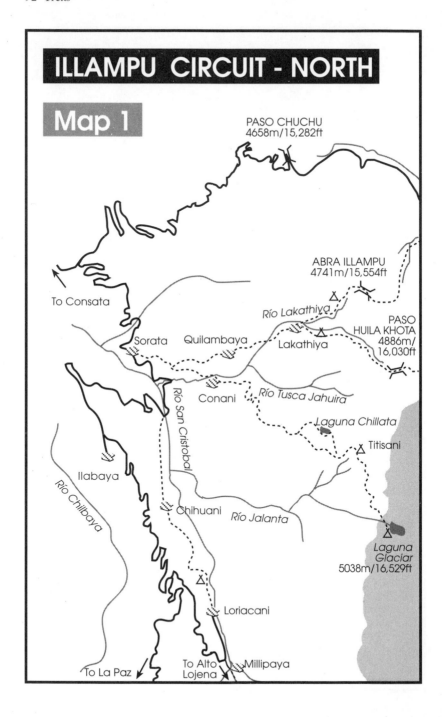

ILLAMPU CIRCUIT - NORTH

Map 1

PASO CHUCHU
4658m/15,282ft

ABRA ILLAMPU
4741m/15,554ft

To Consata

Río Lakathiya

PASO
HUILA KHOTA
4886m/
16,030ft

Sorata   Quilambaya   Lakathiya

Río San Cristobal

Conani

Río Tusca Jahuira

Laguna Chillata

Titisani

Ilabaya

Río Chilbaya

Chihuani

Río Jalanta

Laguna
Glaciar
5038m/16,529ft

Loriacani

To La Paz

To Alto
Lojena

Millipaya

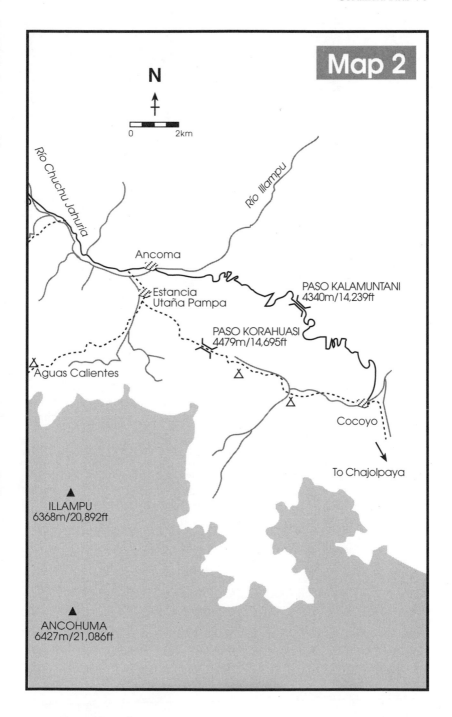

Map 2

N

0   2km

Río Chuchu Jahuira

Río Illampu

Ancoma

Estancia
Utaña Pampa

PASO KALAMUNTANI
4340m/14,239ft

PASO KORAHUASI
4479m/14,695ft

Aguas Calientes

Cocoyo

To Chajolpaya

ILLAMPU
6368m/20,892ft

ANCOHUMA
6427m/21,086ft

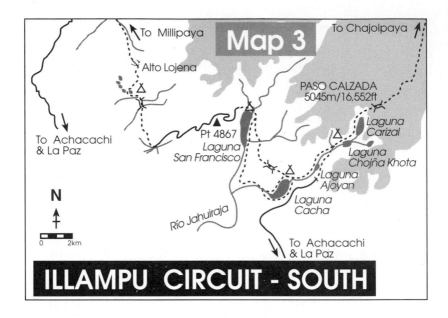

Fresh bread is available and there is a small market selling some fruit and vegetables, but all packaged food should be bought in La Paz, where there is a far greater selection.

It is highly recommended to organize mules from Sorata to Lakathiya at 4,000 m (13,100 ft). Locals (if they are not carrying a load) can get to Lakathiya from Sorata in 2½ hours; mule time is 4 to 5 hours depending on how obstinate the beasts are and how many rests are taken; visitors carrying their own packs take 6 hours or more. Each mule costs US$8 per day and will carry two rucksacks. Mules are available through Residencial Sorata and Hotel Copacabana. Mules will not go more than 1 hour above Lakathiya towards Aguas Calientes; if you want your packs carried, organize porters from Lakathiya to Aguas Calientes (US$8 per porter).

Hiring mules also neatly solves the problem of finding the route out of Sorata. There are myriad paths, as the area is densely populated, by Bolivian standards, and intensively cultivated. Maize is common lower down and potatoes higher up.

La Paz-to-Sorata buses leave from Calle Manuel Bustillos corner Avenida Kollasuyo, two blocks above Cementerio, every day between 6:00 A.M. and 2:00 P.M. Booking is recommended, especially on Fridays. The journey (US$2) takes 4 hours, the same for the return. Sit on the right for the best views of the Cordillera Real. Remember to take your passport for the military checkpoint at Achacachi.

Sorata-to-La Paz buses leave from the main square every day between 5:00 A.M. and 3:30 P.M.

Cocoyo plain, Illampu Circuit

Itinerary

Day 1, to above Lakathiya. Day 2, to Ancoma (or Aguas Calientes). Day 3, to before Cocoyo. Day 4, to above Chajolpaya. Day 5, to Laguna Cacha. Day 6, to Laguna Cacha or the top of the Millipaya valley. Day 7, to Sorata. A fit and acclimatized group could do the trek in 4½ days: Day 1, to Quebrada Illampu (or Aguas Calientes). Day 2, after Cocoyo. Day 3, before Paso Calzada. Day 4, to the top of the Millipaya valley. Day 5, to Sorata.

Maps

DAV Cordillera Real Nord (Illampu) covers the route to Cocoyo and then from the top of the Chajolpaya valley to Paso Calzada and on. Liam O'Brien's map covers the whole route but at 1:135,000. The IGM Sorata 5846 I and Warizata 5846 II sheets cover a similar area to the DAV map but are not as good; the sheets to the east are not available.

Other Trekking Possibilities

Sorata is also the starting point for: trek 6, Lagunas Glaciar and Chillata; trek 8, Camino de Oro; and trek 21, Cordillera Real Traverse, which goes through Chajolpaya. It is an optional start for trek 7, Mapiri Trail.

There are also a number of day hikes from Sorata. Ask Louis Demers, the French-Canadian manager of the Residencial Sorata, who has sketch maps on the walls of the hotel as well as some interesting old topographical maps of the area. Eduardo Kramer, German owner of the Hotel Copacabana, can also provide information.

Route Description

From the main square in Sorata, aim to leave the village heading southeast and upward into the left-hand (northern) side of the Río Lakathiya valley. There are many paths; if you're not sure, keep asking for Quilambaya, at 3,200 m (10,500 ft), which is reached in 1¾ hours. In Quilambaya go around the back of the church, up through a cacti avenue, and continue. Cross the aqueduct and continue up before turning right (east) to contour along to a bridge across the Río Lakathiya in 1¼ hours. From the bridge, stay on the path on the right-hand (eastern) side of the stream for 15 minutes, and then head up (right) through once-cultivated terraces and reach the village of Lakathiya at 4,000 m (13,100 ft) in another 35 minutes. Lakathiya is made up of stone houses, with the more modern corrugated iron roofs replacing the traditional thatch. It is a sign that the area is relatively well-off and close to civilization—every piece of metal has been carried up from Sorata.

From Lakathiya there are two alternatives: Estancia Utaña Pampa via Abra Illampu or Aguas Calientes via Paso Huila Khota at 4,886 m (16,030 ft). The Abra Illampu route is lower and the path is wider and more heavily used than the Aguas Calientes route. But the latter is more direct. The views are better from Abra Illampu, but the camping is better at Aguas Calientes.

Option 1, via Abra Illampu: In Lakathiya, the bigger path drops down (left) to a stream crossing; do not take it. Instead, continue along the narrow path (to the right) contouring through the village, and drop down to cross the stream at a small bridge below the soccer field. Do not follow the path up the broad valley of the soccer field, but take the smaller valley to the left above the bridge. There is excellent camping 45 minutes after the bridge. If you have time and energy, continue up the path on the left-hand (northern, then western) side of the valley until immediately before the stream crossing, for camping at 4,200 m (13,800 ft) in another **hour.**

On Day 2, fill water bottles for the dry ascent to Abra Illampu at 4,741 m (15,554 ft), 1¼ **hours.** The pass gives fantastic views of Illampu and is marked by an apacheta, a pile of stones with small offerings of beer bottles, alcohol potable containers, and pieces of cloth to the earth goddess Pachamama for a safe journey. The descent through Quebrada Illampu to the Sorata-Ancoma-Cocoyo road takes 1½ hours and passes plenty of camping possibilities. Join the road, turn right (southeast), and follow it down for 40 minutes to the turnoff before Ancoma to Estancia Utaña Pampa at 3,877 m (12,720 ft). The Estancia—today a small village rather than a single farm—is also home to a trout farming cooperative.

Camping is possible around Estancia Utaña Pampa, but not recommended due to the proximity of the village. It is preferable to continue on the road to Ancoma, where you can buy basic supplies and camp for US$2 per person. If you want to camp around Estancia Utaña Pampa, head up the Quebrada Ancohuma Jahutra valley as far as possible—but not as far as the climbers who use this valley to Aguas Calientes as one of the approaches for Illampu—and then retrace your steps to Estancia the next morning.

Option 2, via Aguas Calientes: In Lakathiya, cross to the right over the aqueduct and leave the village on the broad path to the right and above the soccer field. After **15 minutes** reach a plain with excellent camping for Day 1.

On Day 2, continue up the right-hand side of the plain to reach a second, smaller plain. Cross the plain, staying to the right of the stream, and follow the clear-cut and marked path, which rises up above the right-hand side of the third plain. Head for the orange-red scree, which takes you to Paso Huila Khota in **3 hours** from the first plain. There are small, intermittently worked copper and wolfram mines dotted around high up the valley sides. From the pass, it takes less than **45 minutes** to descend 200 m (650 ft) to the small plain of Aguas Calientes (despite their name, these springs are merely tepid and greasy) and excellent camping at 4,600 m (15,100 ft), though the frogs croak all night. Aguas Calientes is Camp 2 for climbers attempting Illampu via the normal route up the South-West Ridge. On Day 3, from Aguas Calientes, descend the left-hand side of the valley to reach Estancia Utaña Pampa in under **2 hours.** (If you are using option 2, Paso Korahuasi, described below, cross the valley and head up, right, before reaching Estancia Utaña Pampa.) From Estancia Utaña Pampa there are two routes to Cocoyo.

Option 1: The road continues to Ancoma, where it is possible to buy basic supplies and camp (the local people charge US$2 per person to camp). (Trek 8, Camino de Oro, goes through Ancoma.) From Ancoma, the road continues through the Paso Kalamuntani at 4340 m (14,239 ft) before dropping down to Cocoyo.

Option 2: The preferred route, which is more impressive and hassle-free,

Going through Chihuani, Illampu Circuit

uses Abra (Paso) Korahuasi, 4,479 m (14,695 ft). To reach Abra Korahuasi, take the track down (south) immediately before the road over Río Chuchu Jahuria in Estancia Utaña Pampa. Reach a one-stone bridge across Quebrada Ancohuma Jahutra and then head along the left-hand side of the stream, keeping a lookout for a path heading up, left (southeast). Head up and into the hanging valley and continue to Abra (Paso) Korahuasi, **2 hours.** The descent passes plenty of camping possibilities before the path contours right and out of the valley, giving impressive views down to the Cocoyo plain—wide, long, and flat with steep sides. The path follows a series of zigzags to reach the head of the plain **1¾ hours** after the pass, with excellent camping for Day 3. The valley running into the plain is the climbers' main approach route to Ancohuma.

It is **35 minutes** to the village of Cocoyo, staying on the left-hand (northern) side of the valley. Cocoyo, where the two options rejoin, is at 3,512 m (11,522 ft). There are two shops close to the bridge, one before and one after, where bread, tuna, canned tomatoes, and some other basics are normally available. Cross the Cocoyo bridge and follow the track up and right (southeast) and out of the village. Go around the corner but do not cross the bridge over the Río Sarani. Instead continue up the right-hand (western) side of the valley. Camping is possible 15 minutes above Cocoyo and at many other places along the Sarani valley. After **1½ hours,** a huge, flat boulder forms a bridge across the Río Sarani, taking the path onto the left-hand (eastern) side of the valley. A **couple of minutes** later there is a group of houses on the left. Go toward the houses and then follow the path that rises up left immediately after them. It is possible to continue up along the valley floor, but the climb out is a lot steeper and involves scrambling. There is camping on the flat and sometimes boggy valley floor, but better camping is **15 minutes** along the path up the left-hand side of the valley near a couple of derelict houses. It takes **another hour** to reach Paso Sarani, 4,600 m (15,100 ft). Camping for Day 4 is possible **10 minutes** below Paso Sarani.

Five minutes below the camping area below the pass, cross the stream to the right. **Five minutes** after the stream, follow a good path going right (south), which reaches the valley bottom in **30 minutes.** (If you want to go to or through the small village of Chajolpaya, continue straight down, east, to the valley bottom, looking out for paths going left. Trek 21, Cordillera Real Traverse, can be done from this point by either going through Chajolpaya, or by following the path right to the valley bottom, then crossing the bridge over the Río Chajolpaya and heading up the path on the other side to enter a valley, which leads up southeast from the Chajolpaya valley.)

The Illampu Circuit continues up the right-hand (northwest) side of the Río Chajolpaya. The path is initially rather unclear, as it crosses and goes around a boggy section, but after **20 minutes** it becomes a wide, roughly paved path—the Calzada road. Apparently, this was once a major link between the Altiplano and the Yungas. However, the stone paving is intermittent and not of particularly high quality. It takes **5 hours** to reach Paso Calzada at 5,045 m (16,552 ft). It is a long way, so it's best to get as far up the valley as possible before camping on Day 5. There is excellent camping **35 minutes** up the Calzada road and then **1½ hours** farther up, with views of Calzada to the left and Kasiri to the right. The last good camping before the pass is immediately before the path climbs up, left (southwest) from the valley floor, **4½ hours** after you join the Calzada road.

The Río Chajolpaya is full of sediment, but side streams are clear although spaced apart. The Calzada Pass is broad—it takes 10 minutes to cross from one *apacheta* to the other—and barren. But camping is possible near the numerous small lakes if you want to try sleeping at over 5,000 m (16,400 ft). From the pass, follow the broad path down to the right (west) of Laguna Carizal and on down to Laguna Chojña Khota in **1½ hours.** Turn around for views of Kasiri to the left and Calzada to the right. Camping is possible at the southern end of the lake. The path then crosses Quebrada de Kote to the left (east) and rises up on the other side. Either follow the path and then drop back down to Laguna Cacha, or go cross-country, staying on the right-hand side of the valley, to Laguna Cacha. Either way, you should be at Laguna Cacha in another **1¼ hours,** where camping is possible. From the north end of Laguna Cacha there are two options.

Option 1: Follow the path down and around to the right (west) and then up over a pass to Laguna San Francisco in **2½ hours.**

Option 2: Better, head straight up to the ridge to the northwest. The climb takes **50 minutes** but is worth it for the views of Lake Titicaca, Ancohuma, Kasiri, Calzada, Chearoco, and Chachacomani. From the ridge, descend right (northwest) to follow the lakeshore toward the north end of Laguna San Francisco. From the lake, head up (north) to rejoin the other path in **1¼ hours,** where there is excellent camping. (The flat, green valley continues up to a glaciated pass that is less than 700 m (765 yds) wide, and then the next valley descends to the Cocoyo plain; if glacial retreat continues at current rates, this will be a trekking option in 20 years.)

The two options rejoin at the north end of the lake. The path goes left (southwest) and then bears right (west) across a plain, joining and then leaving the disused road to reach a pile of stones, Point 4867—meters— (15,968 ft) in 1½ hours. Kasiri, Calzada, Chearoco, and Chachacomani are all visible, as is Lake Titicaca 1,057 m (3,468 ft) below. If you think that is a long way down, remember that Sorata is 1,132 m (3,714 ft) below the lake, and that's where you are going. Follow the disused road down for 1¼ hours from Point 4867. As the valley flattens out to the right, the road crosses a small disused aqueduct and a path that cuts back right (north) to a stream. Follow this path, cross the stream, and then 5 minutes later look for a path heading right (northwest). Head north-northwest for Laguna Hualatani (on the DAV map—not marked on Liam O'Brien's map), and then follow the path on the right-hand (eastern) side. The path crosses an aqueduct shortly before reaching an *apacheta* 1 hour after the stream crossing. From this point on, the rest of the trail is almost continually downhill. Camping on Day 6 is possible after the trail crosses a new road 20 minutes below the *apacheta*. (For those doing the trek in 6 days, continue on to Sorata rather than camping here.) The new road is rarely used and is not marked on any available maps.

The descent joins the road shortly before Alto Lojena, which is reached 35 minutes after the road crossing. The road has been washed away at several points. From here, it takes another 40 minutes to get to Millipaya at 3,475 m (11,401 ft). Millapaya has a church bell mounted on some pieces of wood, but no church. There are plenty of trees, and the difference from the high mountain areas of the previous few days is striking. Apart from farming, many of the local men work in small cooperative antimony and gold mines. There are several options from Millipaya.

Option 1: Trucks to La Paz leave irregularly from Millipaya, joining the La Paz–Sorata road above Umanata. If you want a lift back to Sorata, take a ride to the junction and then get a lift heading right (north). There is irregular transport to Sorata along the road on the right-hand (northeastern) side of the valley. Locals may advise you to walk along the road to Sorata, but it takes 3 or 4 hours and you won't see Illampu, Ancohuma, and the other snowy peaks high above the right-hand side of the valley.

Option 2: Go to Loriacani, 25 minutes from Millipaya, which is as far as vehicles can go along the road. Routefinding for the next hour is difficult due to the vegetation and the numerous narrow paths linking fields, going up and over the ridge to the La Paz road, and dropping down to small riverside mines. However, it is worth the effort for the views across the valley and down to Sorata. At Loriacani, cross the stream and head down, following the path through some houses, along a streambed, and out between some cultivated fields. Head up (left) to join a good but narrow path that takes you in and out of a series of *quebradas*. There is excellent camping 45 minutes after Loriacani, up and left from the path.

Option 3: Follow the road down the right-hand side of the valley for 30 minutes until the road drops down to the antimony mine Nueva Austria;

drop down around the mine to a bridge across the river and head up on a good path on the other side to reach Loriacani in another **hour.**

From here the path gets clearer and broader. Across the valley there are fantastic views of the glaciated massifs, Illampu on the left and Ancohuma on the right.

From Loriacani it takes **1½ hours** to reach Chihuani at 3,140 m (10,300 ft), dropping down, right (north), to the village, through the village, and then the path drops more steeply. There are many paths. Avoid either dropping too quickly to the Río San Cristobal or going too high. It is possible to select paths that will bring you out exactly at the point where the La Paz–Sorata road bridges the Río San Cristobal at 2,665 m (8,743 ft), reached in just over **1 hour.** Cross the bridge to the right-hand side of the Río San Cristobal and follow the road to Sorata, reached in **1 hour.**

6. Lagunas Glaciar and Chillata
Sorata to the lakes and back
(4 days)

Short, steep, and beautiful, the route up gives fantastic views of the western sides of Illampu and Ancohuma. Laguna Glaciar is high—5,038 m (16,529 ft)—and has small icebergs. Incredibly, you will also see ducks and hummingbirds, as well as breathtaking sunsets and fantastic views of Illampu and across the Río San Cristobal valley. Laguna Chillata is a sacred lake surrounded by legend and mystery. Local witches *(brujos)* communicate with the lake to cure people of diseases and afflictions. There are ruins in the area, allegedly Inca, and tales of gold in the rocks.

Start and Finish

For information on getting to and from Sorata, plus facilities in Sorata, see trek 5, Illampu Circuit.

Itinerary

Day 1, to Titisani. Day 2, to Laguna Glaciar. Day 3, to Laguna Chillata. Day 4, back down to Sorata.

Maps

DAV Cordillera Real Nord (Illampu) covers this area; IGM Sorata 5846 I; Liam O'Brien's map covers this area but not this route.

Other Trekking Possibilities

It is possible to go directly from Titisani to Paso Huila Khota and Aguas Calientes, and from there pick up the rest of the route for trek 5, Illampu Circuit, which descends toward Ancoma. From Ancoma, it is possible to pick up the rest of the route for trek 8, Camino de Oro.

Laguna Glaciar

Route Description

From the main square in Sorata, head up and aim to leave the village heading southeast and into the left-hand (northern) side of the Río Lakathiya valley. After 45 minutes, at a fork in the trail, head down (right) toward the Río Tusca Jahuira, which you cross to the right **1¼ hours** out of Sorata. Follow paths up and through the strungout village of Conani, and over the ridge above in another **hour.** Cross the flattish section—but do not follow the road, as it takes the long way around—and follow a gently rising southerly traverse. Then turn left and up, following the first decent stream, to reach an excellent spot for lunch in **30 minutes,** with panoramic views of Illampu on the left and Ancohuma on the right. Continue southward and upward, following any of the numerous paths heading for the gap between Illampu and Ancohuma. A notch at 4,400 m (14,400 ft) is reached in **1½ hours** overlooking the moraine, rock, and glacier below Pico Schulze. Mules cannot make the short, steep descent, so you have to carry your packs down and then up to reach the abandoned mine and camping in **25 minutes** at Titisani. Below camp drops the steep Río Jalanta valley.

From camp, head up the right-hand side of the stream that runs through the camp and then follow a rising traverse with views of Sorata 1,700 m (5,600 ft) below, Lake Titicaca, and, way to the north, the glaciated peaks of the Cordillera Apolobamba. The path is normally clear and there are spray-paint marks on the rocks. **Two hours** later, cross streams flowing from the glacial tongue and then head up to the right-hand side of the moraine ridge to arrive at Laguna Glaciar and camping in **another hour.** The main stream from the lake is full of sediment, but there are a number of clear ponds within a few minutes of the camping area.

The descent follows the same route back to the notch above the abandoned Titisani mine, reached in **2 hours** from Laguna Glaciar. **Fifteen minutes** from the notch, at about 4,300 m (14,100 ft), head off to the right, following a series of faint paths, to reach Laguna Chillata at 4,204 m (13,792 ft) in **45 minutes,** where it is possible to camp. The ruins are to the north of the lake.

From Laguna Chillata, head straight down until you meet up with the main path again, or head off cross-country following animal paths to reach the valley of Río Tusca Jahuira above its confluence with the Río Lakathiya. Descend to the river, cross to the right, and follow the good path back to Sorata in **4 hours.**

7. Mapiri Trail
Ingenio to Mapiri
(8 days)

This is a hardcore trek. You will have to battle with thick vegetation, fallen trees, pervasive insects, and, depending on the time of year, ubiquitous mud. The Mapiri Trail starts in the village of Ingenio, northwest of Sorata, and trends northward up to Mapiri. It is extremely remote and there are few reliable water sources en route. You need to carry at least 4 liters (quarts) of water per person for the lower part of the trail, which is dry.

Louis Demers, manager of the Residencial Sorata, has investigated the history of the Mapiri Trail. The trail is neither Inca nor pre-Hispanic, but was built in the nineteenth century to facilitate the transport of quinine out of the Mapiri area. The construction contract required a trail 1.5 m (5 ft) wide in difficult sections and 3 m (10 ft) wide in easier parts. It was predicted that the trail would halve the cost of transporting the quinine. Unfortunately, the trail was finished around 1879, at the same time as quinine began to be industrially cultivated elsewhere in the world, where transport costs were lower. As a result, the Bolivian quinine industry collapsed.

However, rubber was then found in the same area and this injected new life into the trail until the 1950s. In 1906 the explorer and adventurer Colonel Fawcett used the Mapiri Trail to reach the Amazon. After the decline of the rubber trade, the Mapiri Trail fell into disuse and eventually disappeared. But in 1989, it was reopened by miners looking for gold.

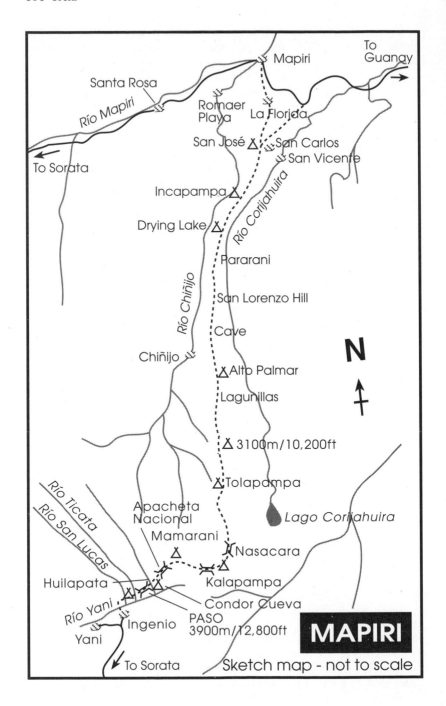

To Guanay

Mapiri

Santa Rosa

Río Mapiri

Romaer Playa
La Florida

San José

San Carlos
San Vicente

To Sorata

Incapampa

Río Corijahuira

Drying Lake

Pararani

San Lorenzo Hill

Río Chiñijo

Cave

Chiñijo

Alto Palmar

Lagunillas

N

3100m/10,200ft

Tolapampa

Lago Corijahuira

Apacheta Nacional
Mamarani

Río Ticata
Río San Lucas

Nasacara

Huilapata

Kalapampa

Río Yani

Condor Cueva

Ingenio

PASO
3900m/12,800ft

Yani

To Sorata

MAPIRI

Sketch map - not to scale

As long as the path has been used or cut recently, routefinding should be relatively straightforward. A stick is useful for knocking the vegetation before you brush through it, and also helps to scare off snakes. Don't wear glasses unless you have to—they reduce your peripheral vision, so you are more at risk of getting a poke in the eye from the vegetation. Start as early as possible each day—cloud normally comes in between midday and 2:00 P.M. and it rains most days during the afternoon.

Take a comb with you—there are *mañu mañu* flies, which do not bite but get stuck in your hair if you stop for more than 5 minutes, and the only way to remove them is by combing them out. (The best way to deal with the *mañu mañu* flies is to urinate into a white bowl—the flies are attracted to the urine and drown in it.) Other pleasures are *tufos/tujos* ants, which eat tents and clothes—do not camp above their underground nests. Check and doublecheck at night by walking around the tent before going to sleep. Wear long-sleeved shirts and trousers to limit your exposure to ticks in long grass and to reduce scratches from vegetation. Watch out for the double-ended brown eistis ant—its bite can cause a whole limb to swell up. Insecticide spray is useful, especially if you are attacked by a bee swarm.

Louis Demers, who has done the route twice, says, "The Mapiri Trail is for the dedicated masochist athlete." Despite this, Mapiri does have some fans. Mules cannot do this trek because there are several sections where you have to crawl under fallen trees. But guides can be hired in Sorata.

Start

Ingenio is a small village at 3,550 m (11,650 ft) with two basic *alojamientos*—the more expensive one (US$1) has beds; the cheaper one (US$0.60) has mattresses on the floor. To reach Ingenio, travel from La Paz to Sorata (see "Start" for trek 5, Illampu Circuit), then take a pickup from Sorata (US$6), a 4-hour trip. Ask Louis Demers at the Residencial Sorata for assistance in getting a pickup. Leave as early as possible.

Finish

Mapiri is a small gold-mining village at 613 m (2,010 ft) with two *alojamientos*, some shops, and an Entel (international) telephone office. Santa Rosa, 1 hour out of Mapiri by pickup, has a good hotel.

To return to La Paz from Mapiri, get a pickup for the 1-hour journey to Santa Rosa. From Santa Rosa it is 11 hours to Sorata by pickup or jeep (US$12 per person). Alternatively, you could take a boat down the Río Mapiri to Guanay (US$6), a 3-hour trip. From here, it is possible to get a bus back to La Paz, or continue downriver by boat to Rurrenabaque (US$20)—see chapter 10, Rurrenabaque and the Western Amazon Basin.

Itinerary

Day 1, to Río Ticata. Day 2, to Mamarani. Day 3, to before or after Nasacara. Day 4, to ridgetop camp at 3,100 m (10,200 ft). Day 5, to Alto

Conflicting path use: sheep on the move below Sorata

Palmar. Day 6, to drying lake below Pararani. Day 7, to San José. Day 8, to Mapiri.

Maps

This area is unmapped at any useful scale.

Other Trekking Possibilities

You can walk to Yani (near Ingenio) from Sorata in 2 days. If you do, you could combine any of the Sorata-area treks with this one.

Route Description

From Ingenio, walk 50 m (165 ft) to the start of the trail running down the right-hand side of the village. Follow the paving down to the Río Yani, cross to the other side, and then cross the tributary Río San Lucas. Follow the trail, reaching a campsite at 3,550 m (11,650 ft) after **1 hour,** just before the Río Ticata.

Cross the Río Ticata and continue up past the last two inhabited houses to a pass in 1¼ hours at 3,900 m (12,800 ft). Drop down, cross a ridge, go through Huilapata (in between Condor Cueva and Apacheta Nacional), and cross a river that runs back to the Río Yani. Camping is possible here. Head up and over another ridge and up to a second ridge in 1¼ hours, which marks the divide between the Río Yani and Río Chiñijo valleys. Below the Condor Cueva at 3,850 m (12,600 ft), there is excellent camping. There is a lake 100 m (330 ft) up (left) from the trail and it is another 30 minutes to the Apacheta Nacional, as it is painted. A well-built staircase drops 120 m (400 ft) down. After the bottom of the zigzags, a path leads off left. Do not follow it; it is probably a failed attempt to reopen a very old path to Chiñijo. Some 45 minutes from the pass, there is another stream and, immediately afterward, good camping at Mamarani at 3,650 m (12,000 ft)—but watch out for the cows.

From Mamarani it is **1¼ hours** to a lake where it is also possible to camp. Another **1½ hours** brings you through an area called Kalapampa, and to the next river and possible camping. A **half hour** on is another stream and camping, and then stone steps up; cross the next stream and reach the top of a ridge at a point called Nasacara at 3,950 m (13,000 ft). Farther on it is possible to look back to the valley of the Río Yani. From here the trail follows the top of the ridge. The river down to the right is the Río Corijahuira.

After **2 hours or so** on the ridge, there is a cave off to the right, and camping before the next river. A **half hour** farther on is Tolapampa, marked by an abandoned house built in 1895 to shelter mule drivers, with a stream and camping. Following the ridge, drop into and rise out of patches of jungle, and after **3 hours** reach excellent camping on top of the ridge at 3,100 m (10,200 ft). Enjoy it, since from here on it is jungle. If this area is dry and parched, seriously consider abandoning the route and walk back to Ingenio, because water will be very scarce below this point. The water sources mentioned below are for average years.

As you enter the jungle, keep a careful eye on the trail and bear right. **Two hours** later there is a small clearing with water and a big landslide. Do not attempt to cross it, as it is easy to slip and slide down. Beyond the landslide is a hilltop at 2,800 m (9,200 ft), **1½ hours** from the clearing. Two more dry hilltops and **4 hours** later, reach Lagunillas. This is the last guaranteed water supply and a good place to camp, but leaves you with a very long waterless next day. Fifty years ago, muleteers used to wade through waist-deep bog across this section when the trail was in regular use and being churned up by mule trains every day. A better alternative is to fill all water containers—you need enough water to get through the whole of the next day—and carry on up for **1 hour** to camp at Alto Palmar at 2,700 m (8,850 ft), which is dry.

The next day, after **4 hours,** when you reach the lowest point, there is a cave to the right of the trail with a seep, which would provide emergency water for a small group. From the cave it is **45 minutes** up to the dry San Lorenzo hilltop at 2,200 m (7,200 ft), where the bees and flies start to swarm in earnest. **Three hours** down, **1½ hours** below an area called Pararani, there is a receding lake, which is the next source of water—8 hours from Alto Palmar and 9 hours from Lagunillas. Camp before the lake.

Exit the jungle and **4 hours** later reach Incapampa and a marsh, which can sometimes provide water in the center if you dig a bit; there is camping shortly afterward. **Three hours** later there is better camping and water at a long-abandoned hacienda site called San José. The water is 300 m (1,000 ft) from the hacienda site following a trail to San Carlos, a hacienda still in use, back up (right).

This area is famed for its long grass, which conceals snakes, ticks, bees, and horseflies. Cows are also a problem—they graze at night, which can keep you awake, and they are inquisitive and will push around, knocking down tents, unintentionally or intentionally.

From San José, continue down for **1 hour** to reach a junction. From here, you can make a run for the road off to the right, which is **1½ hours** away (but unless you get a lift, it is a 4- to 6-hour road slog to Mapiri). A better idea is to continue on through La Florida and from there you can reach Mapiri in **4 hours.**

8. Camino de Oro
Sorata to Llipi or Unutuluni
(6–7 days)

A thousand-year history, dramatic changes in landscape and vegetation, and the impact of a new gold rush combine to make the Camino de Oro, or Gold Diggers' Trail, a unique trek. It begins in the heights of the Cordillera Real and ends in lowland jungle. If you start walking in Sorata, you have to ascend to Abra Illampu at 4,741 m (15,554 ft). But if you prefer, you can skip this and take a jeep up and down to Ancoma. (If you start in Ancoma, you can complete the trek in 3 or 4 days.)

Dating back to pre-Hispanic times, the Camino de Oro served as a trade route between the settlements of the Altiplano and the gold fields of the Río Tipuani valley. Much of the gold used in the buildings of the Inca capital Cusco is thought to have come from the Tipuani fields.

Today, a large proportion of Bolivia's gold production comes from the Tipuani valley. Thousands of migrants have been drawn to the region, seeking their fortune, and this has spawned a road that is gradually pushing up the valley, eating up the ancient trail.

You reach the first mining cooperatives before the halfway point, at Ocara. But don't let this put you off. The trail remains intact as far as the Inca staircase near Puente Nairapi, and although a lot of jungle has been cleared, along

Illampu, Camino de Oro (Andrew North)

the north bank of the Tipuani it is still largely untouched for most of the trail. There is a fascination in the mining operations themselves. There are now plans to drive the road down from Ancoma. Do the trek while you can.

Start

For information on reaching Sorata, its accommodations, and the first stretch to Abra Illampu, see trek 5, Illampu Circuit.

From Sorata, rather than walking to Ancoma you can take a jeep over the pass to Ancoma and start your trek there. Louis Demers, the manager of the Residencial Sorata, can help you find a lift over the pass. There are several locals in Sorata with the necessary four-wheel-drive vehicle or *camioneta*, who will make the 3-hour journey (US$55). The exhilarating journey compensates somewhat for the cost, with spectacular views of Sorata and the Illampu massif. The cheaper, but less reliable, option is to be in the Sorata plaza around 6:00 A.M. and see if any pickups are heading toward Ancoma. You could get a lift to the top of the pass, from where it is about a 2-hour downhill walk along the road into Ancoma.

Ancoma is a settlement of around 100 huts situated in a flat meadow next to the Río Illampu (which becomes the Río Tipuani further downstream), below the route of the trail. It has one or two shops. If you don't

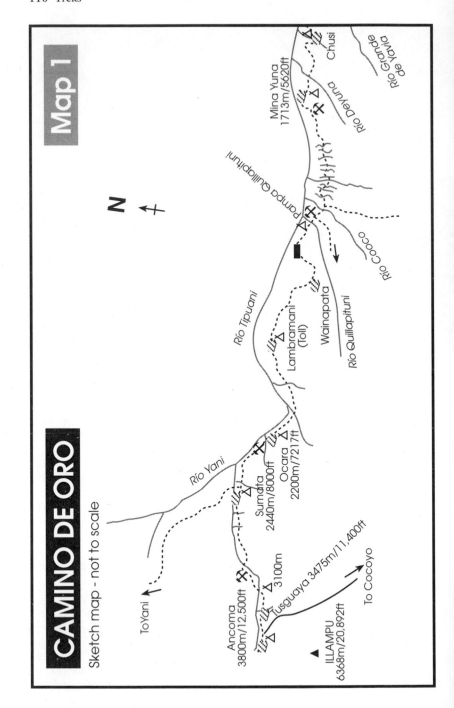

Map 1

CAMINO DE ORO

Sketch map - not to scale

N

To Yani

Río Yani

Río Tipuani

Ancoma
3800m/12,500ft

3100m

Sumata
2440m/8000ft

Ocara
2200m/7217ft

Lambramani
(Toll)

Wainapata

Tusguaya 3475m/11,400ft

To Cocoyo

ILLAMPU
6368m/20,892ft

Pampa Quillapituni

Río Quillapituni

Río Cooco

Mina Yuna
1713m/5620ft

Chusi

Río Deyuna

Río Grande
de Yavia

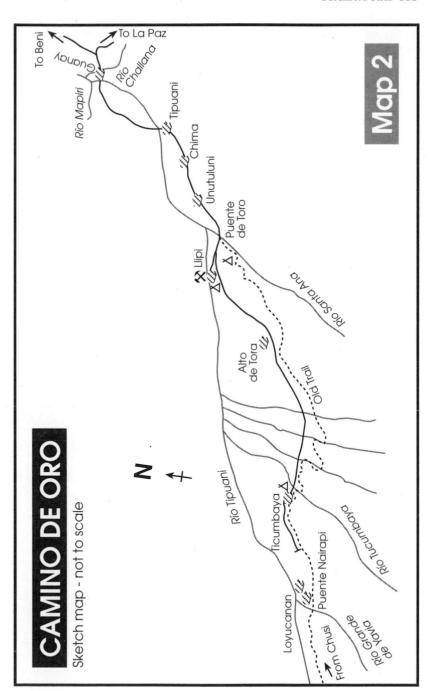

Map 2

CAMINO DE ORO

Sketch map - not to scale

want to go any farther the day you arrive, you can camp on the soccer field or nearby, although you might be charged US$2.

If you want to use mules, you can hire them in Sorata or Ancoma, plus the services of an *arriero* (muleteer) as a guide. One mule can carry two rucksacks. Rates for a mule and guide range from US$8 to $11 per day. If you want mules for the whole trip and the muleteer does not want to travel that far, ask him where you can hire other mules en route. Ocara and Wainapata are two places to try.

Finish

The trail ends at whichever point the road has reached when you do the trek. But you have to get to Llipi to link up with transport out of the region. It is best to get to Llipi as early as possible. There are several *camioneta* services linking up Llipi with the larger mining towns downriver—Unutuluni, Chima, Tipuani, and Guanay—from where there are connecting buses to La Paz. In Llipi, you can also take your chances with one of the private pickups that bring supplies to the mining settlements.

In Unutuluni, there is daily bus service to La Paz, which leaves at 4:00 P.M. The trip takes between 12 and 13 hours (US$14–$15). More frequent services run from Chima, Tipuani, and Guanay. Guanay is an interesting jungle town from where you can take river trips, so you may want to stay there for a couple of days.

Itinerary

Day 1, to Lakathiya. Day 2, to Ancoma or past Tusguaya. Day 3, to Sumata or Ocara. Day 4, to Pampa Quillapituni. Day 5, to Mina Yuna or Ticumbaya. Day 6, to Ticumbaya, or to Llipi or Unutuluni. Day 7, to Llipi or Unutuluni.

Maps

DAV Cordillera Real Nord (Illampu) covers the first part of the trail to Ancoma, as does the IGM Sorata 5846 I. There are no useful maps available for the rest of the trail until after Llipi (IGM Tipuani 5947 II).

Other Trekking Possibilities

See trek 5, Illampu Circuit, for other trek possibilities beginning in Sorata.

Route Description

For the beginning of the trek, from Sorata to Lakathiya and Ancoma, see the first 2 days of trek 5, Illampu Circuit. You can stay the second night in Ancoma, or continue on 1½ hours to camp past Tusguaya.

On Day 3, from Ancoma the trail heads due east out of the settlement and at this point it is still a jeep track. As you leave, with the river below and on your left, pass a shop where you can buy bread, sweets, drinks, and other basic provisions. **Ten minutes** out of the village, the track forks, with the jeep track leading up the hillside to the right. Take the lower path, which heads downhill for a while before climbing again above the river. About **1 hour** of walking takes you to the village of Tusguaya (sometimes written as Tusuaya).

Fifteen minutes beyond, just past a cluster of huts, is a large open meadow above the river, which offers good camping. Look behind you and there is a magnificent view of the Illampu and Ancohuma massifs. Next to the river itself are a couple of smaller patches of open ground which also make good campsites. This is also a good place to try some trout fishing. The trail goes straight across the meadow and then narrows. The vegetation also changes significantly: look for wild rhododendron, bromeliads, and cactuses as you descend, as well as the occasional clump of bamboo. You may encounter large areas of hillside where the vegetation has been deliberately burned by local people. The aim of this destructive practice is to capture small animals.

Twenty to 30 minutes of walking brings you to your first stone staircase, which might or might not have been constructed by the Incas. From here descend through increasingly dense vegetation to Río Tipuani. In another **half hour** you arrive at a meadow and a log bridge across the Tipuani. The path then stays fairly close to the river and there are several steep downward sections. On the rocks below are painted notices prohibiting fishing, put up by the local cooperatives. At various points along the river you may see stone dams that have been built to trap fish. Locals sometimes use dynamite, detonated under the water, to stun the fish and bring them to the surface.

Forty minutes from the first bridge, reach a log bridge back across the Tipuani. Just before you cross, you will see a small miners' encampment. The trail now stays to the right (south) of the Río Tipuani, until the end of the trek. **Twenty minutes** from the second bridge, the vegetation opens out and you have a wonderful view of the tree canopy in the valley below. The trail stays fairly close to the river, before opening out into a clearing, where there are several ruined houses and gravestones. Look for wild strawberries in the forest. **An hour** farther on is Sumata, which consists of two houses and a clearing above the river. You can camp here or continue on to Ocara.

Beyond Sumata is a slippery stone staircase. Soon after come the first signs of the gold mining operations: rockfalls from blasting, miners' shacks, and working mines. The color of the river also changes from its earlier healthy-looking gray-green to a dirty industrial color. It is then a fairly constant descent to Ocara, **an hour** beyond Sumata at 2,200 m (7,217 ft).

After the raw beauty of the mountains and jungle, it is depressing to arrive in this little mining settlement, with electricity pylons and television aerials. Above the settlement, the hillside has been almost totally cleared of trees. Many of the miners are migrants from the Brazilian border region and consequently speak Brazilian Portuguese. Most trekkers stop short and camp at Sumata, but it is possible to put up your tent in Ocara. The village shops stock basic food supplies.

The trail goes through the upper level of Ocara before climbing above the river. Make sure you have sufficient water supplies for Day 4, as you will not see the river again until just before Pampa Quillapituni, some 4 hours later. Below are yet more mines. Twenty minutes beyond Ocara, the trail splits, with one path heading down to a mine. Take the high road. Watch for epiphytic orchids living on the branches of trees, wild begonias, and, as you cross streams, giant prehistoric tree ferns.

About 1½ hours out of Ocara, as you are still climbing, arrive at Lambramani. Its enterprising inhabitants often try to enforce a toll on passing trekkers. If you can, avoid paying, as it will only perpetuate the practice here and elsewhere. From Lambramani, it is just over 1 hour to the hillside village of Wainapata, which is surrounded by banana plantations. Here you can buy big bunches of bananas for US$0.20, and they sometimes have bread. A half hour beyond, the trail splits, with one path going uphill. Take the downhill trail toward the river, which brings you to a tunnel through the rock. Fifteen minutes later, the trail opens into the clearing at Pampa Quillapituni, where the Río Quillapituni joins the Río Tipuani. This makes an excellent campsite and is perhaps one of the most beautiful parts of the trail.

As you continue on Day 5, the trail goes through the clearing and across a small suspension bridge before climbing a steep stone staircase. A half hour farther on, reach a path up to the right; avoid it and continue to the next bridge. Ten minutes later, avoid another small path heading up to the right. For the next 2½ hours, the trail trends upward, although you have to negotiate several steep descents down stone staircases and various high-sided cuts in the mountainside. Four hours from Pampa Quillapituni, reach the mining settlement of Mina Yuna, nestling on a ridge at 1,713 m (5,620 ft). The trail passes across one of the local mines just before reaching the town. (Camping is possible on the soccer field the other side of the village, or you can continue to Ticumbaya.)

An hour farther is Chusi, clinging to the hillside. It's not the most attractive of places, but it does have a good selection of food: pasta, bread, canned tuna, drinks, chocolate, and vegetables. There is no space for camping here, although the villagers allow trekkers to sleep in the school. The trail climbs briefly out of Chusi before descending steeply to the bridge at Puente Nairapi, over 1½ hours away. Stock up on water at the bridge, which crosses a tributary of the Tipuani, because that is the last reliable supply until Llipi, over 4 hours away. Soon after the bridge, the trail joins a well-preserved and very steep staircase. This effectively marks the end of the trail, as the road begins at the top of the climb. It is not yet clear whether this staircase will be obliterated as the road pushes forward. From the top, it is about 1 hour along the road to the small settlement of Ticumbaya. It consists of a few huts and a soccer field on a bluff above the road, where you can camp. Ask one of the residents. There is water **5 minutes** down the road, where it crosses a stream.

On your last day, it is then over **2 hours** of hard, boring slogging along the road to get down to Llipi. There are no campsites in Llipi, but it does have a soccer field. In Unutuluni, 1 hour's pickup truck journey from Llipi or a hard, unpleasant **2- or 3-hour walk,** there is a basic travelers' lodge, the Alojamiento El Amigo. Ask about it at the café on what passes for Unutuluni's main square. Next to the café is the telephone office; you can make international calls from there. After experiencing the town's surreal atmosphere, complete with its resident colony of circling vultures, you might feel like phoning to tell someone!

9. Hichukhota to Condoriri
Lago Khotia to Laguna Chiar Khota
(2–3 days)

This high-level trek skirts the western side of the Cordillera Real before heading into the heart of the range via a spectacular pass with fantastic views of the Cabeza del Condor peak. This trek takes you closer to a glacier than any other trek in the Cordillera Real, and ends at the beautiful Condoriri base camp. The 3-day itinerary means short days, but this is ideal if you are still acclimatizing.

Start

Hichukhota is the name for both a small village and the valley containing the three lakes Khara Khota, Khotia, and Jankho Khota. From Hichukhota you drive to the southern end of Lago Khotia. There is no regular public transport from La Paz to Hichukhota and Lago Khotia. You have to hire a jeep, which takes 2 hours from La Paz (US$120). There are no amenities in Hichukhota.

Finish

At Laguna Chiar Khota is the Condoriri base camp, with plenty of camping but nothing else. From Laguna Chiar Khota, walk down to Tuni, where there is no regular public transport but a prearranged jeep out to La Paz takes 2 hours (US$60).

Itinerary

Day 1, to Laguna Ajwañi or Lago Sistaña. Day 2, to Lago Juri Khota or Laguna Chiar Khota. Day 3, to Laguna Chiar Khota.

Maps

Walter Guzmán's Condoriri-Negruni. IGM Lago Khara Khota 5945 IV, Peñas 5945 III, and Milluni 5945 II. Liam O'Brien.

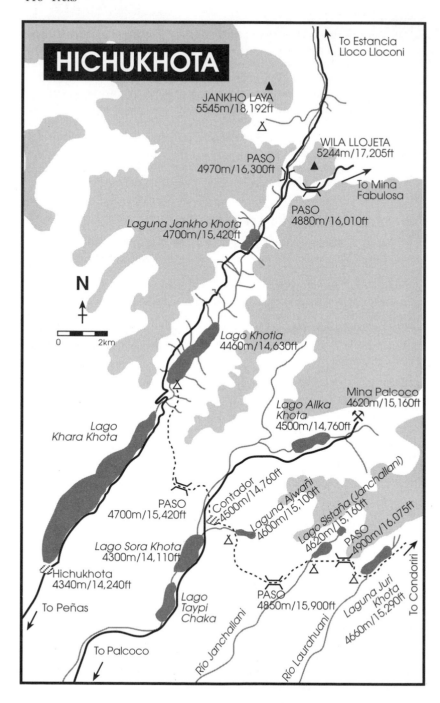

HICHUKHOTA

To Estancia
Lloco Lloconi

JANKHO LAYA
5545m/18,192ft

WILA LLOJETA
5244m/17,205ft

PASO
4970m/16,300ft

To Mina
Fabulosa

PASO
4880m/16,010ft

Laguna Jankho Khota
4700m/15,420ft

N

0   2km

Lago Khotia
4460m/14,630ft

Mina Palcoco
4620m/15,160ft

Lago Allka
Khota
4500m/14,760ft

Lago
Khara Khota

Contador
4500m/14,760ft

Laguna Ajwani
4600m/15,100ft

Lago Sistaña (Janchallani)
4620m/15,160ft

PASO
4900m/16,075ft

PASO
4700m/15,420ft

Lago Sora Khota
4300m/14,110ft

Hichukhota
4340m/14,240ft

To Peñas

Lago
Taypi
Chaka

PASO
4850m/15,900ft

Laguna Juri
Khota
4660m/15,290ft

To Condoriri

Río Janchallani

Río Laurahuani

To Palcoco

Laguna Juri Khota and Cabeza del Condor, Hichukhota to Condoriri

Other Trekking Possibilities

Continue on trek 10, Condoriri to the Zongo valley, where there is reasonably regular transport back to La Paz. The walk out across the Altiplano to the La Paz–Huarina blacktop road is 25 km (16 mi) of not very interesting road slog.

Route Description

From the campsite at the southern end of Lago Khotia, head up the path that rises gently and diagonally up to the east of Lago Khara Khota to reach a flat pass area in **1 hour**. Following animal paths, descend along the left-hand side of the valley—the road on the other side goes to Mina Palcoco—to arrive at the bottom of the valley and a stream crossing in **1 hour**. Follow paths rising up and left through the small settlement of Contador. Do not follow the first stream up but continue on to reach an aqueduct that leads to Laguna Ajwañi, **1¼ hours** from the stream crossing. There are many birds in and around Laguna Ajwañi—including seagulls—and it is an ideal place to camp.

Head up (right) from the lake, cross over the road, and continue uphill before contouring around to the left and up. Cross either of the two passes visible—the right-hand one is lower—both of which have great views of Huayna Potosí. Drop down to ideal camping just below Lago Sistaña (also known as Laguna Janchallani) in 1½ **hours** from Laguna Ajwañi.

Head up, going away from Lago Sistaña, to reach another broad pass area after **35 minutes,** and then drop left to reach Laguna Juri Khota in another **40 minutes,** where it is possible to camp at the southwest end.

Mules and llamas use a path that goes up directly from the southern end of the lake, but it is far more interesting to continue northeast on either side of the lake; fill up water bottles before rising above it. At the northern end of the lake, head up the stone moraine ridge on the right-hand side to reach a rocky viewpoint above the glacier with impressive views of the peaks Ala Izquierda and Cabeza del Condor in 1¼ **hours** from the northern end of the lake. Stay on the left-hand side of the rock and work out a route. (It is not as steep as it first seems.) Arrive at a pass to the northeast of Pico Austria in **45 minutes,** overlooking Laguna Chiar Khota and with views of Huayna Potosí. (It is possible to climb Pico Austria in 45 minutes from the pass.) The descent to Chiar Khota takes less than 1 **hour.**

10. Condoriri to the Zongo Valley
Tuni to Chacapampa
(2–3 days)

Driving across the Altiplano, Condoriri is one of the most striking mountain groups in the Cordillera Real. The three highest peaks together look like a condor lifting its wings before takeoff. According to legend, the largest and most ferocious condors of the Andes live around Condoriri. Peasants leave their babies there to be fed and brought up by the condors. These babies then grow up to be human-condors.

The area was first explored by the British mountaineer Sir Martin Conway (who in 1898 became the first person to climb Illimani). He said that as night fell, "clouds" of condors appeared. While the condors are not nearly so numerous nowadays, it is normally possible to see one or two circling high above the mountains of the Condoriri group. This trek crosses the Cordillera Real near its midpoint.

Start
Tuni is a small village with no shops. There is no regular public transport from La Paz to Tuni, so you have to take a 2-hour jeep trip from La Paz (US$50). It is possible to hire llamas (US$4) or mules (US$8 each) to carry gear for the 2-hour walk in to camp at 4,600 m (15,100 ft) on the far

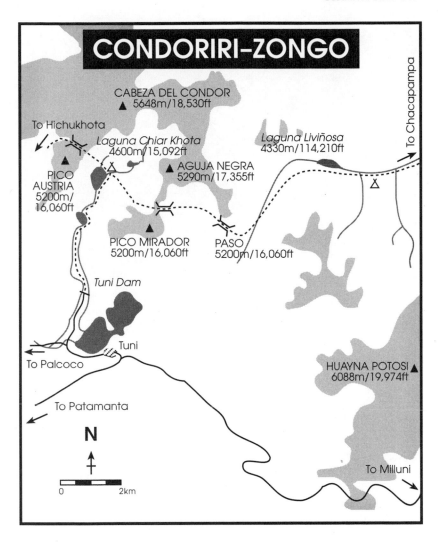

CONDORIRI-ZONGO

To Chacapampa

CABEZA DEL CONDOR
▲ 5648m/18,530ft

To Hichukhota

Laguna Chiar Khota
4600m/15,092ft

Laguna Liviñosa
4330m/114,210ft

PICO
AUSTRIA
5200m/
16,060ft

AGUJA NEGRA
5290m/17,355ft

PICO MIRADOR
5200m/16,060ft

PASO
5200m/16,060ft

Tuni Dam

Tuni

To Palcoco

HUAYNA POTOSI ▲
6088m/19,974ft

To Patamanta

N

To Milluni

0   2km

side of Laguna Chiar Khota, the Condoriri base camp for climbers. Mules and llamas are available at Tuni village and at a place before Tuni known as Plaza de Mulas.

Finish

Chacapampa in the Zongo valley is a small village with no shops. From Chacapampa, the truck from Zongo village to El Alto passes by on Tuesdays, Thursdays, and Saturdays, around 10:00 A.M. to midday (US$2); the truck is difficult to get on; it's 3 hours to Plaza Ballivián in El Alto. There are La Paz-bound jeeps and minibuses at irregular intervals. A jeep takes

Llamas below Abrn Ilampu, Camino de Oro (Andrew North)

2½ hours to reach central La Paz (and costs about US$80 if prearranged).

Itinerary

Day 1, to Laguna Chiar Khota. Day 2, to below Laguna Liviñosa or Chacapampa. Day 3, to Chacapampa.

Maps

Walter Guzmán's Condoriri-Negruni, although the names of most of the Condoriri peaks are wrong. Four IGM sheets are needed to cover the same area as the Guzmán map: Milluni 5945 II, Peñas 5945 III, Zongo 5945 I, and Lago Khora Khota 5945 IV. Liam O'Brien.

Other Trekking Possibilities

Much of the Zongo valley has been destroyed by the construction of hydro-electric installations. It is no longer worth hiking up to the Zongo Pass. Either use transport to get out or head up to the lakes via Estancia Botijlaca and out of the Zongo valley as soon as possible (see trek 12, Lakes).

Route Description

From Tuni, follow the track below the road and then rise up a gentle hill to join the road beyond the Samapa water company gate. Follow the road around the Tuni Dam, and then below and across the bottom of the dam wall and on up to an aqueduct. Stay on the road, with the Cabeza del Condor and its left and right wings in full view, until nearly the end of the aqueduct, where you drop down (left), cross the stream below the concrete wall, and head up following animal paths. Cross the stream back to the right-hand side of the valley via the remnants of a stone bridge, move up a grassy slope, and follow clear animal paths along the side of the valley until you reach Laguna Chiar Khota (in Aymará, "Black Lake"). Camp is at the far (northeast) end of the lake, **2 hours** from Tuni.

On Day 2, head straight up (east-southeast) to the lowest point in the ridge between Aguja Negra and Pico Mirador, which is closer to Mirador and reached in **50 minutes**. The pass area gives great views of the southwest side of Huayna Potosí and back to the Condoriri group. Follow the mule/llama path for a few minutes and then head straight for Huayna Potosí, drop down a short, steep scree gully, and then head down to the valley bottom, with the path up to the next pass directly ahead. Cross the stream **40 minutes** below the first pass and head up for **30 minutes** to reach the next pass, which brings you closer to Huayna Potosí. Cloud tends to come in early—often by midday—on the eastern side of the Cordillera Real, but routefinding is not a problem as you follow the Río Liviñosa valley down from here on. From the pass, descend to the valley bottom and cross the stream to reach the path, which stays on the right-hand side of the stream and becomes increasingly clear, to reach Laguna Liviñosa in **1¼ hours**. Follow the path down the right-hand side of the lake and continue downvalley, cross the aqueduct, and descend through stone-walled fields. Camping is possible near the stream among the stone-walled fields **1 hour** below Laguna Liviñosa, above where the Río Taypi Khuchu joins the Río Liviñosa from the right.

Below this point, virtually all flat land (including the path itself) is cultivated. Stay on the right-hand side of the valley to reach what is now the electricity-generating company village of Chacapampa in **50 minutes.**

11. Milluni Valley
Chacaltaya to Zongo Pass
(1 day)

This high-altitude day trek crosses the 5,345-m (17,536-ft) summit of Chacaltaya, and leads on to many other possible treks. The landscape is barren and bleak but all views north and east are dominated by the 6,088-m (19,974-ft) Huayna Potosí. From Chacaltaya it is possible to see El Alto on the Altiplano and La Paz nestling in the huge canyon below. On the far side of the city, Illimani is visible and on clear days one can see Bolivia's highest mountain, the 6,542-m (21,463-ft) Sajama way over to the west, and also the cobalt-blue Lake Titicaca on the border with Peru.

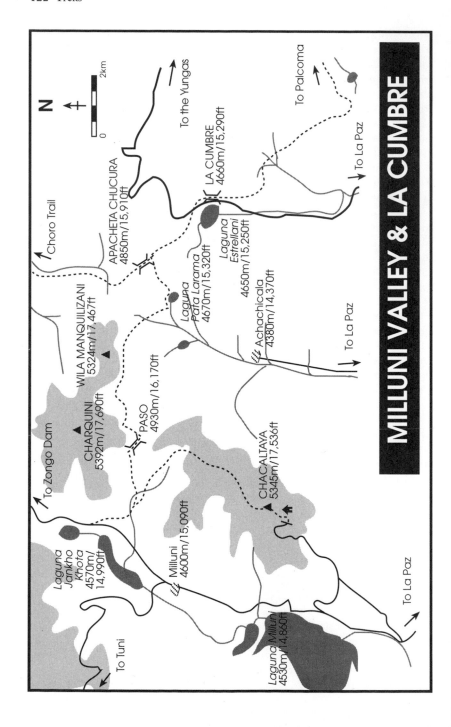

MILLUNI VALLEY & LA CUMBRE

Warning: Do not go to Chacaltaya before acclimatizing for at least a week at the height of La Paz or equivalent, due to the risk of suffering serious altitude sickness.

Start

The Club Andino Boliviano ski hut at Chacaltaya is where this trek begins. On weekends it is possible to have a meal at the hut, if you fancy eating at this altitude. Drinking water is more important for most people. To reach Chacaltaya, the Club Andino sends a bus from outside its La Paz office in Calle México 1648 every Saturday and Sunday at 8:00 A.M. This takes 2 hours. Buy your ticket in advance from the club office (US$10). A jeep takes 1½ hours from La Paz (US$60).

Finish

To use the Huayna Potosí hut at Zongo Pass, it has to be booked. Contact Refugio Huayna Potosí on La Paz 323584 (US$10 per person per night, meals extra, excellent hot shower). To return from Zongo Pass, there is a regular truck (difficult to get on) that comes upvalley from Zongo village on Tuesdays, Thursdays, and Saturdays (reaching the pass around midday), which goes to El Alto's Plaza Ballivian in 2 hours (US$1). From El Alto, there are La Paz-bound jeeps and minibuses at irregular intervals during the season. A jeep takes under 2 hours to get back to central La Paz (US$50).

Itinerary

Day 1, to the Refugio Huayna Potosí at Zongo Pass and back.

Maps

IGM La Paz (Norte) 5944 I and Milluni 5945 II. Guzmán Huauna Potosí. Liam O'Brien.

Other Trekking Possibilities

From Chacaltaya, cross to the Apacheta Chucura towards La Cumbre for the start of the Choro Trail (trek 13), or continue from La Cumbre to Palcoma for trek 14, Hampaturi Trail, to Mina San Francisco.

From the Zongo Pass, you can continue on trek 12, Lakes, and reenter the Zongo valley at Estancia Botijlaca; or you can cross the pass to join trek 13, Choro Trail, at Achura via Uma Palca or Estancia Sanja Pampa.

Route Description

From the Club Andino hut at Chacaltaya, go up to the first summit (**20 minutes**) and then continue to the second summit (**15 minutes**). Go left along the ridge toward an aerial and then drop right to follow the next ridge. Looking back, it is possible to see Titicaca. After **25 minutes,** pick a convenient spot to drop left and descend to the valley bottom in **20 minutes,** then go cross-country toward a wide pass area above a small

Ski lift engine house, Chacaltaya

rock section. The going is easiest to the right **(35 minutes)**. If you hear dull thuds in the distance, they are probably dynamite explosions in the small mines southeast of Chacaltaya.

Descend left into the valley and start heading straight for the impressive bulk of Huayna Potosí's East Face. Cross a track after **55 minutes** and head for the first and then second standing stones. Before you reach the road, contour right and follow animal tracks that join the road after **40 minutes**.

After **15 minutes** on the road, head up and right toward an electricity pylon following an old white granite stone path. Rejoin the road and follow it alongside the right-hand side of the Zongo Dam to reach Refugio Huayna Potosí in **45 minutes**.

The Zongo Dam (and all dams in the area) are for electricity generation. The now deserted small town of Milluni used to house tin miners and their families—up to 4,000 people once lived there—until the collapse of the world tin market in 1985. The peculiar colors of the lakes around Milluni are due to massive chemical and metal contamination.

12. Lakes

Zongo Pass to Estancia Botijlaca
(3 days)

This is a short connecting trek that makes accessible a rarely visited and beautiful area made up of many lakes, dams, and mountains and a few villages unchanged for centuries. The trek is good for acclimatization because it stays fairly high.

Start

The Refugio Huayna Potosí hut at Zongo Pass has to be booked. Contact Refugio Huayna Potosí on La Paz 323584 (US$10 per person per night, meals extra, excellent hot shower). A jeep from La Paz to Zongo Pass takes 1½–2 hours (US$60). A truck from El Alto leaves Plaza Ballivian on Mondays, Wednesdays, and Fridays at midday (US$1), if you can get on it. It is possible to hire a minibus from Plaza Ballivian (about US$8); arrive and haggle with drivers of empty minibuses.

Finish

Estancia Botijlaca is a small village with no shops and nowhere to stay. To return from Botijlaca, hitch a ride or arrange to be picked up.

Itinerary

Day 1, to after the first pass. Day 2, to Laguna Warawarani. Day 3, to Estancia Botijlaca.

Maps

IGM Milluni 5945 II. Liam O'Brien.

Other Trekking Possibilities

From above Uma Palca it is possible to go to Estancia Sanja Pampa in 1 day and then on to Achura on the Choro Trail, and either continue the Choro down to Coroico (trek 13) or go uphill to La Cumbre and back to La Paz. From Uma Palca it is also possible to follow the valley down and right to join the Choro Trail at Choro.

A longer route is to go from Zongo Pass to Apacheta Chucura (see trek 21, Cordillera Real Traverse), drop down to Chucura (see trek 13, Choro Trail), and then go to Sanja Pampa and continue upvalley and then drop to Uma Palca and out.

Route Description

The road above the Huayna Potosí hut heading away from La Paz takes a sharp right bend a couple of minutes from the hut, before starting the steep descent to the Zongo valley. Follow the road for a few meters and start looking to drop left to join the pre-Hispanic path that avoids the zigzags of the modern road. The old path rejoins the road **25 minutes** below. Follow the road, go through the first bend and then leave the road, heading left, after **5 minutes.** Cross a stream to join a well-defined path rising up the hillside. After **45 minutes** the path crosses a stream coming down from the peak Kunatincuta. **Twenty minutes** farther there is a small lake where it is possible to camp. A steady **50-minute** climb brings you to an *apacheta* and **25 minutes** later a pass. From the pass it is only

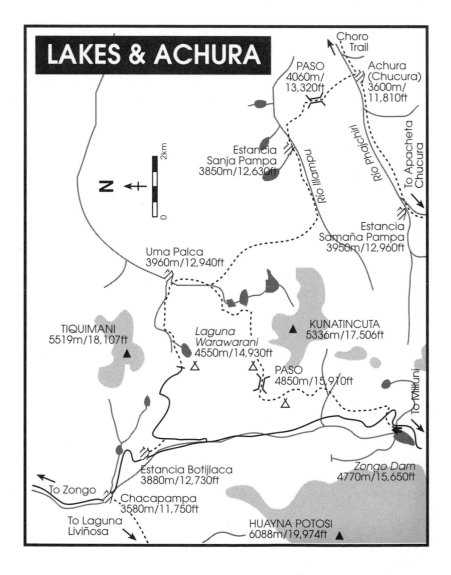

15 minutes to reach the stream in the valley bottom and camping. Avoid the wet patches here.

The first lake is reached in another **25 minutes.** At the far (lower) end of the lake, drop left, pass above two derelict buildings on the shore of another lake, and then head down (left) to reach the shore of a third lake **20 minutes** from the end of the first lake. Follow the path along the left-hand side of the third lake and drop down to the point where the two valleys meet above Uma Palca **(40 minutes).**

Option to Estancia Sanja Pampa and Achura (link to trek 13, Choro Trail): From the point where the two valleys meet above Uma Palca, head right (south-southwest) and up; cross a stream below the first lake after **40 minutes** to reach a campsite above the lake. It can be boggy, but there is a large flat rock to use, if you can get your tent up without using pegs. Follow the path on the right-hand side of the lake, cross the stream to the left, and then cross back to the right before arriving at a second lake **25 minutes** later. Follow the well-defined path up right passing a shelter stone and on to a pass **(35 minutes).** From the pass, descend to a derelict house where it is possible to camp **(10 minutes).** Continue down toward the valley bottom and follow paths that contour left above the valley bottom to reach a series of huge fallen blocks of rock, shelter stones, and camping possibilities after **50 minutes.** Continue along the left-hand side of the valley, cross and recross the stream to reach the photogenic village of Estancia Sanja Pampa in another **50 minutes.** Sanja Pampa has not yet entered the corrugated-iron age—all the roofs are thatched. There are a lot of stone walls dividing up fields—unusual in Bolivia.

In Estancia Sanja Pampa, cross the bridge going right, then cross a smaller stone bridge and rise up right to reach the top of the first ridge in **20 minutes.** Follow the path through immaculately tilled fields to a pass area in another **20 minutes.** Follow the path down, passing good camping possibilities. The path sticks to the right-hand side of the valley and is occasionally rather narrow. Extreme care should be exercised in wet conditions. After **25 minutes** arrive above a lake and **20 minutes** later arrive in Achura. In Achura, you have two options.

Option 1: Cross the bridge and the soccer field to reach a wide path. Turn left and down to follow the Choro Trail to Coroico.

Option 2: Turn right and up to go **3¾ hours** uphill to Apacheta Achura and another **45 minutes** to reach La Cumbre and the blacktop road, and lifts back to La Paz.

For the main route to Laguna Warawarani and Estancia Botijlaca, from the point where the two valleys meet above Uma Palca, continue down to Uma Palca, which is made up of a few small houses, and then follow the path up the left-hand side of the valley coming in from the left. The path goes up to Laguna Warawarani, giving impressive views of the evil-looking and infrequently climbed Tiquimani. There is excellent camping at the far end of the lake, **2½ hours** from Uma Palca.

From the lake follow the path over a small pass and drop down to a new road. Continue along the road until you are overlooking the Zongo valley and the village of Estancia Botijlaca. Do not follow the road down to the valley but descend on a trail directly to the village.

13. Choro Trail
La Cumbre to Coroico
(3–4 days)

Pre-Hispanic paving and a spectacular but savage descent, plus easy route-finding—once you've found the start—make the Choro Trail very popular. The differences in weather, temperature, and vegetation between the

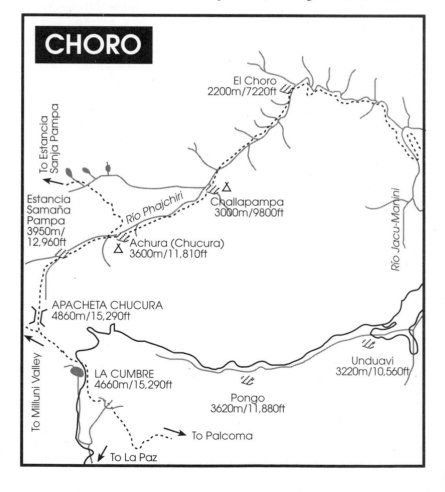

start and finish are extreme. You might start walking across a snow-covered moonscape in a blizzard at 4,800 m (15,750 ft), pass through dense subtropical vegetation, and end up walking alongside citrus plantations at 1,500 m (5,000 ft). There are limited camping places on the trail. Clouds and bad weather are normal at the 4,700-m (15,400-ft) La Cumbre.

Start

La Cumbre is high, bleak, and barren. Get in and get out as quickly as possible. To reach La Cumbre from La Paz, take a bus or *camión* from Villa Fatima. It takes less than an hour to climb the 22 km (14 mi), but make sure the driver knows you want to get off at La Cumbre (US$1). Alternatively, get a radio taxi from central La Paz (about US$12) or hire a jeep (US$30).

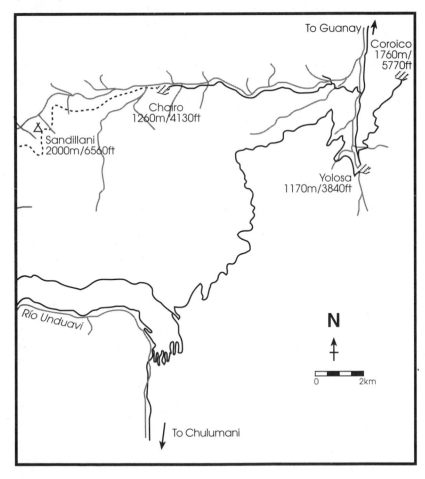

Finish

Coroico ("Gold Hill" in Quechua) is a pleasant town at 1,760 m (5,770 ft) with views of snowcapped Mururata. Coroico is the capital of the Nor Yungas Department, popular with Paceños on the weekends—especially during its main fiesta around October 20—and full of places to stay and eat. The best hotel is the German-Bolivian-run Esmeralda, which has the cleanest swimming pool in town. The owner, Fernando, will save you the 15-minute uphill walk from the town center by picking you up in his jeep. Call on arrival (telephone 6017). Ask Fernando about day-hike possibilities in the area, including the walk up Uchumachi.

You are unlikely to get to Chairo in time to catch the regular transportation out. Rumor has it that there is a truck from Chairo to Yolosa at 6:00 A.M. A truck will go to Yolosa if there are enough people willing to pay US$2.25 each—one of the most expensive truck trips in Bolivia, given the distance (17 km/11 mi), but it is well worth it. From Yolosa it is 8 km/5 mi uphill to Coroico with regular transport for US$0.60 per person.

From Coroico there are hourly minibuses to La Paz through the morning and early afternoon along the infamous Yungas road, clinging to the valley sides. The trip takes 4 hours (US$2.60). Sit on the right-hand side to fully "enjoy" its terrors. The numerous crosses along the side of the road mark the points where fatal accidents have occurred. A number of waterfalls cascade onto the road during the wet season!

Itinerary

Day 1, to Achura or Challapampa. Day 2, to Río Jacu-Manini or Sandillani. Day 3, to Sandillani, Chairo, or Coroico. Day 4, to Yolosa and Coroico.

Maps

Walter Guzmán. IGM Milluni 5945 II and Unduavi 6045 III. Liam O'Brien.

Other Trekking Possibilities

It is possible to start in the Zongo valley and Chacaltaya. See trek 12, Lakes.

From Coroico there are many trekking possibilities: It is possible to trek to the Afro-Bolivian village of Tocaña or to Santa Ana del Vagante in 1 day, with another day for the return. Ask Fernando at the Hotel Esmeralda for more information.

Route Description

Immediately before the blacktop Yungas road drops down from La Cumbre, there is a collapsing plastered brick wall on the left, which marks the start of the trek. However, there are no landmarks to help get you across the 3 km (2 mi) of featureless moonscape to the Apacheta Chucura

Coroico

(1 hour), where the trail proper begins. Follow the jeep track. When you reach a lake, look for a path that rises up (right) to the *apacheta*. Follow the left hand of the statue of Christ, and take a map and compass (or hire a guide) to get you to the start of the trail, which is then well (and pointlessly) marked with paint splashes. The descent from the *apacheta* is spectacular, following a well-built pre-Hispanic road down the left-hand side of the valley. The gradient slackens off once you hit Estancia Samaña Pampa 4 km (2½ mi) farther on and 1,300 m (4,300 ft) farther down. It takes **4 hours** to get to Achura (also known as Chucura) and then another 1¼ **hours** to get to Challapampa (also known as Achapalla Pampa), where it is possible to camp—the locals will ask for money or food. You can also camp in Achura but this will extend an already lengthy second day. There is little to buy in Achura and nothing in Challapampa.

The subtropical vegetation begins, and in **2 hours** and 8 km (5 mi) below Challapampa, reach the Choro bridge. It used to be a regular event for this bridge to get washed away, leaving locals and trekkers alike with a frayed steel cable with which to haul themselves across. The latest bridge appears to be better built than its predecessors. Fill your water bottles—the next **2 hours** and 7 km (4 mi) are dry until you cross the Río Jacu-Manini, which is a nice spot for lunch. Camping space is a bit constricted.

From here it is another dry **3 hours** to Sandillani, where it is possible to camp in the carefully tended garden of Tamiji Hanamura, a Japanese immigrant who has lived in Bolivia for many years. He keeps a book with the names of every passing traveler, and he likes to see postcards and pictures from other countries.

From Sandillani there is good pre-Hispanic paving down to Villa Esmeralda. Continue to Chairo in **2 hours,** where there are limited supplies for sale—bread and canned food. If you've got the money, stay at the five-star Hotel Río Selva; otherwise continue on.

It is 17 km (11 mi), **4 hours,** to Yolosa. The trudge along the road is alleviated by the views of orange, grapefruit, lemon, banana, and coffee plantations, but it is hot. Early in the season the river crossing can be tricky. Take care. From Yolosa it is 8 km (5 mi) uphill to Coroico. Pickup trucks charge US$0.60 per person.

14. Hampaturi Trail
Palcoma to Mina San Francisco or Choquekhota
(2 days)

This is a short trek close to La Paz perfect for acclimatizing or as an alternative start to any of the trails starting at Mina San Francisco. Despite its proximity to La Paz, after Palcoma there are only a couple of farms and you are in the countryside.

Start

In Palcoma there are a few shops selling the basics, but nowhere to stay. To reach Palcoma, get a bus to Alta Pampahasi from the center of La Paz, which takes 20 minutes (US$0.20), or take a radio taxi (US$3). There are regular minibuses from Alta Pampahasi to Palcoma, 45 minutes, but they are often full. Haggle for a price (US$7). A jeep from La Paz to Palcoma takes 1 hour (US$25).

Finish

At Mina San Francisco, there are abandoned mine buildings, plenty of running water, but nothing else. Down the road in Choquekhota, there are a few shops and many begging children. Walk downvalley to Ventilla and take a ride with any vehicle heading toward La Paz.

Itinerary

Day 1, to Laguna Jachcha Khasiri. Day 2, to Mina San Francisco or Choquekhota.

Maps

IGM La Paz (Norte) 5944 I covers the start of the trek, though Palcoma is marked "Estancia Karpani." More useful is Chojlla 6044 IV, which

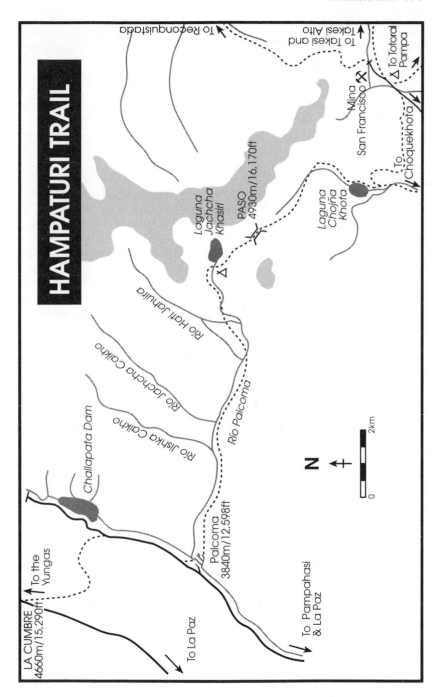

HAMPATURI TRAIL

To Reconquistada
To Takesi and Takesi Alto
To Takesi and Takesi Alto
To Totoral Pampa
Mina San Francisco
To Choquekhota
Laguna Jachcha Khasiri
PASO 4930m/16,170ft
Laguna Chojña Khota
Río Hati Jahuira
Río Jachcha Caikho
Río Jisnka Caikho
Río Palcoma
Challapata Dam
Palcoma 3840m/12,598ft
LA CUMBRE 4660m/15,290ft
To the Yungas
To La Paz
To La Paz
To Pampahasi & La Paz
N
0 2km

covers the main body of the trek and the few routefinding decisions. The
end of the trail to Choquekhota is covered by Palca 6044 III, though this
is as unnecessary as the first sheet.

Other Trekking Possibilities

Mina San Francisco is a possible starting point for trek 15, Mina la
Reconquistada, and trek 16, Takesi Trail and Takesi Alto Option.

It is also possible to continue on to link up with trek 18, Illimani, via
Estancia Totoral Pampa to Lambate, or via Paso Pacuani to Cohoni.

Route Description

From Palcoma at 3,840 m (12,598 ft), cross the river and head up the
valley on the right-hand side. When the vehicle track ends, cross the stream
and follow llama paths up and left, cross a stream, and follow the obvious
contour path up and left below the pointed rock peak. Stay on the left-
hand side of the stream until you reach Laguna Jachcha Khasiri, 4,690 m
(15,387 ft), in **4 hours.** Camp at the far end of the lake.

From the lake, head to the right of the mountain above the lake to a
pass at 4,930 m (16,170 ft) in **1 hour,** with views of Illimani and Mururata
ahead. Descend to Laguna Chojña Khota at 4,200 m (13,800 ft) after **1½
hours** and then continue to the end of the lake in another **15 minutes.**
From the end of the lake there are two options.

Option 1: Follow the path down the valley to arrive in Choquekhota in
under **2 hours** and then follow the road downvalley to Ventilla and hitch a
ride back to La Paz.

Option 2: Do not cross the stream but follow the path up (left) and away
from the lake. The path rises and then contours around to the left until it is
above the Ventilla–Mina San Francisco valley. Descend diagonally (left) along
pre-Hispanic paving to join the road at 4,300 m (14,100 ft) in **1½ hours.**
From here it is **2 hours** down the road to Choquekhota.

15. Mina la Reconquistada
Mina San Francisco to the Sud Yungas road
(2–3 days)

This is an unusual trek because part of it is underground. There is a 200-m
(650-ft) tunnel through the mountain above the abandoned Mina la
Reconquistada, so remember your flashlight. The path from Mina San Francisco to Estancia Totor Pata was rebuilt in 1995 with money from Conservation International.

If you have time at the end of the trek, it is worth visiting the hotel El
Castillo in the village of Chaco. The distinctive round-towered building was
constructed by prisoners taken captive during the Chaco War (1932–35)
with Paraguay. Today, it has its own swimming pool, river, and waterfall.

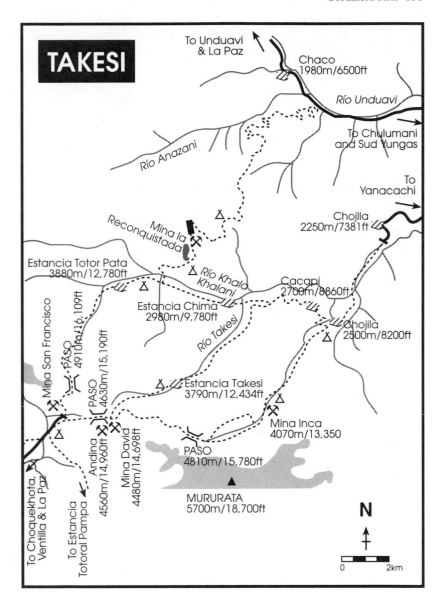

Start

Begin in Ventilla or Mina San Francisco. It is possible to buy some supplies in Ventilla, but easier to bring everything from La Paz. There are regular buses from La Paz to Palca and Ventilla leaving from outside the Comedor Popular in Calle Max Paredes, above the junction with Calle Rodriguez,

Mururata reflected in Laguna Khelluani, Reconquistada

every day at 5:30 A.M. (US$1, journey time 3 hours). You can also hire a radio taxi from central La Paz to Ventilla (US$15).

Other alternatives: In La Paz, get any bus going to Bolsa Negra, Tres Rios, or Pariguaya from Calle General Luis Lara corner Venacio Burgoa, near Plaza Libano, San Pedro. They leave Mondays through Saturdays at 9:00 A.M. It is not possible to buy tickets in advance—there's no ticket office. To ensure a ticket, be there at 7:00 or 8:00 A.M. on the day, or send someone to buy it for you. Drivers may not want to take you just to Ventilla, so you may have to pay more, e.g. up to US$2, which is the fare to Chuñavi.

From La Paz get a micro- or minibus to Chasquipampa or Ovejuyo and try hitching a ride with any vehicle coming from La Paz. If there isn't any transportation available, haggle with drivers of empty minibuses in Ovejuyo; you should be able to get one to go to Ventilla for about US$10.

There is no public or regular transport from Ventilla to Mina San Francisco; you have to hire a jeep from La Paz, which takes less than 2 hours (US$60). Mules can be hired in Choquekhota, midway between Ventilla and Mina San Francisco (US$8 per day plus up to US$8 for the muleteer).

Finish

You come out on the Sud Yungas (La Paz-to-Chulumani) road. To return to La Paz, which is reached in about 3 hours, flag down any vehicle heading left and up. Or flag down any vehicle going down and right if you want to visit Chulumani, which is reached in 2 hours. While the La Paz-to-Chulumani road is statistically a lot safer than the La Paz-to-Coroico road, it is just as impressive and drivers avoid it at night. Therefore, there is little transportation in the afternoons and none once it gets dark. If you can't get a lift or just want to relax, walk up to the El Castillo hotel in the extremely small settlement of Chaco at Km 64 on the Sud Yungas road.

Itinerary

Day 1, to below Totor Pata. Day 2, to below the notch after the tunnel or Sud Yungas Road. Day 3, to Sud Yungas Road.

Maps

IGM Chojlla 6044 IV. Liam O'Brien—but the route does not follow the marked red line from the mine to the pass. That would involve a steep and lengthy drop to the bottom of the valley and a tough climb back out again. Instead, the path contours around as described below.

Other Trekking Possibilities

Alternative starts to Mina San Francisco include trek 14, Hampaturi Trail, and trek 17, Palca Canyon.

Route Description

If you begin walking from Ventilla, 3,200 m (10,500 ft), head upvalley, taking the left-hand road just outside the village. After 1½ hours of following the road up a gentle hill, on the left-hand side of the valley reach the traditional village of Choquekhota. Here, you have to ford the ankle-deep Río Quela Jahuira. The number of children approaching you saying, *"Regálame dulces/plata"* ("give me sweets/money") attests to the popularity of this route. Don't feel special—the kids try it with anyone, Bolivian or foreigner, walking or driving up the road.

Up from Choquekhota, on the right-hand side of the road, is a cemetery. Higher up, a track goes off to the right. Do not follow it unless you want to get really close to the unusually shaped 5,700m (18,700ft) peak of Mururata (see trek 16, Takesi Trail, for more details). Shortly after a river crossing **3 hours** out of Ventilla, reach a disintegrating plaster wall with a map of the trail painted on it. Stay on the road and follow it to its end **30 minutes** later among abandoned mining buildings. The recently rebuilt path continues where the road stops. After **1 hour** there is a lake, where it is possible to camp. It is advisable to fill water bottles here. It takes another **40 minutes** to reach the *apacheta,* with views back of the east side of Illimani, looking far rockier than the normal view of the west seen from La Paz. Camping is possible **20 minutes** below the *apacheta.* It takes another hour to reach the bridge at Totor Pata and the end of the rebuilt path. Stay close to the stream on its right-hand side to reach a *pampa* with good camping at the far end, **45 minutes** from the village.

From the end of the *pampa*, pick up the increasingly distinct path to descend toward the Río Khala Khalani. As you descend, check out the path rising up in zigzags on the other side of the valley. Although it looks prominent, it is not easy finding the start, so remember where it is. After **45 minutes** of descent, there is a wood and mud bridge. Cross it and then leave the path and make your way down (left) to the river. It is possible to find the remains of the bridge and boulder hop to the other side. However, early in the season or after a heavy rain, crossing the Río Khala Khalani can be a risky business involving fast-flowing, waist-deep water.

With the remains of the bridge behind you, head up (right), aiming roughly northwest, to meet up with the path you saw from the other side of the valley. This path is very unclear near the river, but becomes clearer and clearer the higher you get, being cut and paved. From the bridge remains it is **1¾ hours** to reach an *apacheta* and then deserted mine buildings on the side of Laguna Khellhuani, where camping is possible, with great views of Mururata. Follow the path along the right-hand side of the lake to reach the abandoned buildings of Mina la Reconquistada in **45 minutes.** There is a flat area, perfect for camping, but very little—if any—water.

From the mine, it takes **20 minutes** on a zigzag path to reach the tunnel entrance. The tunnel is 200 m (650 ft) long. You cannot see the other end because of bends and a 15-m (50-ft) descent. Immediately before the descent, there is a shaft on the left dropping steeply down. The descent

View to the Yungas from the pass on Reconquistada

is very roughly stepped, but excercise extreme caution. At the bottom, you can see the light at the end of the tunnel. It is possible to avoid the tunnel by going around the mountain. But this is extremely dangerous and slower to boot.

From the tunnel exit, follow the broad road past the abandoned mining equipment to reach an excellent, wide path. This skirts around the valley head before arriving at a narrow pass in 1¼ **hours.** There is an *apacheta* there and deserted mining buildings. The descent is long but easy and takes you from the mountains at 4,080 m (13,390 ft) to the heart of the Yungas at 1,950 m (6,400 ft). After 35 minutes, you can see the Chulumani-to-La Paz road way down to the right. **Five minutes** later, you can see the Coroico-to-La Paz road way off to the left at about the same height. At this viewpoint, there is camping near a lake. Another **15 minutes** farther on is another lake with the last camping and water possibilities.

From the lake it is **3 hours** down to the Sud Yungas road. The path becomes narrow as the vegetation encroaches. There is water in only two places: 1½ hours below the last lake and **30 minutes** below that, from small streams flowing across the path. Come out on the road and flag down any vehicle going up and left toward La Paz.

16. Takesi Trail and Takesi Alto
Ventilla or Mina San Francisco to Yanacachi
(1–3 days)

This short, easy-to-follow trek crosses some of the best-preserved pre-Hispanic paving in South America. From the pass above Mina San Francisco, the trail is all downhill. Certified masochists have attempted this trail starting in the Yungas and heading uphill!

Due to its accessibility, beauty, and shortness—a little over 30 km (19 miles)—the Takesi Trail is extremely popular with visitors and Bolivians. As a result, there is a lot of litter along the trail and four cafes en route. The trail is especially popular with Bolivians on holiday weekends—at Easter up to 2,000 people have been known to do the trek.

The drive in gives great views of Illimani and Mururata as well as passing very close to the strange fluted mud formations of the Valle de las Animas (literally, "Valley of the Souls").

From the Takesi Trail, Mururata is not the flat-topped giant you see from the Altiplano, but has more of a classic mountain shape. There are a number of legends behind this. According to one tale, Mururata was once a proper, pyramid-shaped mountain that looked down on all, including the Great Inca, who took exception to this attitude and knocked Mururata's top off. Another story is that Illimani and Mururata had a fight over who was the most glorious; Illimani won and cut off Mururata's head. A third states that Mururata was taller than Illimani; but Illimani complained to the

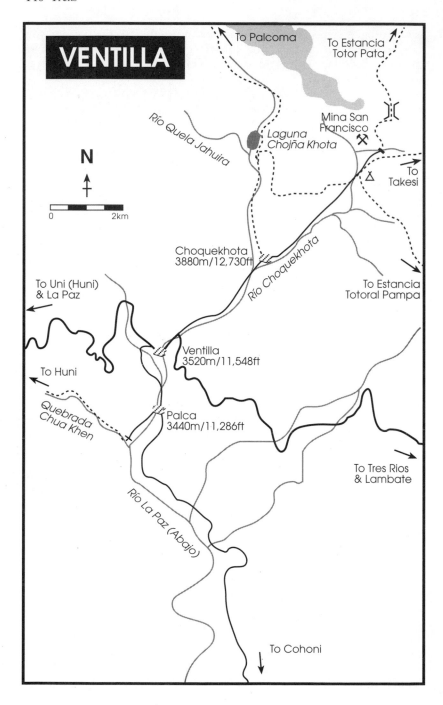

VENTILLA

To Palcoma

To Estancia
Totor Pata

Río Quela Jahuira

Laguna
Chojña Khota

Mina San
Francisco

N

To Takesi

0   2km

Choquekhota
3880m/12,730ft

Río Choquekhota

To Uni (Huni)
& La Paz

To Estancia
Totoral Pampa

Ventilla
3520m/11,548ft

To Huni

Quebrada
Chua Khen

Palca
3440m/11,286ft

To Tres Rios
& Lambate

Río La Paz (Abajo)

To Cohoni

Colonial plastered adobe houses in Yanacachi, Takesi

Great Inca about the supposed injustice. The Great Inca responded by cutting off Mururata's head and told it to go away, using the Aymará word *sarjam*. However it happened, Mururata's head is now said to be Sajama, Bolivia's highest mountain.

The Takesi Alto option is higher and considerably more challenging than the Takesi Trail. But it is rarely attempted, so it is litter-free and you can enjoy complete solitude. The Takesi Alto gives fantastic views of the north face of Mururata. This option makes for a comfortable 2-day trek; but completing it in 1 day is a struggle.

Start

For information about getting to Ventilla, and amenities there, and the route from Ventilla to Mina San Francisco, see trek 15, Mina la Reconquistada.

Finish

Chojlla is an unpleasant mining village with an *alojamiento*. Yanacachi is trying to exploit its tourism potential, with a number of hotels and *alojamientos* around the end of the trail at the top of the village. The center and lower section retain their colonial feel and are very attractive. There are a number of shops, a Cotel telephone office, and some places to eat that are sometimes open and sometimes have food.

From Yanacachi, there are regular minibuses to La Paz at 6:00 A.M. but they are often full; buy a ticket when you arrive, if you can. It is possible to continue down to the Chulumani road in 1 hour from Yanacachi and hitch a ride, but Friday afternoons should be avoided, as all La Paz-bound transport tends to be full. The road is spectacular, following the Río Unduavi to the village of the same name, where it climbs steeply up to the Coroico road. Alternatively, jump on a bus or truck going to Chulumani, capital of the Sud Yungas.

Itinerary

Day 1, to Estancia Takesi or Yanacachi (Takesi Alto, to Mina Inca or after the Río Quimsa Chata). Day 2, Cacapi or after the Río Quimsa Chata, or Yanacachi. Day 3, Yanacachi.

Maps

IGM Chojlla 6044 IV (and, if you want the section from Ventilla to Mina San Francisco, Palca 6044 III). Walter Guzmán. Liam O'Brien.

Other Trekking Possibilities

It is possible to start with trek 17, Palca Canyon. From Palca, walk uphill for 30 minutes to Ventilla and camp the first night before the pass or at Estancia Takesi.

You can also start with trek 14, Hampaturi Trail, which either goes to Choquekhota or more directly to Mina San Franciso. Camp before the pass or at Estancia Takesi for the first night.

Route Description

The first **3 hours** from Ventilla are the same as for trek 15, Mina la Reconquistada (see that route description). When you reach the disintegrating plastered wall with a map, the road continues left to Mina San Francisco and the start of trek 15, Mina la Reconquistada; do not follow it.

From the road near Mina San Francisco, follow the broad path up to the right, over excellent pre-Hispanic paving, to the large *apacheta* at the 4,630-m (15,190-ft) pass in **1 hour**. From the pass, Mururata, 5,700 m (18,700 ft), is visible to the right. The excellent stonework continues below the *apacheta*. When you reach the abandoned camp of Mina David **25 minutes** below the *apacheta*, you have two options.

Option 1, Takesi Trail: Continue down on the good paving toward Estancia Takesi; near the small lakes just below the pass it is possible to camp. Camping is also possible above Estancia Takesi, which is reached in **another hour.**

Below Estancia Takesi, you feel the change in air temperature and rising humidity. The vegetation becomes ever-more dense as the path rises to the

Opposite: *Waterfall, Takesi Alto*

right and above the Río Takesi (fill water bottles before leaving the river). In **2 hours** reach the rather incongruous "CGI" cafe (where the path up from Chima joins the Takesi Trail) and, in another **30 minutes,** "Don Pepe's" cafe in Cacapi, where it is possible to camp. Better camping is found 15 minutes below Cacapi after crossing the Río Quimsa Chata, where the Takesi Alto trail rejoins the Takesi Trail.

Option 2, Takesi Alto: Do not follow the good paving down, but continue along the broad but unpaved path that starts climbing to the right. After **1¼ hours** there is a lake and camping possibilities among derelict miners' houses. There are wonderful views of Mururata to the southeast and of the Cordilleras Takesi and Hampaturi to the northwest. If you arrive here in the early afternoon, it is often possible to look down on the cloud moving up the Takesi valley from the Yungas. Follow the path up to the *apacheta* in **1¾ hours.** Cross the valley to reach the right-hand side and follow the path down to the abandoned mining camp of Mina Inca, **1½ hours.** The seracs along the long north face of Mururata are very clear from here. Camping is possible.

Continue downvalley for another **35 minutes** to reach some more derelict houses and your first views of Chojlla, more than 1,700 m (5,580 ft) below. Unfortunately, the path is missing for the next section—the *paramo* grass has reclaimed it since the mine was abandoned. Descend steeply on the left-hand side of the valley and then work your way back to the stream until you reach a waterfall. From here, it is basically flat and the path magically reappears at the other side of the flat section to the right of the stream. It can take **up to 2 hours** to reach this path, depending on the line you follow and your descending abilities in *paramo* grass. When the trail goes through a series of abandoned terraces, your path-following difficulties are again severely tested: stay on the right-hand side of the valley, gradually moving farther away from the stream. After **1½ hours,** arrive at some houses to the side of a group of mature trees. Relax. Path-finding is straightforward from now on. In fact, you can see the next section below. Follow the path right and cross the pipe-fed stream. You should arrive at a fence across the path designed to stop animals attempting the airy descent on the other side! Climb over the fence and *do not* slip off the path. About **25 minutes** below the houses, you arrive at ideal camping near the stream. At this point the Takesi Alto rejoins the Takesi Trail.

Most of the bridge built over the Río Quimsa Chata has long since been washed away. But there is a dodgy-looking and flexible-feeling three-log bridge over the river. If you don't like the look of that, it is quite easy to boulder-hop slightly higher up. From here it is uphill for **20 minutes** along a clear-cut and paved path to another cafe in what is Chojila. Looking down (left), it is possible to see Chojila's soccer field slowly disappearing under new vegetation. Chojila does not appear to be big enough to field a team of eleven people—perhaps this explains the state of the field. After **40 minutes** of descent over mainly paved path, reach a bridge back over the Río

Takesi. Cross the bridge and follow the path right to reach the start of the aqueduct in **40 minutes.**

If you arrive at this section at dusk, there are hundreds of fireflies. Between the path and the river, there are a couple of clearings where it is possible to camp if you don't feel like finishing the trek in the dark. When you feel concrete underfoot and can see telephone wires overhead, you are close to the village of Chojlla. At the point where the aqueduct ends, follow the road around and, at the junction, head up (left) and go through some mine workings. Stick with the road as it rises up to the right of Chojlla and then starts the descent to Yanacachi, which is reached in **2 hours** from the end of the aqueduct. Shortly before Yanacachi there is a 4-m-high (12-ft-high) gate across the road to control access to the mining settlement of Chojlla. The gatekeeper often asks tourists to register. Do not pay anything for this privilege. At night when the gate is locked, you may have to wake up the gatekeeper and ask him to open it.

From Yanacachi, if you wish to continue down to the Chulumani road, do not follow the road at the top of the village, but walk down to its square. With your back to Yanacachi's Cotel office, leave the square by the downhill (left-hand) cobbled street. A track wide enough for vehicles zigzags down but takes forever. There is a direct path that cuts off the zigzags, repeatedly crossing the track, which will get you down from Yanacachi to the Chulumani road in under **1 hour,** passing through citrus orchards.

17. Palca Canyon
Uni to Palca
(1 day)

The Palca Canyon, which you can explore in a 1-day trip from La Paz, is an amazing, eroded mud valley, surrounded by steep walls and pinnacles. The route follows the bed of the Quebrada Chua Kheri and should not be attempted in the wet season.

Start

Reach Uni (Huni) from central La Paz by radio taxi (US$12). Or take the bus heading to Palca and get off at Uni. From La Paz, the bus leaves from outside the Comedor Popular in Calle Max Paredes above the junction with Calle Rodriguez every day at 5:30 A.M. (US$1). Alternatively, get the micro- or minibus 385 from central La Paz to Chasquipampa or Ovejuyo, and try hitching a ride from there on. If there is no transportation, haggle with drivers of empty minibuses in Ovejuyo—you should be able to get one to Uni (about US$5). Or walk from the end of the minibus route. It takes 30 minutes along the road to reach the pass area near a lake with great views of Illimani and Mururata, and then 25 minutes down to Uni.

View on leaving Palca Canyon

Finish

Palca is a pleasant village that is often full on weekends with visiting Paceños. It has limited accommodations, but many shops. To return to La Paz from Palca, there are regular buses and more on weekends (US$1). Or arrange to be picked up by jeep (US$35).

Itinerary

Day 1, to Palca and back to La Paz.

Map

IGM Palca 6044 III—though it's not really necessary because it is not a complicated route.

Other Trekking Possibilities

From Palca, walk 30 minutes up the road to Ventilla and then up the valley of the Río Choquekhota to Choquekhota and do trek 14, Hampaturi Trail, in reverse.

Or continue upvalley and head across to Estancia Totoral Pampa (see trek 21, Cordillera Real Traverse).

Or continue to Mina San Francisco at the top of the valley for trek 15, Mina la Reconquistada, and trek 16, Takesi Trail and Alto Takesi.

Route Description

In Uni, look for a broad road leading down (right) and follow it, past the school and on. There is pre-Hispanic stone paving before it reaches the canyon floor. Walk through the canyon until it opens out, reached in **2 hours.** Follow the path up and left to Palca, which takes another **30 minutes.**

18. Illimani
Cohoni to Lambate
(5 days)

This is a tour of Illimani, the beautiful triple-peaked mountain that overlooks La Paz. The journey to the start at Cohoni (pronounced "koni") takes you through the southern suburbs of La Paz and continues out along the bed of the city's small and highly polluted river, the Río Choqueyapu ("God of Gold"). Below La Paz it is called Río Abajo ("Low River") and the landscape is unusual even by Bolivian standards. The valley floor is green and cultivated, but on either side are deeply eroded mud and rock peaks. It has a "badlands" feel to it. Just before the road leaves the river bed at Tahuapalca, there is a fantastic view of Illimani's south peak (the highest). The climb up to Cohoni is precipitous but exciting, and gives great views back across the badlands.

Start

Cohoni is quite a big place: it has electricity and plenty of shops, but no official accommodations. Ask around if you want to stay there. There is also a Cotel phone office—when a call comes through, the Cotel worker goes out into the square and shouts out the name of the person receiving the call. The bus from La Paz to Cohoni leaves from Calle General Luis Lara off Calle Boqueron, San Pedro, Mondays through Saturdays at 1:00 and 3:00 P.M., taking 4 hours (US$2).

Finish

Lambate is smaller and less lively than Cohoni. The bus from Lambate to La Paz leaves at 4:00 A.M. and takes 6 hours (US$2.25). Some claim the bus goes back to La Paz Mondays through Saturdays, but experience suggests that it is a less regular and predictable service.

Itinerary

Day 1, to Puente Roto. Day 2, to above Estancia Totoral Pampa. Day 3, to Río Pasto Grande. Day 4, to above Estancia Totoral. Day 5, to Lambate.

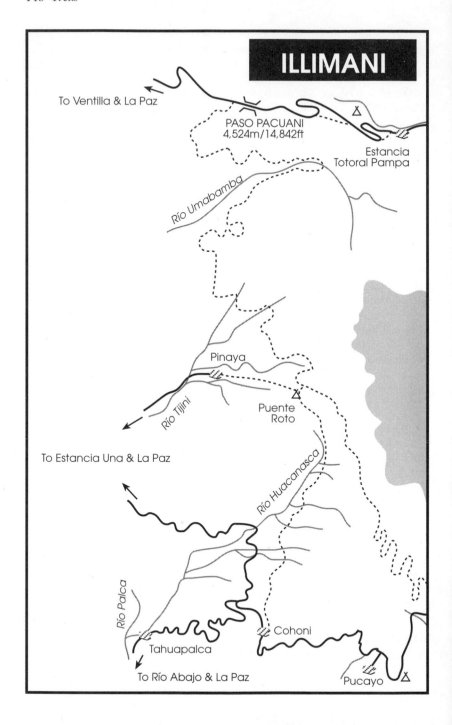

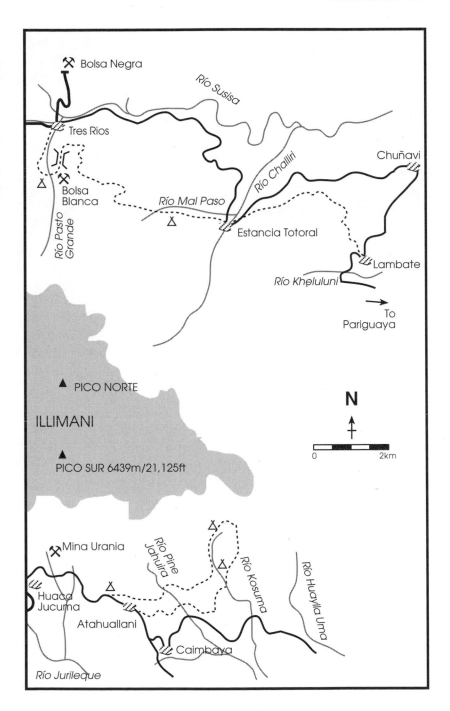

Bolsa Negra

Río Susisa

Tres Rios

Chuñavi

Río Challiri

Bolsa
Blanca

Río Mal Paso

Río Pasto Grande

Estancia Totoral

Lambate

Río Kheluluni

To
Pariguaya

PICO NORTE

ILLIMANI

N

PICO SUR 6439m/21,125ft

0   2km

Mina Urania

Río Pine Jahuira

Río Kosuma

Río Huaylla Uma

Huaca
Jucuma

Atahuallani

Río Kosuma

Caimbaya

Río Jurileque

Puente Roto below Illimani, Cohoni Loop

Maps

DAV Cordillera Real Süd (Illimani). IGM Cohoni 6043 IV and Palca 6044 III. Guzman Illimani. Liam O'Brien.

Other Trekking Possibilities

This trek can be started or finished in Estancia Una, Paso Pacuani, Tres Rios, Estancia Totoral, or Lambate.

The section from Lambate back around to Cohoni, which could be added as a loop trek, involves at least 2 days of road slogging. But the road is rarely used by vehicles—perhaps three a day—and there are great views of Illimani.

It is possible to go on to trek 20, Yunga Cruz, from Lambate or Chuñavi.

Route Description

From Cohoni's square, follow the road down and out of town, heading back toward La Paz. Five minutes down the road there is a broad, roughly paved path leading up to the right—follow it. As you rise above the village, you can see Río Abajo 1,400 m (4,600 ft) below, and see why it took the bus almost **2 hours** to get up here. After **40 minutes** there is a notch through a ridge leading to a view of most of the west side of Illimani.

Continue on up the path, staying to the right of the Río Huacanasca, eventually joining it. Continue until you arrive at a steppe known as Puente Roto ("Broken Bridge")—the bridge must be so broken that it has completely disappeared in 2½ hours. There are plenty of clear streams crossing the flat steppe area, providing ample space to choose your own spot to camp. Illimani's highest peak is the one farthest right.

Above Puente Roto is a disused mining road. Either follow it north or at least keep it in view, and off you go along the whole western side of Illimani until you reach the La Paz–Tres Rios road after **6 hours.** Turn right and up to reach Paso Pacuani. Drop down the other side of the pass, looking for paths to the right to speed up the descent to Estancia Totoral Pampa, which takes **3 hours.** Before the village is a large flat plain—look for somewhere that is relatively dry to camp.

Continue on to Tres Rios in **1½ hours** along the road. From Tres Rios, follow the mining road up the Río Pasto Grande valley toward Bolsa Blanca. From Tres Rios to the pass above Bolsa Blanca takes **3 hours,** but you can camp in the valley floor before starting the ascent.

The trail becomes more obvious as you descend toward the Río Mal Paso and you can camp in the valley bottom **2 hours** from the pass. Continue down the right-hand side of the Río Mal Paso valley to possible camping above Estancia Totoral.

Continue down to Estancia Totoral in less than **1 hour** and follow the road out of the village. After crossing the bridge over the Río Challiri, look for a path on the right and follow it up over a broad pass area, and then drop down to Lambate, **4 hours** from Estancia Totoral.

19. Cohoni Loop
Cohoni to Cohoni
(3–4 days)

This trek takes you into an area little visited by outsiders, foreign or Bolivian. The area is intensively cultivated (so there are a lot of paths), providing a contrast with the heavily eroded and steep mud badlands to the south that plunge down to Río Abajo. This river cuts through the Andes, marking the division between the Cordilleras Real and Quimsa Cruz.

Going in, the path stays high; coming back, it is lower and then follows the road for easier trekking. The valley of the Río Kosuma is beautiful and quiet—the paths built by miners are no longer used, because the small mines at the base of Illimani's glaciers are no longer worked.

Start and Finish

For information on getting to Cohoni and its amenities, see trek 18, Illimani. Buses return to La Paz from Cohoni Mondays through Saturdays at 9:00 A.M. and take 4 hours (US$2).

Itinerary

Day 1, to Puente Roto. Day 2, to the valley of Río Kosuma. Day 3, to the roadside camping above Pucayo or to Cohoni. Day 4, to Cohoni.

Maps

DAV Cordillera Real Süd (Illimani). IGM Cohoni 6043 IV and Araca 6043 I. Guzman Illimani. Liam O'Brien.

Other Trekking Possibilities

You can continue around to Lambate via the road from Caimbaya, in 2 days. This combines this trek with trek 18, Illimani, for a complete circuit of the mountain.

Route Description

For the route from Cohoni to Puente Roto, see the first day's itinerary for trek 18, Illimani.

From Puente Roto, head up toward Illimani and then follow the old mining road right (southeast). As the road starts to drop, shortcut around the bends by following paths to the left of the road until you can see the village of Huaca Jucuma. When you arrive at a point overlooking the village, you can also see the buildings of Mina Urania and a road zigzagging down. Cut across above the village to reach the road below the mine (in **under 3 hours** from Puente Roto), and then follow it left (east) toward Atahuallani.

An hour later, after a wide grassy track dropping down to the right, leave the road and head off left. Cross an aqueduct which passes excellent camping possibilities. When you continue on, fill up your water bottles at the aqueduct. At the end of the cleared area, head for a small notch in the ridge, which gives views of Atahuallani and straight ahead to the Cordillera Quimsa Cruz. Do not follow the path up the ridge, but continue climbing gradually around the next hill. Then drop down to a stream at the exit of a hanging valley with some derelict houses and excellent camping, **1¼ hours** after leaving the road.

From the valley, follow one of the paths heading up the left-hand side of the valley to meet the ridge after **15 minutes.** Contour around a series of ridges, staying above the aqueduct until you come out of the cleared area. Follow paths curving left and go around a corner to find yourself below Illimani once again. Drop down to the aqueduct and follow it, pushing through the vegetation.

After **1 hour,** reach a single flat stone bridge over the aqueduct at the point where the path from below joins. Cross the aqueduct and follow the zigzag path up. Camping is possible near the derelict buildings or higher up, **30 minutes** from the bridge. Traverse across and then drop down, aiming for the path on the other side, which turns out to be a dry aqueduct. Follow this aqueduct around until you find a comfortable place to drop down (right) through the long, coarse grass to the valley bottom. Follow the path along the left-hand side of the valley until you reach a ford of the Río Kosuma, and cross to excellent camping.

Follow the path up to a notch through the ridge **15 minutes** above the ford. Continue on the good path as it contours around through fields and then up to Atahuallani in **2 hours.** From Atahuallani, follow the road back down to below Mina Urania in **45 minutes.** Do not follow the zigzags up to the mine, but cut through fields below Huaca Jucuma, using the numerous paths, to reach the road to the west of the village in under **1 hour.** Follow the road and you will have great views over the badlands to the south. After **1 hour** there is excellent camping to the left of the road, near the point where the road bridges an aqueduct. After that, the road drops down to the Pucayo turn-off.

As you come around the corner, above Pucayo, you can see the huge drop to Río Abajo. Continue along the road to Cohoni in **1¼ hours.**

20. Yunga Cruz
Chuñavi or Lambate to Chulumani
(3–5 days)

This is the most exciting but hardest of the three so-called Inca trails, and therefore less popular. This not only means fewer people, but less litter and begging than on the other treks and more wildlife, such as condors, hawks, and hummingbirds. As with the other Inca trails (trek 13, Choro Trail, and trek 16, Takesi Trail and Takesi Alto), you start high and drop low, going through the full gamut of climate zones. Be prepared.

Water is a major consideration; once you get below Cerro Khala Ciudad, fill water bottles whenever you can. Each person should carry *at least* 2 liters (quarts). Back-up water bags are worth packing, as listed in "Clothing and Personal Equipment" in the "Equipment" section of chapter 2, Pre-departure Preparations.

The option of starting in Lambate allows you to link this trek with others. It normally takes 2 days from Lambate to join the main route, involving a hot and sweaty haul up from the Río Chunga Mayu.

If you plan to stay in Chulumani for a couple of days, check out the Apa Apa Ecological Park, 8 km (5 mi) from town. Call Ramiro Portugal, who speaks English (0811-6106 or La Paz 790381), to arrange a free lift from Chulumani to the park. So far, 360 different plant species have been identified in the 800-hectare (2,000-acre) park—16 completely new to science—and more than 70 different bird species. It is the last area of Yungas forest untouched by modern agricultural activity.

Start
Chuñavi is a small village with limited supplies, as is Lambate. To reach either from La Paz, take the bus going to Pariguaya, from Calle General Luis Lara corner Venacio Burgoa, San Pedro. It runs Mondays through

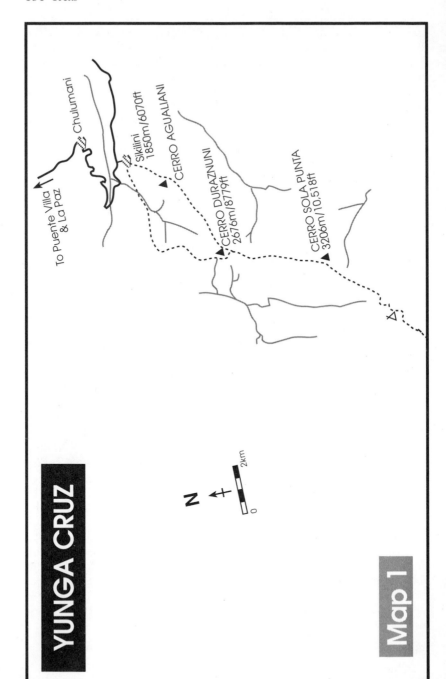

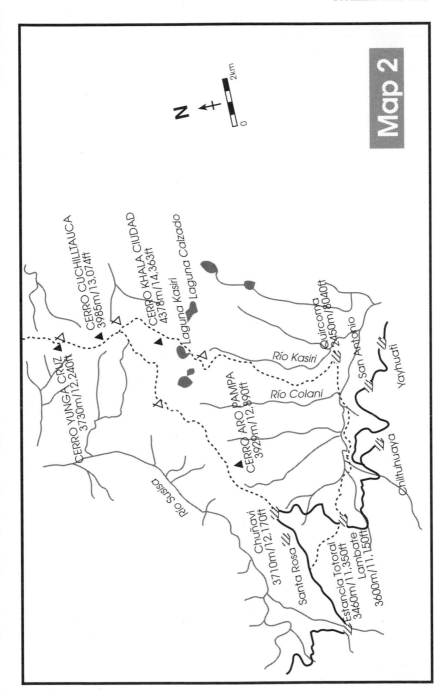

Map 2

Saturdays at 9:00 A.M. The journey takes 6 hours to Chuñavi (US$2), and 6¼ hours to Lambate (US$2.25), 3 km (2 mi) farther on. Buses to Tres Rios and Bolsa Negra also leave at the same time, but they stop well before Chuñavi or Lambate. It is not possible to buy tickets in advance—there's no ticket office. To ensure a ticket, you need to be there at 7:00 or 8:00 A.M. on the day of departure, or send someone to buy it for you. The bus stops at 10:00 A.M. for an hour in the outskirts of La Paz for *almuerzo*.

Finish

Chulumani, the capital of the Sud Yungas Department, is considerably quieter and less developed than its Nor Yungas counterpart, Coroico. However, it is at a similar altitude—1,700 m (5,580 ft)—and is just as warm as Coroico. There are a number of hotels, ranging from cheap *alojamientos* to the five-star San Bartolomé just outside town. However, there are a limited number of restaurants worth eating in. To return to La Paz from Chulumani, there are buses and minibuses every couple of hours through the mornings, for the 4- to 5-hour trip (US$2.50).

Itinerary

From Chuñavi: Day 1, to before Cerro Khala Ciudad. Day 2, to Cerro Yunga Cruz. Day 3, to Chulumani. (A fit group making an early start could get from Cerro Khala Ciudad to Chulumani in one long day.) From Lambate: Day 1, to Quircoma. Day 2, to Laguna Kasiri. Day 3, to Cerro Yunga Cruz. Day 4, to south of Cerro Sola Punta. Day 5, to Chulumani. (A fit group making an early start could get from Cerro Yunga Cruz to Chulumani in one day.)

Maps

IGM Lambate 6044 II and Chulumani 6044 1. Walter Guzmán. Liam O'Brien.

Other Trekking Possibilities

The Yunga Cruz trek is normally started in Chuñavi (3 days) or Lambate (5 days), but it is possible to start higher up the Río Susisa valley in either Tres Rios or Estancia Totoral (see trek 18, Illimani). From Estancia Totoral, follow the right-hand side of the Río Challiri down to Estancia Santa Rosa. Then climb up to Santa Rosa and continue to Chuñavi—a 1-day journey.

From Lambate, the end of trek 18, Illimani, you can combine these two treks.

It is possible to link into this trek from Mina San Francisco (the start of trek 16, Takesi Trail and Takesi Alto) or, farther away, from Palcoma (the start of trek 14, Hampaturi Trail).

There are a number of interesting villages to the north of Chulumani, including Irupana, Ocabaya, and Chicaloma (the main center of the

Afro-Bolivian population). The ruins of Pasto Grande are also north of Chulumani, and can be reached by foot or truck. The best map of the area to the north of Chulumani is painted inside the church on the main square.

Route Description

Option 1, from Chuñavi: follow the path left (east) from the La Paz road, contouring gently up. Pass some small lakes after **1 hour** and reach the deserted shell of a building after another **40 minutes**—camping is possible down to the right. Look back for great views of the east side of Illimani and Mururata. Stay on the left-hand side of the ridge until you reach a stream and camping after **2 hours,** below Cerro Khala Ciudad (literally, "Stone City Mountain"—you will see why).

A good paved stone path continues along and up. After **1 hour,** reach a

Pre-Hispanic stone paving and the east side of Illimani, Yunga Cruz

junction where the path from Lambate and Quircoma comes up from the right to join the Chuñavi path. Camping is possible down to the right.

Option 2, from Lambate: From the village, drop down almost 1,000 m (3,300 ft) to the Río Kheluluni and follow the path along the right-hand side of the river. Here, the name of the river changes to Río Chunga Mayu. Just before its confluence with the Río Colani, cross the Río Chunga Mayu, then the Río Colani, and start the climb to Quircoma, where camping is possible and normally necessary. In Quircoma, start the unrelenting **5-hour climb** toward Cerro Khala Ciudad, staying at first to the left of the Río Kasiri and then contouring right to join it. Camp near Laguna Kasiri.

Go around Laguna Kasiri to the right and up and over a 4,200-m (13,800-ft) pass to the right (east) of the mountain. From here, you descend to join the path from Chuñavi.

From the junction: Regardless of which route you came in on, continue north to Cerro Cuchilltauca. From here, carry on to Cerro Yunga Cruz in **2 hours,** where there is water and camping space.

There is further water and camping space in **40 minutes,** just before the start of the descent to the Yungas. The path deteriorates as it descends, first turning left around a ridge. But it improves just before two stream crossings, the first in cloud forest, the second in the open. This descending stretch takes **20 minutes.** There are three streams within the next **40 minutes,** with camping possible just before the third stream. Fill up with at least 2 liters (quarts) per person—there is no more water for a very long time. There are a number of clearings on the way down but no camping place with water until you reach Chulumani.

The descent is very tiring from this point: the vegetation increases, often obstructing your way, forcing you to duck under bamboo and other plants that form tunnels. A machete is useful, especially early in the season when few people have passed through. After **2 hours** there is a fork amid dense vegetation. Take the right fork and come out into the open on the side of a ridge **5 minutes** later. After another **30 minutes,** come to a clearing where Bolivians regularly camp. At the end of the clearing there are two options: go either left or right of Cerro Duraznuni.

Option 1: It is possible to go left but the vegetation is tough and a machete is recommended. Follow the path down on the left-hand side of the ridge you have been following all the way from Cerro Yunga Cruz. The path then goes up and down but basically contours. The first water is reached **2 hours** from the clearing and then the path becomes clearer. When you can see a broad pass area up right, start looking for a good path that rises up right to reach a flat but waterless campsite on top of the ridge, **1 hour** from the water. Another **30 minutes** brings you to the road to Sikilini.

Option 2: It is harder to find the path going right of Cerro Duraznuni but once you have, the going is easier. From the clearing you head up to the right of the hill and then drop down, reaching the road to Sikilini in under **3 hours.**

Regardless of which trail you took to get around Cerro Duraznuni, the paths join up to descend on the other side, reaching a road into the village of Sikilini. Just before a tennis court on the right, there is a good path leading off to the left to a viewpoint. From here, there is a good view to the left of Huancane. Follow the path—which soon turns into a track—down to the Chulumani *tranca* in 1¾ **hours**.

21. Cordillera Real Traverse
Sorata to Cohoni
(20 days)

This is a challenging and hardcore trek through the entire Cordillera Real: it covers 160 km (100 mi), not taking into account ups and downs; crosses up to twenty passes over 4,000 m (16,000 ft); and involves more than 12,000 m (40,000 ft) of ascent and descent.

The route passes through fantastic mountain scenery. The part of the trek on the eastern side of the Cordillera takes you through areas that are seldom visited by outsiders. The western side brings you up close to some of the mountains you see from the Altiplano.

The first few days are particularly tough because you will be carrying 20 days' food and fuel—the route does not pass any villages with shops. However, you may prefer to hire mules in Sorata for the first 2 or 3 days to Ancoma or Cocoyo. To lighten your load, you could arrange a food drop at the Huayna Potosí hut.

A rest day at Refugio Huayna Potosí provides a welcome break and one of the best showers in Bolivia. Plan for another rest day en route, depending on how you are going and where you want to stop.

It is possible to start the trek in Cohoni and finish with a 2,000-m (6,500-ft) descent into Sorata to recover. But starting at Sorata means you get closer to La Paz every day and so, should you want or need to pull out, it will take less time to get back to civilization.

Start

For information on getting to Sorata and its facilities, see trek 5, Illampu Circuit.

Finish

For information on Cohoni and what facilities it has, plus getting back to La Paz, see trek 19, Cohoni Loop.

Itinerary

Day 1, to Lakathiya. Day 2, to Ancoma/Estancia Utaña Pampa. Day 3, to Cocoyo. Day 4, to below Abra (Paso) Sarani, near Chajolpaya. Day 5, to Chajowara. Day 6, to the pass before Estancia Lloco Lloconi. Day 7, to

Lago Khotia, Sorata to Hichukhota

Laguna Jankho Khota. Day 8, to Lago Sistaña. Day 9, to Laguna Chiar Khota. Day 10, to above Chacapampa. Day 11, to Laguna Warawarani. Day 12, to Zongo Pass. Day 13, rest day at Refugio Huayna Potosí. Day 14, to above Palcoma. Day 15, to Laguna Jachcha Khasiri. Day 16, to Mina San Francisco. Day 17, rest day. Day 18, to the pass southwest of Mururata. Day 19, to Puente Roto. Day 20, to Cohoni.

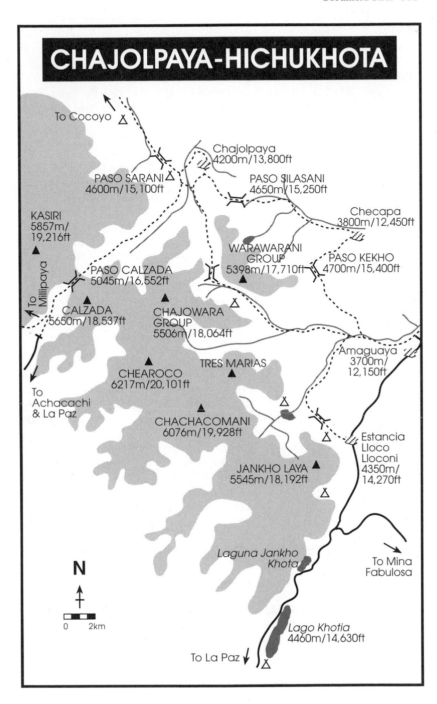

CHAJOLPAYA-HICHUKHOTA

To Cocoyo

Chajolpaya
4200m/13,800ft

PASO SARANI
4600m/15,100ft

PASO SILASANI
4650m/15,250ft

Checapa
3800m/12,450ft

KASIRI
5857m/
19,216ft

WARAWARANI
GROUP
5398m/17,710ft

PASO KEKHO
4700m/15,400ft

To Millipaya

PASO CALZADA
5045m/16,552ft

CALZADA
5650m/18,537ft

CHAJOWARA
GROUP
5506m/18,064ft

TRES MARIAS

Amaguaya
3700m/
12,150ft

To
Achacachi
& La Paz

CHEAROCO
6217m/20,101ft

CHACHACOMANI
6076m/19,928ft

Estancia
Lloco
Lloconi
4350m/
14,270ft

JANKHO LAYA
5545m/18,192ft

N

Laguna Jankho
Khota

To Mina
Fabulosa

0   2km

Lago Khotia
4460m/14,630ft

To La Paz

Maps

Liam O'Brien's map covers the whole route at 1:135,000 and is essential for planning. IGM maps cover the section around Sorata and from Lago Jankho Khota onward: Lago Khara Khota Peñas Cohoni 5945 IV, Pe5945 III, Milluni 5945 II, La Paz (Norte) 5944 I, Chojlla 6044 IV, Palca 6044 III, and 6043 IV—though, again, the DAV Cordillera Real Süd (Illimani) is better.

Other Trekking Possibilities

There is no need to make this trek an ordeal. It is possible to leave, or join, at a number of points where the route crosses or passes close to roads, and get back to La Paz within days. You can either walk downhill to the Altiplano and the Pan American Highway or hitch a lift with a mining truck or bus. "Escape route" possibilities include Paso Mullu near Laguna Jankho Khota, Mina Palcoco, Tuni, the Zongo valley, La Cumbre, Palcoma, and Mina San Francisco. Alternatively, arrange to be picked up or dropped off by jeep at a certain point.

At the end of this trek, it is possible to continue by circling Illimani, going either from Cohoni to Lambate or vice versa. See treks 18, Illimani, and 19, Cohoni Loop.

Route Description

For the first 4 days, from Sorata to Chajolpaya, see the route description for trek 5, Illampu Circuit. For Day 4, camp just southeast of Paso Sarani, before the turnoff to Chajolpaya. At 4,050 m (13,290 ft) it is farther down than you need to go from the Paso Sarani. From the pass, Chajolpaya is down (left), and this trek's route continues down (right) to the river.

On Day 5, cross the bridge and head upvalley (the Illampu Circuit continues upvalley before the bridge). An indistinct path rises up to the left and then crosses a stream to run along the right-hand side of a boggy flat section before a pass area is reached in **2½ hours**. In limited visibility, head for the highest point in the pass area, then head left (south) to reach a pass at 4,950 m (16,240 ft). From the pass it takes **30 minutes** to drop down to a flat area where there is ideal camping, at 4,800 m (15,750 ft). It is just below the glaciered peaks of the Chajowara and Warawarani groups.

On Day 6, follow the path down the right-hand side of the valley, then descend steeply to reach the next valley bottom in **1½ hours,** with views of Chearoco and Calzada. Do not cross the bridge, but continue down until you reach the next valley floor, where there is a stone bridge after **1 hour.** Cross the bridge and, after passing several houses to the right of the path, drop down to 3,900 m (12,800 ft). Then start heading up (right) into the next valley, staying left of the stream. Go through the first flat steppe and up to the second, which is boggy. Then follow the path rising up on the left to head for the pass at 4,800 m (15,750 ft). (If you continue upvalley,

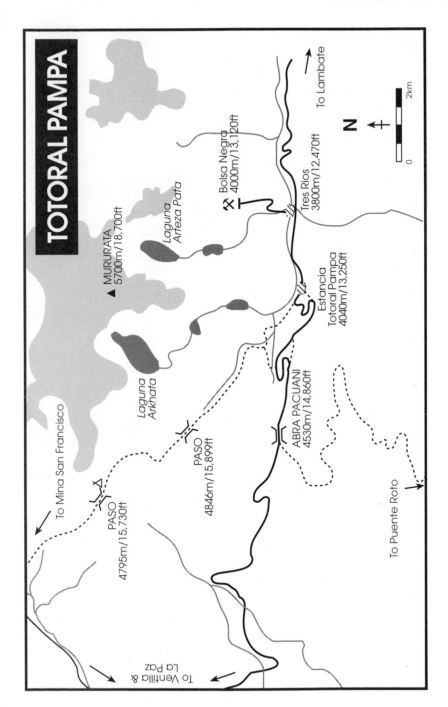

TOTORAL PAMPA

MURURATA
5700m/18,700ft

Laguna
Arfeza Pata

Laguna
Arkhata

Bolsa Negra
4000m/13,120ft

Tres Rios
3800m/12,470ft

To Lambate

N

0   2km

Estancia
Totoral Pampa
4040m/13,250ft

ABRA PACUANI
4530m/14,860ft

PASO
4846m/15,899ft

PASO
4795m/15,730ft

To Mina San Francisco

To Ventilla &
La Paz

To Puente Roto

Pigs below Jankho Khota, Sorata to Hichukhota

you arrive at Laguna Leche Khota, which has excellent camping on its western shores.) Camping is possible around the lake **30 minutes** before the pass. Continue through the pass, **3½ hours** from the entrance to the valley. Leave the path and traverse right to find a stream and camping at around 4,600 m (15,100 ft). Lower in the valley are the houses of Estancia Lloco Lloconi.

On Day 7, descend to Lloco Lloconi at 4,350 m (14,270 ft) in **30 minutes** from the pass. Either ford the Río Amaguaya or scramble up, staying to the right of the river, until you find a crossing point. Most of the pre-Hispanic paved path going up the valley was destroyed in 1995 by the construction of the new road. At points, it is possible to follow the ancient path. It is a much more direct route, especially when the new road goes into zigzags before the pass at 4,970 m (16,300 ft), reached in **2½ hours.** From the pass, descend downvalley to reach Laguna Jankho Khota, where it is possible to camp at the southern end, or continue following the road above Lago Khotia to reach ideal camping between Lago Khotia and Lago Khara Khota.

For Days 8 and 9, from Laguna Jankho Khota to Laguna Chiar Khota, see trek 9, Hichukhota to Condoriri.

For Day 10, from Laguna Chiar Khota to Chacapampa, see trek 10, Condoriri to the Zongo valley.

On Day 11, from Chacapampa, 3,580 m (11,750 ft), with its thatched church, follow the road for a few minutes to reach the main Zongo valley road and turn right. From the road, look for a way up (left) to join the old path above the road. Go around Laguna Viscachani **(2 hours)** and follow the clear path up toward a waterfall, where it zigzags to the right. Then head up to the left to join the road going across the valley. The old pre-Hispanic route leaves the road immediately before the point where the road crosses the stream. Follow this up to a pass at 4,630 m (15,190 ft) and then descend to camp near Laguna Warawarani at 4,550 m (14,930 ft) beneath the steep and evil-looking Tiquimani, 5,519 m (18,170 ft) in **2 hours** from Laguna Viscachani.

On Day 12, from Laguna Warawarani, descend to Uma Palca at 3,950 m (12,969 ft) in **1¼ hours,** cross the stream, and head upvalley to the right to reach Laguna Khota Khuchu in **1 hour.** The path above Laguna Khota Khuchu is not clear. If you arrive at a lake with two modern but abandoned buildings and a large dam wall, it is the wrong one. Pass the smaller building, cross the stream, and then head up (right) and you will reach a smaller lake, and this is the correct one and will take less than **1 hour** from Laguna Khota Khuchu. Head up the valley on the left-hand side to cross a stream after **45 minutes.** Then follow the path up to reach a pass at 4,850 m (15,910 ft) after **another hour,** with views of Huayna Potosí. Descend diagonally left along the stone path that passes a lake and camping after **30 minutes.** From there, continue descending to meet the road at 4,580 m (15,030 ft) in less than **1 hour.** Follow the first switchback going up diagonally right and then leave the road at the bend to follow the ancient paved path. The climb takes **1 hour** and the path comes out 5 minutes before the Huayna Potosí refuge, 4,700 m (15,420 ft) in the Zongo Pass. This is the recommended point for a rest day on Day 13.

On Day 14, from the hut, walk along the road above the Zongo Dam, and head left to follow the old road, which rejoins the new one shortly after. Contour around left into the valley and head up for the obvious pass at 4,930 m (16,170 ft). You should reach it in **2 hours** and it has views of Illimani. Descend below Cerro Wila Manquilizani and then contour to Laguna Pata Larama in **2 hours.** Continue to Apacheta Chucura and then descend to the La Cumbre pass at 4,680 m (15,350 ft) in **1½ hours,** which links La Paz with the Yungas. The highest point of La Cumbre is marked by a statue of Christ with his arms outstretched. Cross the road and head southeast for a col, reaching it in **1¼ hours.** From there, it is **45 minutes** of descent into the valley above the second of two large dams, where there is possible camping. Descend the valley past the higher and lower dams to reach Palcoma (marked on the IGM maps as Estancia Karpani), at 3,850 m (12,630 ft), in **1½ hours.**

For Days 15 and 16, see trek 14, Hampaturi Trail, for the route from Palcoma to Mina Francisco.

On Day 17, below Mina San Francisco, cross the road, and follow the path that contours around on the left-hand side of the valley. Continue on to join the zigzag path going up to reach a small hanging valley in **45 minutes.** Head on up the valley until you reach a pass at 4,795 m (15,730 ft) after **1¼ hours** with views of Illimani and Mururata. Descend to the left for camping near a stream **5 minutes** below the pass.

On Day 18, go back toward the pass and then turn left and go down scree to the valley bottom at 4,502 m (14,770 ft). Cross the stream and then head upvalley on the right-hand side to reach the pass at 4,846 m (15,899 ft) after **2 hours.** Again, there are good views of Illimani and Mururata. Descend and stay on the right-hand side of the valley, and then rise to join the road before Abra (Paso) Pacuani. Descend from the pass and then head left, following the disused mining road to Puente Roto and camping.

On Day 20, from Puente Roto drop down to Cohoni. See trek 18, Illimani, and follow the route description in reverse.

Chapter 8

CORDILLERA QUIMSA CRUZ

By comparison with the Cordillera Real, the Quimsa Cruz is a tiny range. It has around 80 mountains of around 4,900 to 5,800 m (16,000 to 19,000 ft), compared to 600 peaks within that height range in the Cordillera Real. The entire range is just 40 km (25 mi) long and less than 15 km (9 mi) wide. Yet it offers challenging treks and is well served with roads and transportation.

22. Laguna Chatamarca
Viloco to Mina Caracoles
(3 days)

This is a beautiful and seldom-tried high-altitude mountain trek.

Start

The mining village of Viloco had its heyday in the 1920s. Today, it is a rather depressing place, with few shops and no accommodations. You might find some people selling gasoline, though. Buses leave from La Paz to Viloco from Calle Jorge Carrasco between Calle 4 and Calle 5, El Alto, parallel to the Oruro road, on Mondays, Wednesdays, Thursdays, and Saturdays at 7:00 A.M. It takes 10 hours (US$3.30). A jeep from La Paz to Viloco takes 6 to 7 hours (US$275).

Finish

Mina Caracoles is much like Viloco. You might have to stay here while waiting for transportation; or you could walk out to find more salubrious camping. From Mina Caracoles there is allegedly regular transportation back to La Paz. Ask when you get there or arrange a jeep to pick you up.

Itinerary

Day 1, to below the first pass. Day 2, to Laguna Chatamarca. Day 3, to Mina Caracoles.

Map

IGM Mina Caracoles 6143 III.

Other Trekking Possibilities

The Quimsa Cruz is covered in mining tracks and paths. To get around the area, just sit at the side of a road and wait for a lift. And, as Joseph Prem

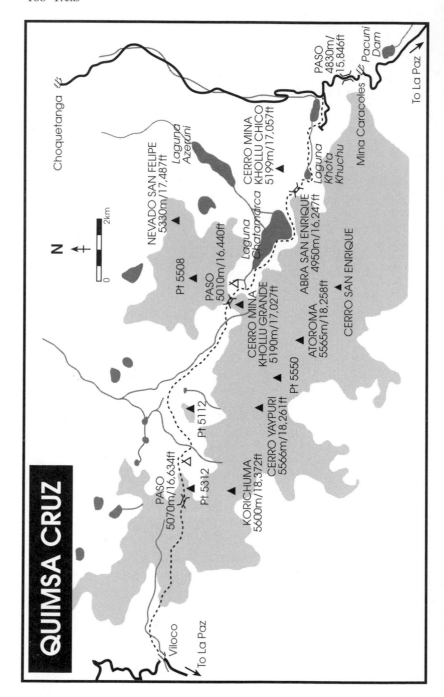

wrote in the *American Alpine Journal* (1943–45), "It is one and not the least of the charms of Quimza Cruz that within a few hours one can go from the Arctic to the Tropics."

Route Description

From Viloco, head upvalley looking for a good path that stays right (south) of the stream. Stay on the path heading for the left (north) of Point 5312, which is reached in **2½ hours.** Drop down to excellent camping in the flatter section of the broad valley below the path, which takes less than **1 hour.**

Head back up to the path and follow it around the valley. Continue up the right-hand side of the next valley, staying to the right of the stream until shortly below Cerro Mina Khollu Grande in **4 hours.** Cross the pass at 5,010 m (16,440 ft). Drop down to camping places at the head of Laguna Chatamarca in **30 minutes.**

Follow the right-hand (southern) shore of Laguna Chatamarca and then head up to Abra San Enrique at 4,950 m (16,240 ft) in **3½ hours.** Drop down to Laguna Khota Khuchu in **45 minutes,** follow the right-hand side of the lake, and then cross over the stream at the far end. Follow the valley down on the left-hand (north) side. Just before the second, larger lake, the path crosses back over to go around the right-hand (south) side of the lake. From the stream, this stretch takes about **2 hours.** Continue to the road and follow it up and over a pass in **1 hour,** and then drop down to Mina Caracoles in under **30 minutes.**

Chapter 9

AMBORO NATIONAL PARK

Amboró National Park is one of Bolivia's greatest ecological treasures. Dominated by a series of steep, jungle-covered ridges, it offers some highly challenging trekking routes, many of them rarely used. However, the park has become trapped in a long-running tug of war between conservationists and colonizers who want to clear the land for agriculture.

Amboró is situated in the lowlands to the west of Santa Cruz. What makes it so special is that it is the meeting point of four distinct ecological zones: the tropical forest of the Amazon basin; the cloud forest of the highland valleys; the Chaco scrubland; and the eastern plains (Llanos Orientales). Altitudes range from less than 300 m (1,000 ft) to over 1,800 m (5,900 ft) further south.

This unusual mix of ecological zones accounts for the park's incredible biological diversity. The bird species count is pushing 800 and includes the Horned Curassow (also known as the Southern Helmeted Curassow). This distinctive bird is an endangered species and is found only in the park and in two small areas of Peru. Among other animals, Amboró has jaguars, pumas, several types of monkey, river otters, peccaries, capybaras, ocelots, and the rare spectacled bear.

Amboró was originally created as a wildlife reserve of 180,000 hectares (444,800 acres) in 1973. In 1984, after the energetic campaigning of British zoologist Robin Clarke, it was given full national park status. Clarke was initially in charge of running the park and in 1990 succeeded in having its area increased to 630,000 hectares (1,556,700 acres). This took the northern boundary right up to the Río Surutú. However, large areas of this expanded northern section had already been colonized by *campesino* farmers who resented the restrictions which appeared to have been imposed on their activities by a foreigner.

There were frequent confrontations between *campesino* groups and the park authorities over subsequent years. *Campesino* leaders accused them of seeking to grab Amboró's resources for exploitation by tourists. Such talk helped create the climate for a controversial decision in 1995 that declared over 200,000 hectares (494,200 acres) of the park as a "multi-use area" (MUA). This effectively reduced its area by a third.

The change has allowed farmers to clear and settle any patch of jungle within the MUA. Some ecologists fear it could lead to all of Amboró's cloud forest being cleared. This could have disastrous consequences for the farming areas south of the park, because most of their water comes from the

Newly cleared rainforest on the edge of Amboró National Park (Andrew North)

park's cloud forest. Even if this does not happen, campaigners fear the MUA has created an irreversible precedent, and the park could be reduced again if political pressure builds up. An estimated 30,000 *campesino* families already live in the area and thousands more are moving in every year, many from the Chapare region.

The exact boundary of the MUA is unclear, but most of it is in a 30-km-wide (20-mi-wide) strip to the west of the Río Surutu, running from the northwest to the southeast, with three smaller patches to the south. But it puts all four northern *guardaparque* (park ranger) stations outside the core park area.

In addition to the alterations to the park boundaries has come a change in the park's management. Fundación Amigos de la Naturaleza (FAN) is supposed to be taking over day-to-day control from the current organization. However, at the time of writing this was still not finalized, causing confusion in planning treks. To get in touch with FAN, see the appendix, Contacts, for their Santa Cruz office.

Despite what appears to be an irredeemably gloomy picture, some believe the MUA may help to relieve the pressure on the park. They point out that although it theoretically opens up the whole area to clearance, in practice only the section of the MUA closest to the road is likely to be claimed for agriculture. As you move southeast of the Río Surutu, Amboró's ridges and hills provide a natural barrier to further expansion. And the only way of getting into these areas is on foot, through thick jungle.

If you want to learn more about the park and its wildlife, visit Robin Clarke. Although he is no longer in charge of the park, he still lives in the area, at Estancia Potrero. He has recently established the Hotel Flora y Fauna there (see "Start," below). Clarke is also creating what he calls a "total forest use" project in the area, with the aim of demonstrating that the jungle can be used profitably without cutting down trees. Other good sources of information are Guy Cox and Jon Heald, owners of the Hotel Amboró.

There are trails all around the park, but some of the most interesting are in the northern section, where it is no longer officially park territory. Most of these begin along the various tributaries of the Río Surutu, including the rivers Cheyo, Pitasama, Macuñucú, Semayo, and Colorado. The starting point for these routes is the town of Buena Vista, the current park headquarters.

Finding a guide with the necessary experience can be difficult. At the time of this writing, there were few locally based guides in Buena Vista, and none had been to the top of Cerro Amboró.

If you are lucky, you may be able to secure the services of the *guardaparques* for a few days. They not only know more routes but also have extensive knowledge of the park's wildlife. However, *guardaparques* are not officially available for hire as guides—they have other priorities, such as protecting what is left of the park. Ask initially at the park office in Buena Vista (telephone 0932-2032), which is open Monday through Saturday; if your route starts at one of the ranger stations, try to make radio contact with the *guardaparques* based there.

Uimpex Travel, a Santa Cruz-based agency, has recently established an office in Buena Vista, and is in the process of training guides. At the time of this writing, none of their guides had been to the top of Amboró, but this should change. Their office is on the main square. Prices are around US$10 a day for guides.

Another option is to ask at the Hotel Amboró (telephone and fax 0932-2054). They can tell you what is happening in the park and may be able to put you in touch with guides. Guy Cox is an expert on the park's birdlife and worked with Robin Clarke on a study of the Horned Curassow.

23. Cerro Amboró
Campamento Macuñucú to the peak and back
(2 days)

The park derives its name from the bulging peak of Cerro Amboró. Beginning along the Río Macuñucú, the trek to the 1,471-m (4,826-ft) summit

Descending from Cerro Amboró to the Río Macuñucú, Amboró National Park (Andrew North)

can be done in 2 days. However, it is extremely hard going, consisting mostly of thick jungle, and a guide is essential. Along the way, you have to climb a 30-m (100-ft) rock face. Keep your gear to the absolute minimum, but bring a machete. You will also find that insects can be a problem.

The trek should only be attempted in the dry season. During the rainy season, not only is transportation to and from the camp unpredictable, but flash floods can hit the Río Macuñucú valley, quite apart from the impact the rain has on the trail.

Start

Campamento Macuñucú consists of three huts and has running water and a toilet. You can wash and swim in the river. The *guardaparques* station has a radio and some bed spaces, costing US$2 a night. But there are plentiful camping spaces. Bring all the food you need. Campamento Macuñucú, the park station, is 47 km (30 mi) by road from Buena Vista.

In Buena Vista, you can hire a jeep to take you to Campamento Macuñucú, although this is expensive—US$45 to US$55 for the return

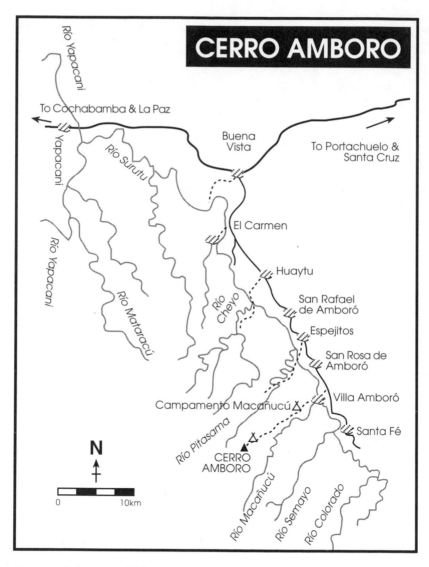

CERRO AMBORO

Río Yapacani

To Cochabamba & La Paz

Río Yapacani

Río Surutu

Buena Vista

To Portachuelo & Santa Cruz

El Carmen

Huaytu

San Rafael de Amboró

Espejitos

San Rosa de Amboró

Río Yapacani

Río Mataracú

Río Cheyo

Villa Amboró

Campamento Macanucú

Santa Fé

Río Pitasama

CERRO AMBORO

N

0   10km

Río Macanucú

Río Semayo

Río Colorado

journey. It is about 35 km (22 mi) down the road from Buena Vista, followed by 12 km (8 mi) along a pitted track. Specify when you want to be picked up when you agree on the price.

A cheaper option is to get the bus down the road to the park from Buena Vista's main square. Ask the driver to drop you off at the turnoff where there is a sign saying 12 KM TO CAMPAMENTO MACUNUCU. You then have to walk to the park station (but that eats up the best part of a day and it is not an interesting walk). From the turnoff where there is a sign saying 12 KM

TO CAMPAMENTO MACUÑUCÚ, the track heads south. After a couple of bridges, you cross the Río Surutu, its depth depending on recent rainfall. When you come to a field and huts, take the left-hand track to the small settlement of Villa Amboró. From here, it is 3 km (2 mi) to the station. The track goes across the soccer field. You then reach a feeder stream which flows into the Río Macuñucú, which flows downstream to the right. The track runs parallel to the river and then comes to a clearing. The track to the left of the clearing leads to the station.

Buena Vista is on the road to Santa Cruz from La Paz, about 3 hours before you reach the city. There is plenty of accommodation in Buena Vista and it is a pleasant place to spend a few days. Just off the main square is the Residencial Nadia, which has rooms for US$5 per person, with bathroom. Breakfast is extra. The Hotel Amboró is a 15-minute walk from the square, on the southwest side of town. Rooms with bathrooms cost US$12 per person, including breakfast. Supper is available. They also have a good library of English books. Further out, Robin Clarke's Hotel Flora y Fauna in Estancia Potrero, offers four self-catering cabins. He might have some kind of restaurant facility in the future. The cabins cost US$40 a night and sleep several people. To get there, take a motorcycle taxi from the main square (US$1), a 15-minute ride.

Buses depart regularly for Santa Cruz from La Paz's main bus terminal, changing at Cochabamba. The trip takes around 18 hours. You can buy straight-through tickets for US$14, with your rucksacks transferred—check that they have been loaded. However, you must get a new ticket at the company's desk when you reach Cochabamba. (Alternatively, you can split your journey in Cochabamba and spend a night there.) Ask the driver to tell you when he reaches Buena Vista.

You can fly to Santa Cruz and get a bus from there to Buena Vista. Lloyd Aero Boliviano (LAB) flies from La Paz to Santa Cruz every day, leaving at 7:30 A.M. and returning every day at 8:00 A.M. (US$91 one way, US$154 return). TAM flies from La Paz to Santa Cruz on Thursdays and Fridays, leaving at 9:00 A.M. They return at 2:30 P.M. on Saturdays and Mondays (US$62 one way, US $106 return).

Finish

From Campamento Macuñucú, jeep back to Buena Vista, or walk to the road and bus back.

The easiest way of getting back to La Paz is to head for Santa Cruz. Buses leave regularly from Buena Vista's main square for Montero, 52 km (33 mi) from the city (US$0.80). Ask to be dropped at the microbus terminal, where there are regular connections to Santa Cruz (US$0.80). Microbuses stop at the main bus terminal, on the southwestern edge of the city center. Alternatively, you can get a bus to Yapacani, west of Buena Vista, and wait for the bus to Cochabamba to pass through. But this can mean a long, boring wait.

Itinerary

Day 1, to campsite below summit. Day 2, to summit of Amboró, then descend to Campamento Macuñucú.

Maps

The 1:250,000 IGM map SE 20-6, Santa Cruz de la Sierra, shows most of the park and Santa Cruz. For more detail, buy the 1:50,000 map of the park, sheet number Cerro Amboró 6840 I. Map Samaipata 6839 III covers the area around Samaipata at 1:50,000. Or you can buy the 1:250,000 map SE 20-10.

Other Trekking Possibilities

The most popular trek from Campamento Macuñucú is to follow the course of the river. At least for the first few days, this is feasible without a guide. The route is rich in wildlife and it is worth stopping for at least a few hours to watch. The hours around dusk and dawn are the most rewarding and you might catch sight of a jaguar coming down to the river to drink.

Uimpex Travel (René Moreno 226, Santa Cruz city center, Casilla 3845; telephone 0-0-3-336001, fax 3-330785) runs a number of treks to this area from their Santa Cruz base, but they are not cheap. A 2-day/1-night trip to the park is US$189 per person. This includes guiding, transportation from and back to Santa Cruz, food, and camping equipment. Ask for Miriam Melgar, who has extensive experience of the park.

You can continue and climb up to the source of the Río Macuñucú, which is at least a 7-day trek. For this, take a guide.

Similarly, you can trek up the other tributaries of the Río Surutu. If you want even greater challenges, continue from one of these tributaries into the center of the park, which has rarely been explored. Ask for advice from park headquarters before contemplating such a route.

Few people have attempted it, but there is a route down from Cerro Amboró which takes you to the Río Pitasama, before rejoining the Río Surutu. There are also some trekking possibilities from the Río Mataracú, which flows into the Río Yapacani, to the west of Buena Vista. Take a bus heading for Yapacani to get there, or hire a jeep.

The main southern access point to the park is at Samaipata and there are a number of good treks from there, including one to the ruins of an Inca fortress. Ask the park authorities for details.

Route Description

From the station, the first part of the trail follows the Río Macuñucú upriver and is fairly easy going. Head southwest out of the clearing and into the jungle, along a path to the left of the river. **Ten minutes** later, the trail crosses the river. Depending on the water level, you will have to criss-cross the river several more times until you reach a long pool. From here

continue on upstream along the middle of the river and there are sheer canyon walls on either side. When water levels are high, you will have to wade.
Just before the river turns a corner, there is another long pool and a cave
on the other side, formed by an overhang in the rock. It is a good spot for
a swim. Look for the tracks of jaguars and other animals, as they often come
to drink here. Around the bend in the river, on the north side of the canyon, is a feeder stream, about **1½ hours** from the campamento.

Fill up with water here, because from now on it is a hard uphill slog and
water supplies are unpredictable. There is no trail as such. You simply pull
yourself up the hillside to the left of the stream, using trees and vines.
Twenty minutes of struggle with the vegetation brings you to the foot of
a small cliff face, about 30 m (100 ft) high, which you must climb. There
are plenty of trees and vines growing out of the cliff to provide hand- and
footholds, but the rock can be a bit flaky.

From the top, bear west to southwest through the forest, to the crest of
a ridge. Look for monkeys in the trees and the Horned Curassow. Head
west along the ridge and, about **1 hour** from the top of the climb, descend
steeply into a ravine, again clinging to the vegetation.

Go straight up the other side of the ravine, through dense vegetation,
bearing west, before descending to another smaller ravine about **20 minutes** later. From here, climb for the next **30 minutes,** at points fighting
through thick ferns, until you reach another ridge where the vegetation is
less dense—a good place to collapse for a rest. Head northwest from here,
along the ridge, and then climb up through thick vegetation which thins
when you reach the hilltop.

Just before the trail drops again into another ravine, to the west, there is
a small campsite that has been cleared by the *guardaparques*. This is your
stop. To the southwest, you can see Cerro Amboró. To the northeast, there
is a wonderful view across Amboró's northernmost band of ridges. If it is a
clear day, you might be able to see Santa Cruz over to the east, but you can
normally pick out the city's lights when night falls. You can get water from
the stream at the bottom of the ravine.

Next day, leave everything (except your water bottles) at the campsite
for the climb to the summit. Scramble down the ravine and climb up the
other side, initially heading west and then turning to the southwest. **Fifteen minutes** from the ravine, reach a more open patch of hillside and head
southwest across it to avoid the heaviest of the vegetation. From the top,
head west along the hill and down to join the ridge which curves round
and joins the northern side of Amboró. The first part of the climb takes
you up the very edge of the mountain, with an almost sheer drop on your
right. There is a short patch of dense bush before the top, which consists
of a small clearing and a few graffiti-covered rocks. There is a little space to
sleep here without tents, but watch out for the ants.

To get down, just follow the route in reverse. At a steady pace, you can
get back to Campamento Macuñucú in under **5 hours.**

Chapter 10

RURRENABAQUE AND THE WESTERN AMAZON BASIN

Rurrenabaque is situated on the Río Beni, at the western edge of the Amazon basin. Aesthetically, it is a bit of an eyesore. But it has become the premier destination for tourists doing short trips into the jungle by river, or to the *pampas* lands to the east. According to a Conservation International survey, there was a 350 percent increase in tourist visitors to the town between 1994 and 1995. One of the reasons for this boom is the best-selling book *Back from Tuichi* by the Israeli Yossi Ghinsberg, describing his experiences when he got lost in the jungle around the Río Tuichi in 1985. However, the river treks you can do from Rurrenabaque rarely penetrate into the same areas.

Logging operations are an increasing threat to the local environment, particularly downstream of Rurrenabaque. Some environmentalists hope that ecotourism may grow big enough to force the loggers to stop. There are a growing number of trekking agencies and conservation organizations operating from Rurrenabaque.

In Rurrenabaque, there is a range of hotels and hostels (ranging from US$3 to $10 per night) and many restaurants and cafes serving freshly caught Río Beni fish. For a tranquil eatery, try the Club Social on Calle Commercio. It has a shaded terrace overlooking the river and is separated from the hustle and bustle of the town. Fried fish and chips or yucca costs US$3. There are several restaurants at the bottom of Avenida Santa Cruz, near the river. If you want to escape that oppressive jungle heat and you don't fancy the Río Beni, swim in Rurrenabaque's public pool. It is at the far end of Avenida Santa Cruz as you walk away from the river, and it costs US$2.

TAM flies to Rurrenabaque from La Paz on Mondays and Saturdays at 10:00 A.M. (US$42 one way, US$84 round trip). The return flight on Saturday departs at 11:15 A.M. On Monday it leaves for La Paz at 12:15 P.M. There is a TAM office in Rurrenabaque, on Avenida Santa Cruz. There is also a LAB flight on Sunday.

There are three bus companies operating services from Rurrenabaque to La Paz: Trans Totaí, Flota Yunguenas, and Turbus Totaí. All of these buses leave from the Villa Fatima area of La Paz around 8:30 A.M. Returning from Rurrenabaque to La Paz, Trans Totaí (on Avenida Santa Cruz) and Flota Yungueñas (on Calle Abaroa) leave every day at noon. Turbus Totaí on

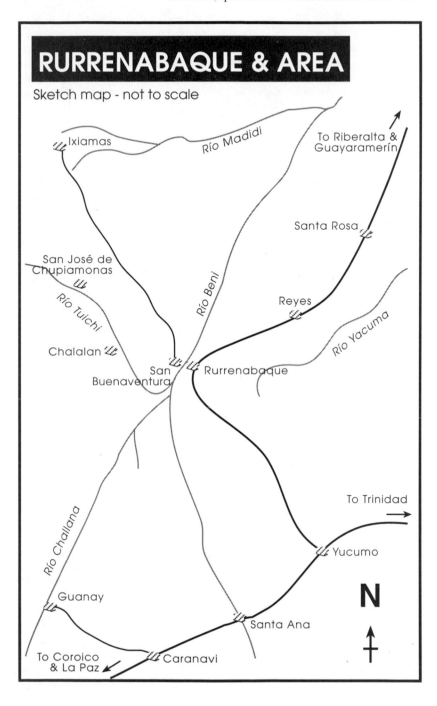

RURRENABAQUE & AREA

Sketch map - not to scale

Ixiamas

Río Madidi

To Riberalta &
Guayaramerín

Santa Rosa

San José de
Chupiamonas

Río Beni

Reyes

Río Tuichi

Río Yacuma

Chalalan

San
Buenaventura

Rurrenabaque

Río Challana

To Trinidad

Yucumo

N

Guanay

Santa Ana

To Coroico
& La Paz

Caranavi

Avenida Santa Cruz leaves every day except Tuesdays at 7 A.M. All three charge around US$11 for the trip. In the dry season, it should take 16 to 18 hours, but rain can slow things down. If you want to try getting a lift with a truck heading back to La Paz, they park at the north end of Calle Commercio. From Rurrenabaque, you can also get buses to other Beni towns, such as Trinidad, Riberalta, and Guayaramerín.

Trips with Tour Agencies

There are a number of tour agencies in Rurrenabaque that offer trips into the jungle *(selva)* by boat and jeep trips into the *pampas*. Every agency offers a standard package of a 2- to 5-day motorized longboat trip up the Río Beni (known as the Alto Beni above Rurrenabaque) and then up the Río Tuichi, followed by a trek into the jungle. But other locations are covered, too. One of the highlights of the Alto Beni trips is the macaw nesting cliff, the only one of its kind in the world. All Alto Beni trips make use of the trails and facilities established by the EcoBolivia Foundation (see below).

Food and equipment such as tents, blankets, mosquito nets, and life jackets are provided. All trips are guided, and larger groups get their own cook. Some agencies organize night walks in the jungle to watch nocturnal animals. Jungle trips of up to 15 days are possible, and some agencies can provide translators if needed.

Pampas trips focus on the Río Yacuma area, a 100-km (62.5-mi) jeep journey from Rurrenabaque. Most companies say that 2 to 3 days is enough time to do the *pampas*, although they may accept bookings for longer trips. *Pampas* trips generally stop altogether from November until December because of the swarms of mosquitoes that plague these areas during this period.

Prices depend on the season, but they are regulated by the municipal authorities. In the high season, from March to September, expect to pay between US$20 and US$25 per person for jungle trips and US$25 to US$30 for *pampas* trips. In the low season, rates drop by around US$10. Shop around to find the best price. All the agencies are within 5 minutes' walk of each other, and you may be able to find space on a trip that is leaving that day. None of the Rurrenabaque agencies had their own phone or fax numbers at the time of this writing. But you can contact them for bookings via the town's Entel office (telephone 0832-2205, fax 0832-9999).

EcoBolivia Foundation: The conservation group EcoBolivia Foundation has two research stations to the north of Rurrenabaque—Caquiahuara on the Tuichi and Charque on the Alto Beni—as well as 35 km (22 mi) of interpretative trails. Included in them is the macaw nesting cliff. All these sites are within Madidi National Park, which EcoBolivia was instrumental in establishing.

EcoBolivia is planning to start its own ecotourism trips to these areas, and will have an office in Rurrenabaque in the future. Treks will take in the Río Beni and Alto Beni, as well as the Tuichi, Hondo, and Quiquibey Rivers. EcoBolivia is working with the indigenous Tacana, Chiman, and Moseten people to help them establish and run their own ecotourism projects. Part of this involves training guides, and they also plan to develop an accommodation, offering the possibility of trekkers staying in local houses.

EcoBolivia's director, Rosa María Ruiz, speaks fluent English. In Rurrenabaque, contact Aura Haensel at the Hotel Berlin. For EcoBolivia's La Paz office address, see "La Paz Agencies" in the "Getting Around in Bolivia" section of chapter 3, Traveling in Boliva.

Agencia Fluvial Tours: This is the longest established agency in Rurrenabaque and is part of the Hotel El Tuichi; the office is on Calle Abaroa. The manager is Tico Tudela. As well as a variety of jungle and *pampas* trips, fishing is an option. They set a minimum of three people per trip. One guide accompanies groups of three to six people. With groups of over six they send two guides and a cook. You can book trips in advance or just turn up at the office and see if there is space on the next trip.

Nahama Tours: This agency offers both jungle and *pampas* trips. The office is on Calle Abaroa. If it is closed, ask for information at the Hotel Santa Ana opposite. Leo Janko is the agency's guide.

Eco Tours: They offer similar jungle and *pampas* packages to the other agencies. The office is on Calle Commercio, just near the center.

Other Trekking Options

This is a brief outline of treks that can be done from Rurrenabaque.

Tumupasa to San José de Chupiamonas (1–2 days): From Rurren-abaque you can either hitch a ride (2–3 hours) or hire a motorbike and driver (1–2 hours) to Tumupasa, where the trek begins. Tumupasa is an indigenous village where you can camp (US$1). Alternatively, ask if anyone has a spare bed in their house; expect to pay US$1 to US$2. You can buy basic food such as bread, pasta, and rice in the village.

In the first **2 hours** you climb about 458 m (1,500 ft). At the top there is a fantastic view aross the Amazonian plains. You can also camp nearby, next to a small river. On arrival in San José, try to find Lars Hafsktolo, a Norwegian agroforestry worker. He will help you find a campsite or bed in the village. He can also find you guides to explore the area around San José and up the Tuichi.

To make a round trip, you could return to Rurrenabaque along the Río Tuichi and Río Challana, which is about a 4-day trip by *balsa* raft. This can be made in a day (US$40) but you need to take two guides (US$10 per day) per raft. If you are a large group, you might prefer to hire a motorized canoe. These craft can get from San José to Rurrenabaque in 1 day. They cost US$200 to hire, but fit fifteen people. You might also like to visit Chalalan, en route.

Chalalan (1 day): Between San José and Rurrenabaque, at Chalalan, a new ecotourism project is being set up and is due to open in April 1997.

It is being managed by Conservation International, in conjunction with the local community, and aims to provide an alternative income to hunting and logging. All the cabins (for two to four people) will be designed locally and made of local products. The maximum carrying capacity of the area has been estimated at twenty-four visitors. There will also be a Nature Interpretation Center. Local guides are being trained to give guided tours. The village is aiming to cater to bird-watchers, with a series of marked interpretive trails around a lake and different jungle areas. Visitors contribute to the monitoring of flora and fauna during their stay. Eventually this project will be run by the local community. However, at present, if you are interested in visiting or obtaining more information, contact the coordinator, Joseph Vieira (see appendix, Contacts, at the back of this book). A full-board, 3- to 4-day stay is about US$100. Chalalan is only accessible by river from Rurrenabaque. There are plans to get inflatables for this trip. Alternatively, you could hire a dugout canoe.

Ixiamas to Cuartel de los Incas (2 days): The base for the trek is Ixiamas, a jungle town of several hundred people 120 km (75 mi) northwest of Rurrenabaque. There is some basic accommodation in town and you can buy some odds and ends of food. Ideally, you should hire a guide for the trek in Ixiamas (US$8), but there is a map of the area: IGM Ixiamas, 3243 H632. There is no direct bus to Ixiamas from Rurrenabaque, but you can get a truck from San Buenaventura, on the other side of the Río Beni (US$5). There is also a bus to Ixiamas from La Paz, leaving Fridays. This takes 20 to 24 hours (US$20).

From Ixiamas, you must get a bus or jeep to the Río Tequeje, around 12 km (7½ mi) south of Ixiamas. From there it is about **5 to 6 hours** to the ruins, where you can camp. The ancient ruins of Cuartel de los Incas cover an area of 160 by 80 m (530 by 260 ft) and hold a commanding position on a sheer cliff face. Some believe the Cuartel was built by the Incas. To get back, retrace your steps to Ixiamas. For the return trip to Rurrenabaque, you may have to get a lift on a forestry truck unless you can arrange a pickup before you leave San Buenaventura. From Ixiamas, there are also some trekking routes to San Antonio, Puerto Heath, and Cobija. The latter is 10 to 20 days away.

Opposite: *Unloading llamas, Plaza de Mulas, Tuni-Condoriri*

SECTION III
THE COUNTRY AND ITS PEOPLE

Jungle trekking after the rain, Pelechuco to Apolo (Andrew North)

Chapter 11

PHYSICAL ENVIRONMENT

Although it is dwarfed by its eastern neighbor, Brazil, Bolivia is a vast country, covering 1,098,575 sq km (425,050 sq mi). From north to south, it is over 1,400 km (875 mi) at its widest point and from east to west 1,200 km (750 mi).

There does not seem to be any agreement among the experts on the geographical division of Bolivia. But as a good general starting point, you should think in terms of four broad geographical regions: the Altiplano and the Andes Cordilleras (mountain ranges) in the west, the Yungas and the highland valleys in the middle, and the lowlands in the east. The lowlands also have their own distinct subregions (see below).

Geography and Climate
The Altiplano and the Cordilleras

The Altiplano, which means "high plain," and the peaks of the Andes dominate western Bolivia. This region accounts for less than 15 percent of the country's area, but some 60 percent of the population live there. It includes the administrative capital La Paz, although the city is sometimes classified as being in a highland valley zone. A large proportion of the treks described in this book start in the Altiplano/Cordilleras region.

Ranging in height from 3,500 m (11,480 ft) to over 4,000 m (13,100 ft), the Altiplano stretches across the Argentine border in the south and over into Peru in the northwest. It is a relatively barren land, with little vegetation and cold, remorseless winds. At its northern end is the vast expanse of Lake Titicaca, commonly dubbed the highest navigable watercourse in the world. In the southern Altiplano, which is much drier, there are huge salt flats, including the Salar de Uyuni.

The Cordillera de los Andes (the Andes mountain chain), which runs virtually the length of South America, does a kind of split when it reaches southern Bolivia. It runs on either side of the Altiplano until rejoining further north in Peru. In the eastern ranges, such as the Cordillera Real, the mountains rise to over 6,400 m (21,000 ft). To the west are the volcanic peaks of the Cordillera Occidental, straddling the border with Chile. Among them is Nevado Sajama, Bolivia's highest mountain at 6,542 m (21,463 ft). To the northeast of Lake Titicaca is the isolated Cordillera Apolobamba. Its glaciers provide much of the water for the rivers of the northern lowlands, which in turn feed the Rió Amazonas (Amazon River).

Overall, this is a dry region with average rainfall of less than 500 mm (20 in) a year. The rainy season lasts 3 or 4 months, from December to March. Temperatures average less than 10°C (50°F) and drop well below freezing in the mountains. Days are cold, with freezing nights. In La Paz, the temperature seldom rises above 19°C (66.2°F).

The Yungas

Immediately east of the Cordillera Real is the Yungas. This is the name given to the subtropical mountain valleys. It is a transition zone, where the heights of the Altiplano and the Andes give way to the lowland, tropical jungle of the Amazon basin.

Altitudes range from 1,000 to 3,000 m (3,300 to 9,800 ft) and rainfall and humidity are much higher. Clouds moving westward from the tropical jungles are trapped by the high peaks of the Cordillera Real just to the west and so dump their load on the Yungas. Rainfall averages 800 mm (31.5 in) per year across the whole region, but rises to as high as 5,000 mm (195 in) in some parts, supporting dense vegetation. Temperatures average around 17 to 24°C (63 to 75°F) in the lower Yungas and 10 to 14°C (50 to 57°F) above 2,700 m (8,860 ft).

It is in the Yungas that many of Bolivia's cash crops are grown, such as coffee, cocoa, sugar, tobacco, bananas, and various tropical fruits. This is also the official, legally sanctioned coca-growing area. See "Coca and Cocaine" in chapter 13, The People and Their Cultures.

The Highland Valleys

The highland valleys (*valles*) begin just south of the Yungas. This region is also a transition zone—in this case, between the Altiplano and the Chaco scrublands in the south and the savanna areas to the west. It includes parts of the Cordillera Central at its northern end and stretches southward through the departments of Chuquisaca and Tarija to the Argentine border. It is a mixed region of forested valleys, basins, hills, and mountains.

The climate here is far more hospitable than in the Altiplano, with warmer average temperatures and plentiful rainfall. Good soils mean this is an important agricultural area, producing such crops as wheat, maize, nuts, olives, and grapes The major cities are Cochabamba, Sucre, and Tarija.

The Lowlands

Around two-thirds of Bolivia's area is classified as lowland, although there are wide variations in height within this region. The average is 200 to 250 m (650 to 820 ft). But the altitude drops as low as 100 m (330 ft) in the far east and rises above 1,000 m (3,300 ft) in places like Amboró National Park, which lies just east of the highland valleys. Lowland temperatures aver-

Opposite: *Ancohuma massif from across the Río San Cristobal, Illampu Circuit*

age 25°C (77°F), but in the dusty, impenetrable Chaco, they rise to over 45°C (113°F).

Broadly speaking, the lowlands cover the departments of Santa Cruz, Beni, and Pando, and parts of La Paz, Chuquisaca, and Tarija departments. Much of the northern and central lowlands are within the basin of the Río Amazonas. Part of the southeastern lowlands are drained by the tributaries of Argentina's Río de la Plata.

There are five main ecological zones within the lowlands. Subtropical prairie or *pampas* predominate in central Beni. This gives way to tropical Amazon rain forest in north and northeastern Beni, Pando, and north La Paz. Subtropical forest and swamps cover much of the eastern plains of Santa Cruz department (Llanos Orientales). But in western Santa Cruz, there are extensive savanna or *pampas* areas. Bolivia's southeastern corner is dominated by subtropical thornbush and scrubland, known collectively as the Chaco. This region stretches across Chuquisaca, Tarija, and south Santa Cruz departments and continues into Argentina and Paraguay. It is the least densely populated part of Bolivia, and this has allowed wildlife to thrive.

Depending on which part of the country they are from, Bolivians refer to the lowlands in different ways. Highlanders often talk of the whole region as being the Oriente (literally, the East). But many lowlanders only use this to mean the Llanos Orientales. To confuse things further, some books on Bolivia refer to the whole lowland region as the Llanos Orientales.

Queara, Pelechuco to Apolo (Andrew North)

The rivers of the northern lowlands are a key source of water for the Río Amazonas. The main river is the Río Beni, into which several major tributaries drain, including the Madidi, the Tuichi, and the Mapiri. The Beni joins up with the Río Itenez and flows into the Río Madeira in Brazil, before joining the Amazon.

The lowland river basins are extremely fertile and provide most of the vegetables and fruit you see on sale in La Paz. The basins also produce key crops such as rice, soya, cotton, and sugar cane. The tropical forests produce many of Bolivia's agricultural exports, such as cocoa, rubber, musk, indigo, and brazil nuts. The forests are also a source of much sought-after hardwoods such as mahogany *(mara)*.

On the Moxos Plain, 140,000 sq km (87,500 sq mi), in eastern Beni, there are large cattle ranches. But cattle farming in Bolivia is nowhere near on the same scale as in its neighbors, Brazil and Argentina.

Geology
by Dennis Moore

Bolivia is made up of six geomorphological subdivisions that trend approximately northwest to southeast. From west to east, they are: the Western Cordillera or Cordillera Occidental, the Altiplano, the Eastern Cordillera or Cordillera Oriental, the Sub-Andean Zone, the Beni-Chaco Basin, and the Pre-Cambrian Shield.

Cordillera Occidental

The Cordillera Occidental occupies the border with Chile and is composed of 65 million-year-old Cenozoic volcanos, domes, flows, ignimbrites (huge, hot ash flows—you wouldn't want to be around when one erupted), and sedimentary rocks derived from these volcanics. The main phase of volcanism was during the Miocene period, about 22 to 25 million years ago.

The area contains many salt lakes *(salares)* and fumerolic sulfur deposits. The region's main economic activity is the exploitation of borates (some are used for soap) from lake deposits in the southern part of the cordillera, although mining companies are exploring the altered stratovolcanoes for gold and silver.

There have been no volcanic eruptions recorded within Bolivia. Only one of its volcanoes is classified as active—the 5,870-m (19,258-ft) Ollague southwest of Uyuni. A very active fumerol can usually be seen venting gases on its southern flank. The volcanoes in the Sajama area are very recent, with well-formed summit craters. Although they are not considered active, they are by no means extinct.

Altiplano

The Altiplano is an elongated basin situated between the two main mountain ranges and stretching from southern Peru to North Lipez, south of the Salar de Uyuni. In the recent geological past (i.e., millions of years ago), the Altiplano was a giant canyon or fracture that has since been filled with sediments derived from the two cordilleras. At the end of the last ice age, the area hosted a large inland sea of which Lakes Titicaca, Poopo, Coipasa, and Uyuni are the remnants.

Cordillera Oriental

The eastern Cordillera Oriental includes the Cordilleras Real, Apolobamba, and Quimsa Cruz. These are composed primarily of sedimentary rocks from the Paleozoic and Mesozoic eras (225 to 600 million and 65 to 225 million years ago, respectively), with some more recent intrusive and volcanic centers. The whole range of sedimentary rocks is present, including sandstones, siltstones, shales, limestones, and quartzites. Volumetrically and economically, Ordovician and Silurian back shales and siltstones are probably the most important sequences (formed 440 to 500 million and 395 to 440 million years ago, respectively).

The cordillera is a classic location for studying structural geology: several cataclysmic deformation episodes have helped form it. Low-angle thrust faults occur throughout the area—these decapitate entire ranges and move massive amounts of rock several kilometers.

The Cordillera Oriental is one of the most highly mineralized mountain chains in the world. Historically, this has been the center of Bolivia's metallic mining industry. The mines and deposits show strong mineralogic zoning, with a wide, heavily exploited tin-silver belt running down the western side of the cordillera, followed by a gold-antimony belt to the east. The latter is flanked on the west by a lead-zinc-silver belt. These belts are only tens of kilometers wide but are hundreds of kilometers long, running northwest to southeast. There are a number of theories as to the cause of this zoning but none fully explain the phenomenon.

The highest peaks of the Cordillera Oriental, such as Illimani, Illampu, and Huayna Potosí, are intrusive massifs (primarily granodiorite) punched up through the sediments during the

Mud and rock pinnacle, Palca Canyon

Triassic era (early dinosaurs, 195 to 225 million years ago). Intrusive rocks such as granite and granodiorite are much more resistant to erosion than the shales and siltstones, and therefore usually form the cores of the highest mountains. The entire Cordillera Quimsa Cruz is composed of granodiorite, forming a towering massif over the surrounding sedimentary rocks.

Sub-Andean Zone

The Sub-Andean Zone can be thought of as the foothills of the Eastern Cordillera. It is a narrow physiographic province running down the eastern side of the cordillera and is composed primarily of Paleozoic and Mesozoic sediments (from 225 to 600 million and 65 to 225 million years ago, respectively). It is a beautiful, rugged, and often wet area that is agriculturally well developed in the wider valleys. Parts of the Sub-Andean Zone southwest of the city of Santa Cruz host significant petroleum reserves.

Beni-Chaco Basin

The Beni-Chaco basin is a low-lying alluvium-covered area containing many rivers. It forms the upper parts of the Amazon basin in the north and center, and the Plata River basin in the south and the Chaco. This is where the jungle begins, or used to begin, particularly in the north. In the western Beni, the sediments are underlain by Paleozoic rocks, while farther east the sediments are thought to be underlain by Pre-Cambrian (Proterozoic and Archean) metamorphic rocks formed more than 600 million years ago.

Pre-Cambrian Shield

The Pre-Cambrian Shield in Bolivia is part of the much larger Brazilian Pre-Cambrian Shield. It is underlain by Proterozoic schists, gneisses, amphibolites, and other metamorphic rocks. Around the center of the shield is the Jurassic Ricon del Tigre alkaline igneous province. The Pre-Cambrian topography varies from flat or gently rolling to jungle-covered, low mountains.

Along with the far northern Peruvian frontier area, the Pre-Cambrian is one of the least explored areas in Bolivia. Jesuit missionaries came up from Paraguay in the seventeenth century and established a series of missions along the southern and western margins of the Pre-Cambrian at places such as Concepción, San Javier, San Ignacio, and San Miguel. The area was worked during the colonial era for both hard rock and alluvial gold at San Ramon and San Simon, but was largely ignored until the past 20 years when logging and modern exploration surveys were carried out. In the past 10 years, two of Bolivia's newest gold deposits have been discovered at San Ramon and Don Mario.

Dennis Moore is a Santa Cruz-based geologist.

Chapter 12

NATURAL HISTORY

The wide variations in terrain and altitude and therefore climate mean that the wildlife in Bolivia is extraordinarily diverse. Low population density and lack of economic development mean that many parts of the country, especially in the lowlands, are relatively untouched by human activity—almost half the country's 1,098,575 sq km (425,050 sq mi) remains wooded. Much of its natural heritage remains to be discovered—the Herbario Nacional de Bolivia has 30,000 unidentified specimens and receives around 5,000 new specimens a year.

Highland Flora and Fauna
Animals

There are 319 known species of wild mammal in Bolivia. The most visible highland animals are the camelids—llamas, alpacas, and vicuñas—the largest native South American mammals, which live at altitudes of up to 5,500 m (18,000 ft).

Llamas were domesticated thousands of years ago. They are used primarily for meat that is very low in cholesterol. You don't see llama steaks on the menu (the Spanish declared it dirty), but many dishes which include unidentifiable meat such as *chorizo* and *salchichas* are made with llama. Llamas are also important for their wool, predominantly white with brown/black, and they are worked as pack animals—a large llama can carry 40 kg (88 lbs), though they are rarely loaded to half this weight.

With their big, round eyes and woolly coats, llamas look cuddly, but they seem to be in a permanent bad mood. When annoyed, they flatten their ears and can spit farther than 10 m (30 ft). They fight each other by standing on their hind legs and neck-wrestling, trying to get a grip on one another's ears—llamas without ears are a relatively common sight. They chase each other and try to bite the hind legs of the other to bring it down. They also chase off dogs.

It is common to see hillsides crisscrossed with hundreds of llama tracks, resulting from their habit of grazing and walking in a long line spread out along an entire hillside.

Alpacas, which have smaller noses and thicker coats, are smaller than llamas. They tend to be a uniform dark brown, almost black. Alpacas provide high-quality wool but are not eaten as often as llamas and are not used as pack animals. Alpacas are more choosy about what they eat and tend to stay near wetter pastures. They look very odd if they have not been shorn—their coats continue growing until they touch the ground and so, with their legs out of sight, they appear to glide over the Altiplano.

Vicuñas (called *huari* in Aymará) are smaller than both llamas and alpacas, and their hair is much shorter—they look more like antelope. They do not spend their lives in herds like the other Bolivian camelids but in families of two to twelve with one male adult *(macho)* leading female adults *(hembras)* and youngsters *(jovenes)*. Single males live in separate groups which tend to be much larger, ten to sixty strong.

Vicuñas refuse to breed in captivity and so have never been domesticated. But their extremely fine wool is much sought-after and has made them a popular target for hunters. Estimates suggest there were over 1 million vicuñas in Bolivia during pre-Inca times. The first laws to protect vicuñas in Bolivia were passed in 1918 but by the 1950s numbers were down to 400,000. In 1965, just 6,000 were left.

The area now covered by the Reserva Nacional de Fauna Ulla Ulla to the west of the Cordillera

Vicuña, Reserva Nacional de Fauna Ulla Ulla

Apolobamba counted 97 vicuñas that year. But since the foundation of the reserve, numbers have risen to over 5,700 vicuñas with perhaps 12,000 in the whole country. It is illegal to kill vicuñas but illicit hunting goes on—hunters using rifles with silencers have killed vicuñas in sight of the Ulla Ulla reserve headquarters. Outside Ulla Ulla, the other main place you are likely to see them is in the Cordillera Occidental around Sajama.

Viscachas are cat-sized rodents with bushy, squirrel-like tails. They live in colonies in rocks near water, lakes, or streams, and run like kangaroos. The best time to see them is at sunrise and sunset. They are shot and eaten by locals, who also use their fur for clothing.

In theory, it is possible to see the endangered spectacled bear *(oso anteojos)* in the Eastern Cordillera, but sightings are extremely rare.

Another inhabitant of this area is the puma, important in native mythology, which is rare and even harder to see—it hunts alone at night and moves quickly and silently. Pumas have also been seen in the Sajama and Ulla Ulla areas.

Andean foxes *(zorro andino)* are smaller than their European and North American counterparts and look more like coyotes than the average fox.

Wild armadillos *(quirquincho)* are endangered. Natives of the Altiplano south of La Paz and still seen in the Sajama area, they are hunted to make the bodies of *charangos,* traditional guitarlike instruments (see "Handicrafts and Artifacts" in chapter 13, The People and Their Cultures), and stuffed for souvenirs.

Wild chinchillas are believed to have been hunted to extinction in Bolivia for their coats—there have been no reported sightings in 50 years—despite the fact that they were the first protected species in the country. In 1832 hunting was banned for 3 years and, after two more temporary bans in 1850 and 1863, hunting was permanently prohibited in 1906. Other laws banned their live export and the export of their skins. Until 1900, Bolivia was exporting 500,000 chinchilla skins to Chile annually. The chinchillas lived in the Cordillera Occidental.

High altitude pig, Puente Roto below Illimani, Cohoni Loop

Birds

Of the 1,358 bird species so far identified in Bolivia (43 percent of all species found in South America), 120 species are found in the Altiplano and Andes regions of the country.

Condors, the national symbol, avoid areas of human habitation but can be seen in many mountain areas, especially on the eastern side of the Eastern Cordillera. Condors are spectacularly big, with wingspans of up to 3 m (10 ft) and live by scavenging. The great birds do not flap their huge wings in flight, but circle around, making use of thermal air currents. However, their grace and power when airborne disintegrates when they land—they hop around in a clumsy, uncoordinated way. And they frequently gorge themselves on carrion to the extent that they cannot fly until they have digested the feast. This makes them an easy target for hunters, who bait them with carcasses, lie in wait, and then pounce after the birds have eaten. (Hunting condors is illegal.) They have a white ruff and bald red heads.

The Mountain Caracara (María) is the most beautiful bird regularly seen in the highlands. It has a yellow beak, red face, black head and neck, white body, and yellow claws. On seeing a María bird, superstitious Bolivians say, "Suerte María" three times, which is meant to bring luck for the journey. It is another scavenger and often follows vehicles looking for squashed carrion.

The black and white Andean geese (*ganzo andino, ganzo salvaje,* or *huallata*) seem to spend all their time in pairs—partnership is for life—and at times they are very noisy.

However, they're not as noisy as Andean gulls (*gaviota Andina*), which live on very high lakes—gulls have even been seen over the summit of Huayna Potosí at 6,088 m (19,974 ft).

Other high flyers are hummingbirds (*picaflores* or *colibris*), which are found over 4,000 m (13,000 ft). The highest living variety of hummingbird, the Andean hillstar, actually stands on flowers rather than hovering in the thin air. It survives the nights by dropping its body temperature from 39.5°C (103.1°F) to 15°C (59°F) and lowering its heartbeat from over 1,200 beats a minute to under 40.

Andean lapwings have marked, angular, V-shaped white stripes on their wings that are not visible when they are on the ground.

Torrent ducks (*pato de torrentes/de las torrenteras*) rarely fly but have an amazing ability to swim against the current. They are seen on the eastern side of the Eastern Cordillera, including the Pelechuco valley in the Cordillera Apolobamba. But they are threatened by deforestation, mining pollution of rivers, and competition with trout for food. The fish were artificially introduced to Bolivia at the start of the twentieth century and have thrived.

Andean tinamou (*perdiz*) look and behave like Scottish ptarmigans or partridges, living most of their lives on the ground and squawking and flapping furiously to fly away when surprised. High Andean *perdices* are the size of chickens but apparently taste better.

The ostrichlike Lesser Rhea (*suri*) lives in the Cordillera Occidental and is in danger of extinction: it is hunted for its feathers, which are used for dusters and carnival clothes. It is also eaten and its eggs are collected.

One of the more bizarre sights in Bolivia are the pink flamingoes that live on the shores of Lake Titicaca and to the south of Sajama and the *salars*. There are three types in Bolivia: Chilean (*flamenco Chileno*), Andean (*Parina Grande*), and Puna or James (*Parina Chica*) which was assumed to be extinct until 1957. Mining pollution of lakes and egg collection threaten the long-term survival of the Andean and James flamingoes.

Flora

From a layperson's perspective, the Altiplano is pretty bleak. The vegetation appears to consist mainly of scrubby bushes and scrubby grass, apart from in cultivated areas. Some of the 200 kinds of potato found in Bolivia are grown in this region, as well as other tubers and the high-protein grain quinoa. The coarse grass that grows in clumps and is eaten by llamas is called *ichu*; *thola* and *yareta* grasses are used for fuel. On the shores of Lake Titicaca, *totora* reed grass grows. It is used for the traditional *balsa* boats and was also employed by Thor Heyerdahl to construct the *Kontiki*, which was built on the Bolivian side of the lake.

The Altiplano around La Paz was covered in small bushes 40 years ago, but these have been cut down and used for firewood. Trees are rare, taking a long time to grow in the dry Altiplano, and no time to chop down! Eucalyptus, pine, and poplars are common but non-native trees. However, in the area between Sajama and the Payachatas in the Cordillera Occidental, the indigenous red-barked keñua tree survives in large numbers. The stubby bushlike trees grow at greater heights than any other tree in the world, surviving at altitudes of up to 5,200 m (17,000 ft).

There are a variety of flowers—like the red-flowered *cajophora horrida*, which stings if you touch it—and small cacti, which also hurt. Short-stemmed needle-grass is a common nuisance, because it sticks in your boots or body, and will also puncture air mattresses through ground sheets.

Valley Flora and Fauna

The more humid and warmer parts of the Yungas have similar types of flora and fauna to the Amazon, while the higher and drier parts are similar to the highlands. Birds are the most visible fauna, with noisy parakeets, often bright green, a frequent sight. They often fly in big groups. Parrots and hummingbirds are also common. It is also possible to see condors in the higher parts of the Yungas.

The Yungas boasts the most diverse flora in the country, because of its transitional nature. Cedar, colorado pine, mahogany, walnut, and jacaranda are widespread, but much sought-after by loggers. Plants such as coca, coffee, sugar, and tobacco are cultivated in the Yungas. It is also an important source of citrus fruits, as well as local fruits such as chirimoya, papaya, guava, and mango. Perhaps the most impressive Yungas plants are its giant cacti, many over 2 m (6 ft, 6 in) high. Most annoying for trekkers is bamboo, which forms tunnels on a number of trails in this book and seems to respond to machete work by growing back even faster!

Lowland Flora and Fauna
Animals

Monkeys are found throughout Bolivia's tropical and subtropical forests. The spider monkey *(marimono)* has long, thin limbs and is heavily hunted for its meat. The red howler monkey *(maneche rojo)*, as its name suggests, has a deep, long howl that you will possibly hear early in the morning. You might also see large groups of squirrel monkeys *(chichilo)*, with their prehensile tails and childlike faces.

Squirrels, coati *(tejon)*, and sloths also live in the trees.

At dusk, look out for bats *(murcielagos)*, of which there are hundreds of species. The vampire bats are not popular with ranchers, since they attack cattle and spread disease.

If you are lucky you might see a giant armadillo, protected by its forty-two bands of armor, or the rare giant anteater. There are porcupines, wild boar, and collared peccaries. These piglike creatures are found all over Bolivia, but due to heavy hunting they are now an endangered species. They forage in groups on the forest floor and you may hear their grunting. While the small and elegant agouti deer *(ochi)* is very shy, you are likely to see its droppings on the path. There is also the red brocket deer *(venado)*, which looks like the North American white-tailed deer.

Other large animals include the tapir *(anta)* which is the largest hooved animal in the forest at 240 kg (528 lbs), the spectacled bear—another endangered species—and the jaguar. There are also several smaller cats such as the black jaguarundi and the ocelot.

Bolivia's lowlands are also home to a large variety of snakes, ranging from giant pythons to small vipers. Poisonous species include the green tree-dwelling lora, the fer-de-lance, the bushmaster, and the yellow and black coral snake.

Coral snake near Río Macuñucú, Amboró National Park (Andrew North)

Fish

Over 3,000 species of fish have been identified in Bolivia's rivers, including giant catfish weighing over 36 kg (80 lbs). However, the use of dynamite fishing techniques and pesticides have severely depleted stocks in some areas. Some fishermen also use the poison from the root of the legume *Lonchocarpus sp.* to catch fish.

The rivers also hold freshwater turtles, caimans *(largato)*, which can grow to 2.5 m (8 ft), giant water otters *(Lobos del río* or "river wolves"), pink dolphins, and anacondas. Piglike capybaras *(capiwara)*, the largest amphibious rodent in the world, frequent the riverbanks. They live on fruit and can weigh up to 65 kg (143 lbs).

Birds

As with other rain-forest wildlife, new bird species are still being found in Bolivia's lowlands. In river areas, you might see cormorants; Amazon, giant, or pygmy kingfishers; herons; storks; and pure white cattle egrets. If you are lucky, you might catch sight of an ibis, distinguished by its large

Jungle near Pata, Pelechuco to Apolo (Andrew North)

curved, yellow beak. Grebes, coots, plovers, ducks, and teals are common. Watch out too for flycatchers and swifts skimming river surfaces to grab insects or catch a drink.

Under the forest canopy there are giant woodpeckers, tree creepers, warblers, finches, pigeons, and doves. On the forest floor there are tinamou (*perdizes*).

You are likely to hear groups of chattering parakeets and possibly catch sight of the bright red or blue flash of a macaw. Six species of macaw are threatened in Bolivia, partly because of habitat destruction.

Tiny hummingbirds (*picaflores/trochilidae*) hover near flowers. Their wings beat an astonishing seventy times a second. There is also the rather comical cow-bird (*serere*), so called since it is solely a herbivore and can only fly for very short distances. They are very distinctive, with a crest of feathers above the head.The colorful toucan (*tucanes*), which boasts a powerful beak for cracking nuts, is symbolic of the rain forest. At night, you might see barn or screech owls, or even the elusive nightjar.

Insects
In sunny spots or near water, look for butterflies. You cannot fail to hear the distinctive scraping sound of cicadas (*chicharra*). Sometimes it is almost deafening. These insects survive the heat of the day by tapping into trees and pumping sap over their bodies. Mosquitoes, horseflies, and midges are unpleasantly common. There is an astonishing variety of ants in the jungle, including the 4 cm-long (1.57 in) "fire-ant" (*abuna*), whose bite can cause severe pain for 24 hours. Termite mounds are common and, on fallen logs, you should see millipedes and centipedes or the prehistoric trilobite.

Flora
Take time to look at the liana creepers, epiphytes, bromeliads, and orchids growing in the trees. That is the mark of the rain forest—everything is growing on everything else. You might come across trees that have been completely taken over by the strangler fig (*matapaio*), so called because it suffocates its host to death. Watch out too for the small achiote tree (*urucu*), which has heart-shaped leaves. Its spiny pod contains red seeds, which Indians traditionally used for body paint. Among the giants of the forest flora is the mahogany tree, which grows to over 50 m (164 ft) high. The kapok tree (*mapajo*) grows to over 40 m (131 ft) high and is characterized by buttress roots and white fiber-covered seeds.

If you are sure you can recognize the plant (or ask your guide), you could try some forest foods, including wild lemons and almonds, tamarind, nutmeg, tree tomatoes, garlic and onions, yucca tubers, and palm hearts.

Chapter 13

THE PEOPLE AND THEIR CULTURES

There is evidence that the Altiplano was first inhabited 15,000 years ago. The first Bolivian peoples to leave any evidence of their existence were the Tiwanacotas, based around the south end of Lake Titicaca. They are believed to have emerged around A.D. 600 and lasted until around 1200 when, for unknown reasons, they disappeared, possibly due to drought. Their center, Tiwanaku, is no longer a lakeside city. Some archaeologists have suggested that Tiwanaku was a city of 70,000 people and controlled an empire stretching from Southern Peru to Northern Argentina, including most of Chile. Agriculture was advanced, using a system of raised fields surrounded by irrigation channels.

The Aymará kings succeeded the Tiwanacotas, ruling for 300 years until the Incas invaded from the north during the mid-fifteenth century, taking over most of what is now Bolivia.

The Incas did not have much time to enjoy their spoils—the Spanish arrived, the Inca capital of Cusco fell in 1535, and the conquest of what the Spanish called Alto Peru began. By sword, disease, and exploitation, the *conquistadores* killed hundreds of thousands of natives—by the seventeenth century, the Indian population in what is now Bolivia had been halved.

In 1545 silver was discovered in Potosí, and Bolivia became the main source of the metal for the Spanish empire, leading to a well-organized system of exploitation. At first, resentment against Spanish rule provoked only localized Indian protests. But in 1780–82, there were simultaneous and apparently synchronized revolts in Peru (led by Tupac Amaru) and Bolivia (led by Tupac Katari). In 1809, anti-Spanish elements in Bolivia, taking advantage of the fact that Napoleon had invaded Spain, declared independence. This was the first declaration of independence made in Latin America. However, Bolivia was the last country to gain actual independence from Spain. This came in 1825, following 16 years of intermittent anti-colonial wars, with armies from Peru and Argentina wading in on various sides of the conflict.

Bolivia is named after the Liberator Simón Bolívar. It was a sop to him because independence fighters here, as elsewhere in South America, did not share his vision of one Panamerican republic. Bolívar was made the first president, but he was only in the country for 6 months before returning to his native Venezuela.

200

Perfectly preserved pre-Hispanic paving, Takesi

Since independence, Bolivia has fought all its five neighbors and lost half its territory. What really hurt was the loss of its Pacific coast to Chile during the War of the Pacific, 1879–84. As a result, the two countries still do not have full diplomatic relations.

After the war, Bolivia succeeded in moving from silver mining, which was in decline, to tin. Exports of tin earned more than silver for the first time in 1902. Tin mining was concentrated in the hands of three families,

Patiño, Aramayo, and Hochschild, who exercised political power indirectly through a system known as La Rosca ("the Screw").

Politically, an event possibly more important than the loss of the seacoast was the pointless and bloody war with Paraguay over a large stretch of useless scrub called the Chaco where some oil had been found. The war lasted from 1932 to 1935, left 55,000 dead (Bolivia had a total population of 2 million at the time), and ended in deadlock, with Bolivia ceding almost all the area to Paraguay (though no oil has ever been found in the Paraguayan Chaco). The impact of the defeat and the bloodshed was massive—25 percent of the Bolivian combatants were killed, deserted, or died. It sowed the seeds for the social and political changes that culminated in the 1952 national revolution, the defining event of post-colonial Bolivian history.

In 1951 Movimiento Nacionalista Revolucionario leader Víctor Paz Estenssoro was elected president. He was due to take office the following year. But before Paz could assume power, the military announced it was taking over. This provoked the popular or national revolution of April 9, 1952, when miners took to the streets armed with dynamite and were supported by students, Indian peasants, the urban working class, and lower middle class. After 3 days of fighting, the army surrendered.

The immediate results were dramatic: the army was purged; agrarian reform gave the peasants the land they worked; the tin mines were nationalized; universal suffrage was introduced; and colonization of the eastern lowlands was encouraged.

The death of the Argentinian Ernesto "Che" Guevara in Bolivia has taken on much greater importance outside the country than within, where he made virtually no impact. His attempt to start a revolution in 1966 was a complete and utter failure. Following the 1952 national revolution, agrarian reform gave the peasants their land, thereby creating an ultra-reactionary group who were not interested in risking their land for the sake of some woolly ideas about communist revolution.

Che attempted a Cuban-style campaign, moving around the countryside in the east of the country gathering support. However, this was an uphill struggle in an area where so few people live. About 2,000 Bolivian soldiers—some trained by the U.S. army—were sent to the area to hunt Che down. His small band was split in two and finally in October 1968 he was captured and executed in Vallegrande by the Bolivian army.

Political stability was enforced by Colonel Hugo Banzer following his coup in 1970. He ruled until 1978 in what is termed the *banzerato*. Tens of thousands of Bolivians were imprisoned or forced into exile for their political views, and trade unions and political parties were banned.

In the period 1978–82, there were three presidential elections, five coups, and nine presidents. They included Latin America's first woman president, Lidia Gueiler and the notorious cocaine dictatorship of General Luís García Meza, who employed the Nazi "Butcher of Lyon," Klaus Barbie, to help run death squads. The blatant criminality of García Meza's regime was too much for the military, who replaced him with a junta. But this failed and the military went back to barracks. Hernán Siles, hero of the national revolution 30 years earlier and winner of the anulled 1980 presidential elections, came to power and democracy was restored.

By 1982 Bolivia had broken world records with 187 coups since independence.

The political anarchy of 1978–82 was followed by economic chaos during the mid-1980s, with inflation hitting between 20,000 and 24,000 percent in 1985. In the same year, the world tin price collapsed—a body blow to the Bolivian economy. As a result, between 21,000 and 28,000 miners' jobs were lost. Just 7,000 working tin miners were left.

Today, Bolivia has one of the lower inflation rates in South America, but it is still one of the poorest countries in the Western Hemisphere after Haiti and Nicaragua, and suffers from endemic underemployment.

However, Bolivia has established itself as a stable democracy with its fourth consecutive democratic elections in 1997. It is a symbol of Bolivia's commitment to democracy that the former dictator García Meza is serving a 30-year sentence in the maximum security Chonchocorro jail on the Altiplano.

Peoples and Major Settlements

The Bolivian population is estimated at 7.4 million—the last census failed to establish exactly how many. Native Amerindians make up 55 percent of the population, mixed Spanish-Amerindians 35 percent, whites 8 percent, and blacks/Far-East Asians/Middle East 2 percent. The Amerindians are split into three groups: Aymarás, descended from the Tiwanacotas; Quechuas, descended from the Incas; and the lowland groups who were not conquered by anyone. Many of the latter group still live on the fringes of modern life.

The Aymarás are basically highlanders, coming from the Altiplano down to Potosí, while the Quechuas are from the valleys (though the Cordillera Apolobamba is Quechua).

Popularly, the highlanders are called *Kollas* and the lowlanders *Cambas*. Highlanders have adapted physiologically to the altitude over the last 10,000 years—they have bigger lungs and hearts than lowlanders (leading to the typical barrel-chested appearance), allowing them to cope successfully with the low pressure.

Highlands

About 60 percent of the Bolivian population lives above 3,000 m (9,800 ft), most of them in La Paz (713,000) and El Alto (officially 406,000 but closer to 800,000). Also significant are the mining centers of Oruro (183,000) and Potosí (112,000) in the southern Altiplano.

El Alto is situated above La Paz, on the Altiplano. Apart from the airport, it did not exist 30 years ago. But today it is the fastest-growing city in

Traditional house Curva,
Apolobamba South

South America, filling with immigrants from the countryside so rapidly that many houses do not have electricity or water.

El Alto is poor and hard. Living conditions are much lower than in La Paz below. The sewage freezes on the street at night during winter. Crime, prostitution, and drug abuse are more prevalent here, leaving La Paz below relatively free from such afflictions.

While La Paz's poor are concentrated in El Alto and around the rim of the canyon, the rich live in the southern suburbs of La Paz, 1,000 m (3,300 ft) lower, where the temperature is noticeably warmer. This is known as the Zona Sur.

Outside the cities, people live in villages scattered across the bleak Altiplano, normally without electricity or telephones. The *campesinos* traditionally live off *chuño, tunta, papa, quinua,* and llama.

Highland Valleys

The largest city of the highland valleys is Cochabamba, with a population of 408,000. Until Santa Cruz overtook it, it was Bolivia's second-largest city, although it is still expanding rapidly. The valleys are also home to Bolivia's legal and official capital Sucre (administrative power rests in La Paz). It has some 113,000 people and many regard it as the country's most beautiful city.

Lowlands

Only 20 percent of the population live in the lowlands, but it is the fastest-growing region of the country. There are thirty Indian groups among the inhabitants of the lowlands. They can be broadly divided into the Panos, Araucos, Chapacuras, Botocudos, and Guaranís, the largest single group.

Since the national revolution of 1952 successive governments have put a lot of money and effort into developing the lowlands. But nowhere has benefitted more than Santa Cruz de la Sierra, the largest city in the lowlands and the second-largest in Bolivia. Industry and agri-business are now thriving in the area, and oil discoveries have provided a further boost to its economy. Santa Cruz's population has ballooned from 100,000 in 1950 to around 900,000 today. Compared to the centers of the Altiplano and highland valleys, it is far more cosmopolitan.

Trinidad, in the department of Beni, is the second-largest city in the lowlands. It has grown to over 60,000 people and has become the de facto capital of Bolivia's Amazon basin region. It is also the cattle ranching center of the country.

Demographics and Social Change

In common with many third-world countries, Bolivia is undergoing rapid demographic change. It has one of the fastest growth rates in South America, at 2.6 percent. If this continues, its population could double to 15 million people by 2025. The cities are growing at twice this rate, fueled by migration from the declining rural areas. However, it was only in the 1980s that the proportion of people living in urban areas crossed the 50 percent threshold, a key indicator of economic change. Most South American states made this transition much earlier.

In common with other fast-growing but poor states, Bolivia also has a very young population. Over 40 percent of its people are under 15 according to United Nations figures, with just 4 percent over 65.

Despite this rapid growth, population densities remain low. The national average is 7 people per sq km (18 per sq mi). Even when you exclude uninhabitable areas, such as the mountains, the density is 50 per sq km (124.5 per sq mi) in the Altiplano and 5 per sq km (12.5 per sq mi) in the eastern plains.

The country's socioeconomic structure remains very skewed. There is a tiny percentage of super-rich above a small middle class, but the vast majority of Bolivians work in low-paid occupations, or are either underemployed or unemployed. Many people survive on far less than the average per capita income of US$900 per year. But there is a further gap between the socioeconomic conditions of urban and rural inhabitants. A 1992 United Nations survey found that 97 percent of Bolivia's rural population lived in "extreme poverty." One indicator is illiteracy rates: it is estimated that over 80 percent of rural dwellers are illiterate, compared to just 9 percent in the cities.

Until the 1952 revolution, there was apartheid in Bolivia. Indians were not permitted to walk on the pavement in La Paz but had to use the gutters; neither were they allowed in the same theaters, cafes, or parks as whites; and a medieval labor system little better than slavery (*ponguaje*) prevailed. The revolution not only put an end to these practices, but banned the use of the term *indio*.

Today, one of Bolivia's national slogans is *"Unidad en la Diversidad"* (unity in diversity). However, racism remains prevalent in all levels of society, and people of pure Indian descent still tend to be the poorest and have the worst jobs.

However, there have been some important victories for indigenous peoples. In 1989, an Aymará woman, Remedios Loza, was elected to congress. Four years later, another Aymará, Victor Hugo Cárdenas, was elected Bolivia's vice president.

One of the first things visitors notice on the streets of La Paz are the *chola* women, perhaps selling small items from pavement stalls or walking along carrying their babies on their back in a multicolored blanket *(ahuayo)*. *Cholas* are women of Indian or Indian/Spanish descent. They are always dressed in the same fashion—multilayered skirts *(pollera)*, blouse, and shawl *(manta)*; centerparted, twin-plaited hair; and small bowler hat. On the other hand, there is no traditional dress for *cholo* men.

There is no one explanation for the uniform *chola* attire. One story is that King Carlos of Spain decreed this dress code during colonial times. The prevelence of bowler hats is generally attributed to a group of French or Italian hat makers in the nineteenth century who were caught with a surplus of the tiny bowler hats when fashions changed. Consequently they offloaded their stock in Bolivia!

To be a *chola* or *cholo* no longer applies only to those of Spanish-Indian parentage; it has become a term to reflect an attitude and reflection of economic position—business people, ranging from street vendors to store owners and distributors, are *cholo* or *chola*.

Religion and Superstition

While 95 percent of Bolivians claim to be Roman Catholic, there is a rich mixture of beliefs and practices, some with their roots in ancient, pre-Christian traditions. On a journey you might notice the Bolivian driver cross himself when passing a church and later stop at an *apacheta* (cairn) to sprinkle alcohol on the stone altar and make an offering to the Earth Goddess Pachamama.

Conversion following the Spanish conquest led to overt acceptance of Catholic customs and the building of many churches. But the lack of priests throughout much of the *campo* meant that the peasants were generally left to themselves.

Evelio Echevarría wrote in the *American Alpine Journal* in 1959: "Four centuries of christianising effort by the Catholic church have absolutely failed; usually the Indian, after attending services in the little village church, strolls to some hidden place where he has erected an *apacheta* (cairn) and prays to Vira Cocha, the god who emerged from Titicaca to bring order and prosperity to mankind. Often tourists notice that the Indians place a cross on top of the pointed roof of their huts, or that they wear icons with the image of Saint Bernard hanging around their necks; this must not be attributed to Christian zeal, but to the Indian belief that the cross deviates lightning, while the appeal of the icon is based upon the fact that Saint

Bernard is often pictured herding a flock of sheep—an important factor in Indian economy."

The political power of the church was smashed immediately after independence in 1825 when all small religious houses were closed down and huge amounts of land confiscated by the new state.

A number of pre-Hispanic traditions are vigorously followed today. One of these is the *cha'lla,* which Bolivians perform to "protect" new buildings. It generally involves a llama fetus being buried in the foundations. You see these fetuses on sale in markets throughout Bolivia. Larger buildings require grander ceremonies and sometimes a whole llama is sacrificed.

A less elaborate *cha'lla* is often performed each year inside existing buildings. All women must leave, except for the woman performing the ceremony, to avoid making Pachamama jealous. The *dulce mesa* is set up with coca leaves, alcohol, and a llama fetus and then incense is burned.

Cha'llas are also performed in mines as an offering to Tío, the god of the underworld. There are many stories, never proved, that drunks and street kids have been sacrificed in the *cha'lla* and their remains buried in the foundations or thrown down mine shafts.

Spring is marked in September by burning vegetation, especially in the Yungas. This is done in the belief that smoke creates clouds which in turn create rain. Despite increasing efforts by the government to stop this custom, Illimani often cannot be seen from La Paz for much of September because of the smoke.

Fiestas

With so many religious, local, regional, and national fiestas, most places have an excuse to party at least once a month. The Catholic church adopted many of the local fiesta dates to ensure greater support for its Christian celebrations. Fiesta has many elements. They incorporate religious beliefs both ancient and modern, nationalism (there is a Day of the Sea—lost in 1880), and an awful lot of alcohol. They are great expressions of vitality, local costume, and music. But fiesta times can be very inconvenient for visiting trekkers—transportation, including mules, may be suspended and hotels fully booked.

In the drab Altiplano, fiestas are supported with great color and energy. The classic example is in the city of Oruro: for 11 months of the year it is a drab and depressing place, but then it stages the most amazing carnival celebrations during February. Carnival in the lowlands is just as enthusiastically celebrated. Across the country, the whole of February is spent chucking water-filled balloons at passersby. Be prepared to get wet, as gringos are popular targets. Other noteworthy fiestas include:

During *Alasitas* in late January, miniature versions of desirable objects are sold and blessed before Ekeko, the Aymará god of abundance. Favorites include vehicles, houses, and US$100 bills, but anything goes—miniature

Curva fiesta, Apolobamba South

cellular telephones, beer crates, tools, degree certificates. People hope the offering will bring them the real thing.

Gran Poder in late May or early June has become a huge carnival through the streets of central La Paz, similar to the Oruro carnival.

Aymará New Year on June 21 is celebrated at Tiwanaku where people keep fires alight all night to help the sun recover from the longest night of the year.

Día de San Juan on June 24 is now the biggest firework event of the year.

For *Virgen de Urkupiña* on August 15 in Quiacollo, Cochabamba, thousands of pilgrims come and offer flowers, candles, and money to the Virgin.

Todos los Santos on November 2 is marked by parties in the cemeteries to keep company with the dead.

Coca and Cocaine
To many Westerners, and particularly the U.S. Drug Enforcement Agency, the coca plant means just one thing: cocaine. Bolivia produces some 30

percent of the world's coca leaves, and many of the leaves do indeed end up as the white powder drug. But as Bolivians will never tire of telling you, coca is not just the raw material for cocaine. It has many other, positive uses and has mystical significance—the plant has played a central role in traditional life for centuries.

People have been chewing the leaf for its mildly stimulating effects for thousands of years in Bolivia. Carvings at least 1,000 years old at Tiwanaku show figures with the characteristic pouched cheek of the habitual chewer. The Incas kept coca for their rulers. The Spanish encouraged the practice among miners to make them work longer in the appalling conditions underground because the coca juices dull feelings of hunger and tiredness.

Miners are still among the heaviest chewers of coca leaves today, but the practice is also widespread among peasant farmers and other laborers. However, people of all classes drink coca tea, *mate de coca*. You will find it in the most expensive restaurants. There are coca markets; people wander around the Prado, La Paz's central street, selling bags of the green leaves.

Many Bolivians also believe coca has healing properties. You often see people with a coca leaf stuck to their forehead to cure their headache. Coca shops sell tonics and creams derived from the plant to cure rheumatism and skin rashes. In addition, it is often used as an offering to Pachamama.

Coca for these traditional uses mostly comes from the Yungas area. However, since the 1970s a more bitter type of coca has been cultivated in the Chapare region around Cochabamba, specifically for cocaine production. Little refined cocaine is actually produced in Bolivia. Instead, most Chapare coca is turned into paste and sent to jungle processing laboratories in Peru or Colombia. Neither is there much demand for cocaine within Bolivia and therefore the country has only limited experience of the social problems associated with the drug in the United States and Europe.

The United States has maintained constant pressure on the Bolivian government to eradicate the coca fields and each year audits the progress of the operation. If the United States is not happy with the results, economic aid to Bolivia, from the U.S. government and from U.S. aid agencies, could be cut back or even stopped. For South America's biggest recipient of foreign aid this is a serious threat, and an impossible situation given the difficulties involved in eradicating coca/cocaine production. In 1995, 5,493 hectares (13,568 acres) of coca plantations were eradicated, eight tons of precursor chemicals confiscated, and 2,000 processing centers and laboratories destroyed.

However, despite these figures, the eradication has not been effective. Peasants are paid US$2,500 per hectare (about US$1,000 per acre) of coca destroyed. But because this money is not paid until 70 percent of a plantation has been eradicated, coca growers face an unbridgeable income gap. Many simply plant a new crop of coca elsewhere and so production continues.

The coca-cocaine industry is the Bolivian government's permanent economic dilemma. They know it brings endless trouble but if they put an end to all cocaine-related production, the country would lose external earnings estimated at between US$300 million and US$700 million a year (23 to 43 percent of all exports). Around 200,000 people would also lose a substantial or total part of their livelihood. In such a poor country, it would be impossible to fill that gap quickly.

The whole debate has become fraught with emotion. Bolivians tend to see the issue as another example of Uncle Sam throwing its weight around and punishing Bolivia for America's abject failure to control the huge demand for the drug within its own borders.

Do not consider taking cocaine in Bolivia. There is a straight 8-year jail sentence for possession, which you would probably serve in the notorious San Pedro jail in La Paz.

Do not take coca tea bags or any other coca product to the United States—it will be confiscated by customs officials.

Handicrafts and Artifacts

Outside La Paz, the choice of handicrafts and artifacts is limited, so you are better off making your purchases in the capital.

However, you will find a wide range of woodwork, leather products, and basketry in Santa Cruz. Amazonian products include carvings from ivory palms, hammocks from Chambira palm, and hats and baskets from the Panama Hat palm (not in fact a true palm). In Sorata, there is a small *artesanal* cooperative on the main square.

La Paz's artifacts center is Calle Sagárnaga, to the left of Plaza San Francisco, and the surrounding streets. There are scores of shops and stalls, selling everything from textiles to leather bags, carvings, and jewelry. The quality is high, with very little in the way of mass-produced tourist tack. Prices are reasonable, but shopkeepers expect you to bargain. There are a few, more expensive shops on the Prado.

The mainstay of the market is textiles, which come in a dazzling range of colors and designs, drawing on a tradition of weaving that goes back thousands of years. If you are interested in finding out more about the history of Bolivian textiles, there are some examples of antique cloths in the Museum of Art and Popular Culture.

The older, finer woven cloths, with characteristic animal motifs, come from the south and Potosí region. You will also find the more brightly colored, modern cloths that *campesino* women use to carry their babies and belongings.

You can also buy jackets, ponchos, jumpers, and waistcoats, made of either cotton or wool. The latter is usually a mixture of llama and alpaca wool. Pure alpaca is extremely soft but slightly more expensive. You may also find angora (*conejo de abolengo*) items. In addition, you can find various clothing items for trekking. Lightweight cotton trousers and long-sleeved shirts go for around US$4 each. You can find woollen scarfs, gloves, and various types of hat for US$3 or $4.

Silver products range from jewelry (with or without semiprecious stones) to paper knives and tea sets. In leatherware there are bags, satchels, and wallets. Other miscellaneous items include wall hangings, wrist bracelets, fiesta outfits, and even the small bowler hats worn by *chola* women.

Music buffs will find an interesting range of instruments in the Sagárnaga shops, including several types of panpipe. The *zampoña* is made of several pipes of different lengths and widths. The *tarka* looks like a recorder with six holes. *Quenas* are soft-sounding bamboo or cane pipes. By far the largest panpipe is the *erke*, a single tube of 3 to 6 m (9 to 18 ft) long with a bell at the far end. You will also see two types of small guitar with five pairs of strings, known as the *charango* and *bandurria*. The *bombo* is a large leather drum that Bolivians beat with hammers.

Bolivian music gained worldwide popularity with Simon & Garfunkel's adaptation of "El Condor Pasa" and, more recently, the spread of the lambada dance. There are record stores around the city selling local music on cassette or compact disc.

Avoid purchasing any hardwood products, musical instruments made of armadillo or other animal carapaces, and viscachaya fur items (now an endangered species).

Descending to Sorata, Lagunas Glaciar and Chillata

FURTHER READING

History, Politics, and Culture

Banco Mercantil. *Masks of the Bolivian Andes*. La Paz: Quipus, 1993. Coffee-table book with glossy photographs of colorful Bolivian masks and costumes.

Crabtree, John, Gavan Duffy, and Jenny Pearce. *The Great Tin Crash—Bolivia and the World Tin Market*. London: Latin American Bureau, 1987. Detailed account of the 1985 tin price collapse and the catastrophic impact this had on Bolivia's main legal source of foreign currency.

Cramer, Mark. *Culture Shock! Bolivia*. Portland, Ore.: Graphic Arts Center, 1996. A personal view of modern-day Bolivia, written by a U.S.-born journalist who has interviewed many of the country's movers and shakers.

Dunkerley, James. *Rebellion in the Veins: Political Struggle in Bolivia 1952–1982*. London: Verso, 1984. Heavy-going political history packed with dates, facts, and initials.

Hendel, Fred. *Revolutions in Bolivia*. Ypsilanti, Mich.: Aventura Press, 1992. A personal view of key events in Bolivia by an Austrian physics professor who lived in Bolivia from 1939 to the 1960s.

Klein, Herbert. *Historia de Bolivia*. 2d ed. La Paz: Juventud, 1990. A readable general history (in Spanish).

Van Lindert, Paul, and Otto Verkoren. *Bolivia in Focus*. London: Latin American Bureau, 1994. Short and very readable study of Bolivia's people, history, politics, culture, and geography.

Travelogues and Novels

Doyle, Sir Arthur Conan. *The Lost World*. 2d ed. London: Buccaneer Books, 1977. A science fiction novel about the rain forest, which was based on Colonel Fawcett's description of the Bolivian forests in 1910.

Fawcett, Colonel Percy Harrison. *Exploration Fawcett*. London: Hutchinson & Co., 1953. Reprint: Century, 1988. Classic adventure compiled from the explorer's papers and diaries after he disappeared in the Mato Grosso.

Ghinsberg, Yossi. *Back from Tuichi*. New York: Random House, 1993. A true story of an Israeli's survival alone in the Bolivian rain forest for 3 weeks.

Guevara, Che. *The Motorcycle Diaries—A Journey Around South America.* London: Verso, 1995. Che Guevara's shoestring trip across South America when he was a young, not-so-politically-correct man.

Hoffman, Gert. *Before the Rainy Season.* London: Mandarin Paperbacks, 1991. Set in 1968, a young German couple visit a remote Bolivian farm which is run by an eccentric fugitive.

Parris, Matthew. *Inca Cola.* London: Weidenfield & Nicolson, 1993. Very funny—a must-read for anyone traveling in the Andes.

Natural History

Armonía, ed. *Lista de las aves de Bolivia.* 4th ed. Santa Cruz: Armonía, 1995. A straight list—no illustrations—of every species of bird found in the country, with names in English, Spanish, and Latin.

Ergueta, Patricia, and Cecile de Morales, eds. *Libro rojo de los vertebrados de Bolivia.* La Paz: Centro de Datos para la Conservación, 1996. A clearly laid-out guide to 250 threatened animal species in Bolivia (in Spanish).

Forno, Eduardo, and Mario Baudoin, eds. *Historia natural de un valle en Los Andes—La Paz.* La Paz: Instituto de Ecología, 1991. Illustrated guide covering the area around the city of La Paz, which includes the vast majority of highland flora and fauna (in Spanish).

Killeen, Timothy, Emilia Garcia, and Stephan Beck, eds. *Guía de Arboles de Bolivia.* La Paz: Herbario Nacional de Bolivia/Missouri Botanical Garden, 1993. Comprehensive, illustrated guide aimed at the specialist (in Spanish).

Plotkin, M. J. *Tales of a Shaman's Apprentice.* London: Viking Press, 1993. How to look for and use medicinal plants in the Amazon.

Rocha, Omar, and Carmen Quiroga. *Aves de la Reserva Nacional de Fauna Andina Eduardo Avaroa.* La Paz: Museo Nacional de Historia Natural, 1996. The Eduardo Avaroa animal reserve in Potosí is a relatively small area of Bolivia. But 100 of the 120 species of highland birds live in the park, so this illustrated and well-written guide is far more useful than its title suggests (in Spanish).

Medical

Wilderness Medical Society. William Forgey, M.D., ed. *Practice Guidelines for Wilderness Emergency Care.* Indiana: I.C.S. Books, 1995. Comprehensive guide which includes chapters on various types of injury, high-altitude illness, hypothermia, heat-related illnesses, water disinfection, fluid replacement, animal attacks, reptile and spider bites, ticks, etc.

Trekking

Bradt, Hilary, and Jon Derksen. *Backpacking and Trekking in Peru and Bolivia.* 6th ed. London: Bradt Publications, 1995. The first trekking guidebook to the area.

Sanjines, Gonzalo Silva. *La Cordillera Real de los Andes.* La Paz: Juventud, 1996. The only guide to cover some of the many short trekking possibilities around La Paz, although it does have some mistakes and omissions (in Spanish).

General Travel Guides

Boero Rojo, Hugo. *Discovering Bolivia.* 2d ed. La Paz: Los Amigos del Libro, 1994. Small handbook giving a brief introduction to the ecology, people, and culture of Bolivia. Available in bookshops in La Paz.

Box, Ben, ed. *South American Handbook.* Bath: Footprint Handbooks, annual. Most up-to-date general guidebook. (A *Bolivia Handbook* is planned for January 1998 and every couple of years thereafter.)

Kunstaetter, Robert, and Daisy Kunstaetter, eds. *The Latin American Travel Advisor.* Quito, Ecuador: Latin American Travel Consultants. (Casilla 17-17-908, e-mail: rku@ecnet.ec, quarterly). Travelers' intelligence newsletter covering public safety, health risk, economics, politics, and travel costs for Bolivia and sixteen other Latin American countries.

Swaney, Deanna. *Bolivia: A Travel Survival Kit.* 3d ed. Australia: Lonely Planet, 1996. The most detailed general guidebook to the country.

CONTACTS

International code for Bolivia + 591
La Paz city code 2
Santa Cruz 3

Inside Bolivia

Conservación Internacional (Conservation International), Avenida Arce No. 2081, Edificio Montevideo, Departamento 204, Casilla 5633, La Paz; telephone/fax 356529; e-mail: ci-bolivia@conservation.org. Coordinator: Joseph Vieria.

Friends of the Earth, Avenida del Libertador 17, P.O. Box 2270, La Paz; telephone/fax 783757.

Fundación Amigos de la Naturaleza (FAN), Santa Cruz office, telephone/fax 533389 or 333806.

Fundación EcoBolivia (EcoBolivia Foundation), P.O. Box 8505, La Paz; telephone/fax 315974; e-mail: ECOB@megalink.com. Director: Rosa María Ruiz.

Museo Nacional de Historia Natural, Calle 27 Cota Cota, Casilla 8706, La Paz; telephone 795364. A small museum with a wide selection of stuffed animals and birds, which will give you an idea of what to look out for on your treks.

Outside Bolivia

Birdlife International, Welbrook Court, Girton Road, Cambridge, CB3 0NA, UK; telephone 01223 277318. Specializing in bird species worldwide.

Green Flag International (UK office), telephone 01223 890250. Works with the travel industry and conservation bodies. Provides an ecotourism guide and advice on selected destinations.

Latin American Bureau, 1 Amwell Street, London EC1R 1UL; telephone 0171 278 2829; fax 0171 278 0165; e-mail: lab@gn.apc.org. An independent research and publishing organization working to broaden public understanding of issues in Latin America and the Caribbean.

Tourism Concern UK, telephone 0181 944 0464. Pressure group campaigning for sustainable tourism around the world.

Traffic International (UK office), telephone 01223 277427. For information about C.I.T.E.S and regulations regarding the export of flora/fauna.

SPANISH FOR TREKKERS

Phrases

Hello, Good day/afternoon	*Buenos días/Buenas tardes*
Good bye, good night	*Hasta luego/Buenas noches*
(*"Hola"* is for friends, as is *"Ciao")*	
How are you? (to a friend)	*Como está? (Como estás?)*
Yes/No	*Sí/No*
Please	*Por favor*
Thank you/No thank you	*Gracías/No gracías*

(However, if someone asks "Would you like some more?" and you say *"Gracías"* it is taken as "No thank you." If you want more, say *"Sí, gracías"*)

Courteous reply to "Thank you"	*De nada* (It's nothing) or *Por que* (For what)
Excuse me (to get past someone)	*Permiso*
Excuse me (after making a mistake)	*Discúlpame*
That's fine/OK	*Está bien*
Where is . . . ?	*Dónde está . . . ?*
Where are you going?	*Dónde va?*
When does the bus/lorry/transport leave?	*Cuándo sale el bus/la camión/la mobilidad?*
Where does the bus leave from?	*De dónde sale el bus?*
How long does it take to get to . . . ?	*Cuántas horas son hasta . . . ?*
Stop	*Pare*
Is there/are there . . . a shop/bread /somewhere to stay/lunch/dinner/ toilet/shower	*Hay . . . una tienda/pan/ alojamiento/almuerzo/cena un baño/una ducha?*
How much is/are . . . ?	*Cuánto es/son . . . ?*
Could you please spell it for me?	*Puede deletrearlo para mí?*
Can we . . . camp here?	*Podemos . . . acampar aquí?*
Yesterday/tomorrow	*Ayer/mañana*
Next/last week/month/year	*próximo(-a)/último(-a) la semana/el mes/el año*
now/really now/really, really now	*ahora/ahorita/ahora mismo*
I don't understand	*No entiendo*
I don't know (a fact)	*No se*
I don' know (a place or person)	*No conozco*
I am vegetarian	*Soy vegetariano, -a*
I don't eat meat/chicken/fish	*No como carne/pollo/pescado*
What is your name (to a friend)?	*Como se llama? (Como te llamas?)*
My name is . . .	*Me llamo . . .*
Where do you come from (to a friend)?	*De dónde es? (De dónde eres?)*
I come from . . .	*Soy de . . .*
What do you do (to a friend)?	*Que hace? (Que haces?)*

I am . . .	Soy . . .
I want to hire a mule/llama /porter/guide	Quiero alquilar mula/llama/porteador/ guía
How much does it cost a day?	Cuanto cuesta por día?
Can I take a photograph?	Puedo sacar una foto?
Help	Socorro
Can you help me?	Puede ayudarme?
I am ill	Estoy enfermo, -a
My...head/lungs/legs/feet hurt(s)	Me duele el/la/los/las...la cabeza/los pulmones/las piernas/los pieds
It hurts here	Me duele aquí
It's cloudy	Está nublado/nuboso
It's cold	Hace frío
It's foggy	Hay niebla
It's hot	Hace calor
I'm going (now)	Me voy
Let's go	Vamos
We'll see each other—i.e. Goodbye, See you later	Nos vemos

Glossary

bridge	el puente	road	la carretera
cloud	la nube	river	el río
countryside	el campo	stream	el arroyo
field	el campo, la pampa	summit	la cumbre
fog	la niebla	snow	la nieve
glacier	la glaciar	sun	el sol
lake (small)	el lago (la laguna)	tent, cover	la carpa
mountain		transport	la mobilidad
(with snow)	el cerro (el nevado)	valley (small)	el valle (la quebrada)
pass	el paso, la abra	village	el pueblo
pass marker		water	
(cairn)	la apacheta	(drinkable)	el agua (potable)
path	el sendero	waterfall	la cascada
rain	la lluvia	wind	el viento

Common Mistakes

casado, -a	married
cansado, -a	tired
comprometir	to promise, not compromise
embarazo, -a	pregnant, not embarassed
ropa	clothes, not rope (cuerda or pita)
sopa	soup, not soap (jabon)

INDEX

Page numbers for maps are in italics.

ABOUT THE AUTHORS

While recovering in the intensive care unit of Chamonix hospital in 1994 following an 800-m (2,600-ft) fall in the French Alps, **Yossi Brain** (pictured), decided to quit his job as a political reporter for an evening newspaper in Britain and take up trekking and climbing full-time. He moved to Bolivia where he works as a trekking and mountain guide, runs the Ozono adventure travel agency in La Paz, and is climbing secretary of the Club Andino Boliviano. He spends as much time as possible trekking and climbing and also indulges in a bit of freelance journalism. He is resident Bolivia correspondent for the *South American Handbook*. Born in 1967, he has trekked and bogtrotted on three continents, extensively in Ecuador where he goes to avoid the Bolivian wet season.

(photo by Gerry Avcari)

Andrew North is a freelance journalist based in London and a keen walker and cyclist. He was born in Britain in 1969. Before going freelance, he was deputy editor of *Geographical Magazine* and worked as a photographer for British and American newspapers. His travels have taken him across the Middle East and Asia, as well as to Latin America. Andrew currently divides his time between working for BBC radio and British newspapers such as the *Independent*. Among other things, he writes about the Internet, and it was through the 'Net that he and Isobel received the request from Yossi Brain to write the lowlands section of the book.

Isobel Stoddart was born in Lancaster, Britain, in 1969, and has lived in Africa, Asia, and Latin America. She has undertaken several adventurous trips around the world, including a 3-month cycle trip across Mongolia. She has also organized several expeditions in Tanzania, Zambia, and northern Namibia. She now works for Sustrans (Sustainable Transport), a British charity that is coordinating the development of Britain's 6,500-mile National Cycle Network.

Yossi met Andrew who met Isobel at University College, London where they studied history, geography, and anthropology, respectively.